Entry Denied

Entry Denied

Controlling Sexuality at the Border

Eithne Luibhéid

University of Minnesota Press

Minneapolis / London

Chapter 4 was originally published as "Looking Like a Lesbian: The Organization of Sexual Monitoring at the U.S.–Mexico Border," *Journal of the History of Sexuality* 8, no. 3 (1998): 477–506. Copyright 1998 by the University of Texas Press. All rights reserved.

Published by the University of Minnesota Press
111 Third Avenue South, Suite 290
Minneapolis, MN 55401-2520
http://www.upress.umn.edu

Library of Congress Cataloging-in-Publication Data

Luibhéid, Eithne.
 Entry denied : controlling sexuality at the border / Eithne Luibhéid.
  p.   cm.
 Includes bibliographical references and index.
 ISBN 0-8166-3803-9 (HC : alk. paper) — ISBN 0-8166-3804-7 (PB : alk. paper)
 1. Women immigrants—Government policy—United States—History.
 2. United States—Emigration and immigration—Government policy—History.
 3. Sex and law—United States—History.   I. Title.
 JV6602 .L85 2002
 325.73'082—dc21

                                                              2002006067

Printed in the United States of America on acid-free paper

The University of Minnesota is an equal-opportunity educator and employer.

12 11 10 09 08 07 06 05 04 03 02   10 9 8 7 6 5 4 3 2 1

Contents

Acknowledgments

This work could not have been completed without generous support from many individuals. I am enormously grateful for the encouragement and critical feedback of my distinguished Ph.D. dissertation committee at the University of California, Berkeley: Elaine H. Kim, David Lloyd, Judith Butler, and Michael Omi. Thanks to Jean Molesky Poz, who introduced me to immigration scholarship and taught me what collegiality means. Thanks to the four fabulous divas with whom I participated in a dissertation-writing support group: Nerissa Balce Cortes, Susan Lee, Sandra Liu, and Caroline Streeter. Thanks to other Berkeley Ethnic Studies colleagues, especially Grace Chang, Arlene R. Keizer, Jasbir Puar, and Isabelle Thuy Pelaud, for continual friendship, intellectual support, and practical assistance. Obeisance to Leslie Minot, who introduced me to the literature on prostitution, roundly debated Foucault over tea, and offered valuable comments on several chapters. Thanks to members of the Interdisciplinary Queer Studies Research Group at the Humanities Research Institute at the University of California, Irvine: Robyn Wiegman, Madelyn Detloff, Carla Freccero, David Gere, George Haggerty, Lisa Rofel, Nayan Shah, and Sandy Stone. The book substantially benefited from engagement with the group.

At Bowling Green State University, I profited from the friendship and assistance of many talented faculty. Special thanks to Vicki Patraka, who made sure that the dissertation actually became a book rather than becoming consigned to the closet. Thanks to the Faculty Writing Group at the Institute for the Study of Society and Culture, especially Rachel Buff, Rob Buffington, Radhika Gajjala, Liette Gidlow, Hai Ren, and Val Rohy, who generously read and carefully commented on drafts of various chapters. Thanks also to the faculty of the Ethnic Studies department, particularly Michael Martin and David Wall, for their support of this project. Phil Terrie graciously commented on a chapter and draft revisions. Taeyon Kim and Julia Mason provided meticulous and thoughtful research assistance. Rachel Gustwiller kindly retyped the appendix after the computer ate it.

Many thanks to Martin F. Manalansan IV and Roger Rouse, whose revision suggestions significantly enhanced the manuscript. Thanks also to the University of Minnesota Press's editorial and marketing staff, especially Carrie Mullen, for superb assistance at every stage of the process.

Many activists and organizers generously provided vital information for the project. They include Sydney Levy and Dusty Aráujo of the International Gay and Lesbian Human Rights Commission in San Francisco; Cathi Tactaquin, José Palafox, and Sasha Khokha of the National Network for Immigrant and Refugee Rights in Oakland; and Shannon Minter of the National Center for Lesbian Rights in San Francisco. Civil rights lawyer Albert Armendáriz shared his files about Sara Harb Quiroz's case. Jesus Romo, who also labors on the side of justice, provided information about Blanca Bernal's case. Roberto Martínez, director of the U.S./Mexico Border Program of the American Friends Service Committee, generously shared news clippings and information about rape at the border. Nancy Kelly of Greater Boston Legal Services made time to answer my questions about refugee and asylum law. Professor Carolyn (Patty) Blum and Colleen Coughlin patiently explained aspects of immigration law. Heartfelt thanks for your support and inspiring examples of activism.

Thanks to the Boston foreign lesbians who told me to write "our story"—you know who you are. Huge thanks to Sylvia Organ for making sure that I stayed in school and did my homework; there would be no degrees without you. Thanks to Nina Payne for introducing me to the craft of writing. Thanks to Berni Smyth for wonderful editorial assistance and the usual insouciance. Thanks to Allison Heather and Joe McInerney for continual support and wackiness. Thanks to the many people whose fierce dreams and everyday acts to create a different world made this work possible. *Buíochas le mo chroí* R. H. for rich intellectual and emotional companionship during the book's final stages and beyond.

The research was partly funded by a Chancellor's Dissertation Year Fellowship and two Vice-Chancellor for Research Awards from the University of California, Berkeley.

Introduction

Power and Sexuality at the Border

I once lectured to an undergraduate class about how the United States excluded lesbian and gay immigrants until 1990, and a student inquired, "How would the Immigration and Naturalization Service (INS) know if someone was gay, anyway?" The question could have been the expression of a democratic belief that there was nothing particularly distinctive about lesbians and gay men. But it could equally have been a homophobic query, implying that the INS could not know if someone was lesbian or gay *unless* the individual revealed the fact—flaunted it, as the homophobes like to say. In that case, following the (il)logic of homophobia, it was the individual's own fault for being excluded. If s/he had been less militant about proclaiming identity, s/he would not have been excluded.[1]

I did not know which meaning the student intended. But as I later reflected on the question, it came to mark for me how dominant groups and institutions construct the intelligibility of lesbian, gay, and other minoritized lives in specific ways but then deny their own implication in social inequalities.[2] For it was not lesbians and gay men who initially sought to be recognized by the immigration service. On the contrary, it was the immigration service that sought, in sometimes bizarre and frightening ways, to identify and penalize lesbians and gay men who tried to enter the country. The fact that the immigration service initiated these efforts is deeply revealing of how sanctioned sexualities become consolidated by delineating and penalizing categories of "others." In this sense, lesbian and gay exclusion is less the history of a minor group than of self-constituting actions by the powerful who then erase the traces of their own production while stigmatizing and policing others. But "How would they know?" denies that dynamic and dismisses histories such as the one I was reconstructing.

"How would they know?" also raised a series of other crucial issues to which this book is, in some sense, a response. At a literal level, the immigration service *didn't* know if a woman was a lesbian, or a prostitute, or being "brought to the United States for immoral purposes," or "arriving in a state of pregnancy," or any of the other categories that have made women excludable on the basis of sexuality. Nonetheless, the immigration service was charged with *trying* to know. So the book's key questions became: how did the immigration service try to know if a woman belonged to any of these categories? What questions did they ask her, in order to (try to) find out? What means did they use not just to uncover her past history but also predict her sexual future, based on factors "of which the individual [her]self might be unaware"?[3] To what regimes of inspection did they subject her? What information might be deemed to constitute a ground for suspicion? How did these regimes of inspection and interrogation change over time and location?

Asking how the immigration service tried to know about immigrant women's sexual acts, identities, tendencies, and possibilities situated my analysis within the literature on social construction, which argues that sexual identities and categories are never transhistorical, essential, fixed and self-evident but rather are constructed within social relations that change over time and by location. As Ellen Ross and Rayna Rapp write, "the bare biological facts of sex do not speak for themselves; they must be expressed socially. Sex feels individual or private, but these feelings always incorporate the rules, definitions, symbols, and meanings of the worlds in which they are constructed."[4] These authors describe how powerful social formations, including the family, community, church, and state, give definition to sexual categories and identities. Within a constructionist framework, the question "How would they know?" suggests the need to shift the analysis away from individual immigrants' lives, interesting though they are, and toward the actions of the immigration service. It identifies the immigration control apparatus as a key site for the production and reproduction of sexual categories, identities, and norms within relations of inequality.

This book therefore investigates how the U.S. immigration control system has served as a crucial site for the construction and regulation of sexual norms, identities, and behaviors since 1875.[5] While both women and men have been targets of immigration control based on sexuality,

this book focuses on women's experiences, since women's bodies historically serve as the iconic sites for sexual intervention by state and nation-
making projects.[6] Immigration laws and procedures that differentiated
women into categories such as wife, prostitute, and lesbian reveal the role
of immigration control in regulating admission on the basis of sexuality.
Historically, laws and procedures granted "preferred" admission to wives,
while mandating the exclusion of lesbians, prostitutes, and other "immoral" women. Yet these distinctions did not simply derive from pre-
existing identities that immigrant women already "had." Rather, this
book argues that in seeking to ascribe these identities the immigration
service centrally contributed to constructing the very sexual categories
and identities through which women's immigration possibilities were
then regulated. The policing of immigrant women on the basis of sexuality also enabled the discursive production of exclusionary forms of nationalism that took concrete shape in immigration laws and procedures,
but extended well beyond the border to produce particular visions of the
U.S. nation and citizenry.

To date, immigration and sexuality scholars have devoted limited attention to analyzing how immigration control actively participates in the
reproduction of sexual identities, categories, and norms.[7] By contrast,
there exists a well-developed scholarship about how immigration control
has reproduced racial, ethnic, and class distinctions. Some of that scholarship goes beyond the important work of describing histories of immigrants' unequal access on the basis of these distinctions to also explore
how immigration control actively contributed to producing these categoric distinctions in the first place. For instance, the research literature
makes clear that, although Chinese immigrants were targeted for exclusion since the inception of federal immigration control, deciding who
was Chinese was never simply a matter of empirical fact—it was always a
moment of social construction.[8] Immigration officials initially relied on
the notion that Chinese people came from the country "China" in order
to enforce the Chinese exclusion law of 1882. But they eventually had to
reckon with the fact that Chinese people also came from the Americas,
and they had to decide whether to admit people who claimed Chinese
ancestry but South or Central American nationality (since the former
were prohibited but the latter were not). Officials also had to decide how
to classify and process immigrants with one Chinese and one non-
Chinese parent.[9] The immigration service's changing constructions of
Chinese identity drew on existing U.S. racial taxonomies. But they also

helped to extend and rework these taxonomies in particular ways and served as a site where people challenged such racial taxonomies and the inequalities that they sanctioned.

Chinese exclusion was also organized on the basis of class, with laborers excluded after 1882, while merchants were allowed entry until 1924. Consequently, U.S. officials and courts ended up sorting out (and, in the process, imposing particular definitions of) these class distinctions. For instance, the 1893 McCreary Amendment established strict guidelines for determining who was, and was not, a Chinese merchant for purposes of immigration. The amendment became law despite the fact that Californians petitioned for the exclusion of all the Chinese on the grounds that "there is no 'merchant class' in the sense we use the word" among them.[10] In turn, the amendment contributed to the construction and elevation of a distinctive merchant class within Chinese immigrant communities in the United States.

The history of Chinese exclusion makes clear that the immigration-control system actively contributed to manufacturing the racial, ethnic, and class categories around which admission and exclusion were organized.[11] Feminist scholarship has similarly traced how immigration control reconstructed racialized, class-differentiated forms of patriarchy that determined which women were permitted to enter the United States and the terms on which they entered.[12] But despite a wealth of articles, no book-length study has addressed how immigration control was also organized to respond to sexuality considerations and, in the process, to construct sexual identities and norms. When sexuality has been addressed, it is generally conflated with gender or racial disenfranchisement rather than analyzed as a distinct axis through which the admission and exclusion of immigrants have been organized.

Entry Denied: Controlling Sexuality at the Border therefore explores how U.S. federal immigration control has been organized around sexuality, in ways that intersect with gender, race, and class criteria without being reducible to them.[13] The work of French philosopher Michel Foucault, especially his books *The History of Sexuality* (volume 1) and *Discipline and Punish,* offers particularly useful tools for examining these relations of power. Granted, Foucault never wrote directly about U.S. immigration control.[14] He has been justly criticized by Ann Laura Stoler for failing to attend to the nation-making and imperial processes through which the histories of sexuality that he traces emerged—a criticism that is directly relevant here, since nation-making and imperialism are integrally related to U.S. immigration control and the construction of sexual identities at U.S. borders.[15] Stoler, like other critics, also indicates the limitations of Foucault's writings on race and gender.[16]

Despite such criticisms, I find Foucault's work very useful in thinking through the connections between U.S. immigration control and the construction of sexual categories, identities, and norms. Foucault's basic account of sexuality, which I have extended to indicate links to U.S. immigration control, suggests that in the nineteenth century the "calculated management of life" emerged as a key objective of liberal governments.[17] The calculated management of life represented a break from earlier rationalities of state that were driven by concepts of divine ordering or the power of monarchs to take life or let live.[18] It necessitated attention and intervention into the life of both the individual and the species or population group. Sexuality was particularly targeted because, as Foucault describes, "on the one hand, it was tied to the discipline of the body . . . on the other hand, it applied to the regulation of populations."[19]

Immigration control is clearly one key dimension of the calculated management of life, because immigration is one of four ways that the United States has acquired new population. The other three ways have been slavery, annexation/colonization, and "natural reproduction." People seeking to immigrate were evaluated both as potential elements of the larger population group called "American" and as individual bodies to be disciplined.[20] Racial and ethnic barriers have always constrained who could be considered an actual or potential "American." Therefore, immigration officials considered (and thereby helped to construct) the racial, ethnic, and class identities of intending immigrants. At the same time, they considered what would happen if these various immigrant groups gave birth to significant numbers of children or had sexual relations or intermarried with "Americans." As Havelock Ellis expressed the concern, "the question of sex—with the racial questions that rest on it—stands before the coming generations as the chief problem for solution."[21] As these chapters show, since sexual behavior was a crucial nexus through which the racial and ethnic order could become altered, immigration was regulated accordingly. But this history also makes clear that the calculated management of life, which necessitated attention to sexuality, was always designed to foster only certain populations while other populations remained unfostered to the point of death.[22]

Sexuality was tied not only to questions of population but also to creating disciplined individuals. According to Foucault, modern forms of state power have assumed a disciplinary cast and operate by initially targeting the body. Sandra Lee Bartky explains that "more is required of the body now than mere political allegiance or the appropriation of the products of its labor: the new discipline invades the body and seeks to regulate its very forces and operations, the economy and efficiency of its movements."[23] Discipline involves detailed behavioral regimes, systems of ongoing surveillance, and normative standards against which every action or aspect of one's being is continually evaluated. The result is the production of docile, disciplined bodies and individuals who are not just subjects but subjected. Sexuality became a particularly effective locus for the production of disciplined individuals, as experts in areas including medicine, psychiatry, and law began to focus on it, analyze it, classify it, and "insert [it] into systems of utility."[24] These experts' activities facilitated the use of sexuality as a means for the "specification of individuals" in ways that then suggested how these individuals could be managed.[25]

Foucault's most famous example of these processes concerns homosexuality. Sodomitical acts had long been known and variously judged. But in the nineteenth century, experts began to suggest that those who engaged in sodomy were distinct "types" of people who belonged in a category called "homosexual" (rather than random individuals who had committed a particular act). As a result,

> the nineteenth century homosexual became a personage, a past, a case history, and a childhood, in addition to being a type of life, a life form, and a morphology with an indiscreet anatomy and a possibly mysterious physiology. Nothing that went into his total composition was unaffected by his sexuality . . . the homosexual was now a species.[26]

The delineation of "the homosexual" as a distinct type legitimated efforts to identify such persons, keep them under surveillance, and attempt their rehabilitation.

As subsequent chapters show, the immigration apparatus sought to identify and control not just "homosexuals" but also other categories of people to whom Foucault refers as the "peripheral sexualities," each of whom was deemed to threaten the nation.[27] Chinese women coming to engage in prostitution were the first of the peripheral sexual figures to become delineated by the U.S. immigration apparatus. Efforts to police Chinese women laid the groundwork for the subsequent delineation and surveillance of a whole host of other "dangerous" peripheral sexual figures. Yet the example of Chinese women also shows that "peripheral sexuality" at the U.S. border was delineated within a broader framework than the homo/hetero binary and focus on orientation that frames much contemporary thinking on sexuality. Immigrants were excluded not only on the basis of sexual orientation but also on the basis of particular sexual acts, when these acts became known to immigration officials. For instance, bigamy, sex outside of marriage, and adultery have at various times been a basis for exclusion. Furthermore, various officially designated identities—not just sexual, but also gendered, racial, ethnic, and class-based—were treated as evidence that undesirable sexual acts would likely occur. The historic practice of barring (or making extremely difficult) the entry of working-class Chinese women, because their intersecting gender, class, ethnic, and racial identities led to suspicion that they were likely to engage in prostitution, offers a paradigmatic example of how racialized gender identities were treated as presupposing particular sexual acts.[28] Even when these acts had not actually taken place, the fear that they might occur was grounds for exclusion. Thus, peripheral sexual figures at the U.S. border included the racialized prostitute, the amoral and despotic pimp, the fecund woman whose reproduction was uncontrolled, the gold-digging hussy intent on snaring an American husband, and the foreigner who threatened miscegenation.

Experts' methods for specifying individuals within sexual taxonomies particularly hinged around examination, a procedure that "combines the techniques of an observing hierarchy and those of normalizing judgment."[29] This book shows that examination lies at the heart of immigration control, as immigrants' bodies, documents, biographies, and appearances are examined, and they are required to answer any questions put to them by immigration officials. According to Foucault, "what was involved [in these procedures] was the very production of sexuality itself."[30]

The production of sexuality through examination processes not only individuated each woman but at the same time tied her into the wider network of surveillance that Foucault vividly described as the "carceral archipelago" of modern society.[31] The description of modern society as a carceral archipelago draws attention to the ways that disciplinary power does not inhabit any one institution (though it is deployed through institutions) but rather works between and across institutions. Indeed, Dreyfus and Rabinow write that disciplinary power "does not replace other forms of power which existed in society. Rather, it 'invests' or colonizes them, linking them together, honing their efficiency."[32] The term "archipelago" refuses a theory of the centralized state and its institutions, even while it draws attention to the ways that procedures utilized by institutions like the immigration service intersect with the functioning of other state institutions.[33] Foucault's image of the carceral archipelago makes clear that even when the processing of immigrants resulted in their admission, it also situated them within larger relations of power to which they remained subjected after entry.

Several examples illustrate this point. Processing generally confers legal status ("legal residency") on immigrants. Yet legal residency is not the same as citizenship.[34] Legal residents always face restrictions on employment, entitlements to public benefits, voting rights, and possibilities for political activism.[35] A concrete illustration of how immigrants become situated within networks of surveillance, based on their status, is two recent bills, the Anti-Terrorism and Effective Death Penalty Act and the Illegal Immigration Reform and Immigrant Responsibility Act, both signed into law in 1996. These bills greatly expanded the crimes for which legal residents of the United States can be deported, regardless of how long they have lived here. The bills also stripped immigration judges of the power to consider mitigating circumstances, such as length of residence or family and community ties. Legal residents had previously been deportable for serious crimes such as murder, rape, and various drug and firearm trafficking offenses. But since 1996 they have also become deportable for any crime that carries a sentence of one year—even if the sentence is suspended—and for "crimes of moral turpitude."[36] Activities such as shoplifting, writing bad checks, consensual sex with someone under eighteen, drunk driving, or hotwiring a car are now also potential grounds for deportation. Since the law applies retroactively, people have found themselves deportable for such incidents that occurred long ago. Along with murderers and drug dealers, the people being deported nowadays include Jesus Collado, who, in 1974, at the age of nineteen,

> was convicted of a misdemeanor offense for having sex with his teenage girlfriend. He was not sentenced to any period of incarceration. In the twenty-three years since, he has maintained a clean record, married a U.S. citizen, and had three citizen children. One week after the new immigration law went into effect, Mr. Collado returned from a three-week visit to the Dominican Republic—only to be detained and placed in removal proceedings for his 1974 conviction.[37]

Other potential deportees include more than five hundred legal immigrants who were rounded up in Texas for having at least three drunk-driving convictions.[38] They also include "Ana Flores," who bit a habitually abusive husband after he sat on her and hit her. In January 1999 two INS agents came to her house and arrested her for deportation because she was charged with biting her husband during a domestic dispute.[39]

The fact that legal residents now find themselves potentially deportable for such wide-ranging but often mundane activities has prompted widespread criticism, including that by the INS. Several bills to change the law were introduced into Congress, and on 25 June 2001 the Supreme Court ruled "that the INS could not apply the 1996 immigration laws retroactively to immigrants who pleaded guilty to crimes committed before the laws were passed. The court also ruled that the right of judicial review of the INS's interpretation of law survived the 1996 immigration statutes."[40] On 28 June 2001 the Supreme Court ruled that immigrants who committed crimes that rendered them deportable cannot remain in indefinite detention, either.[41] While the Supreme Court's June 2001 decisions provided some measure of relief from detention and deportation for legal immigrants, the events of September 11 of that year resulted in new, sweeping changes to U.S. immigration law. The USA PATRIOT Act of October 2001 included provisions that strengthened the government's ability to detain and deport immigrants.[42] The names of and charges filed against immigrants who have been detained in connection with the September 11 incidents are still unclear. There have been reports that some detainees have been held in facilities that also house convicted criminals and have been subjected to abuse and ill treatment by inmates or guards who feel that "they are doing something for their country" by abusing detainees—including detainees who have no connection to the events of September 11.[43] Clearly, inspection at the border is not a one-time experience but is rather, as Foucault's image of the carceral archipelago suggests, a process that situates immigrants within lifelong networks of surveillance and disciplinary relations.[44] Nowadays, the carceral archipelago also operates in a very concrete form. Not only can immigrants be detained and expelled at borders—they are the fastest-growing incarcerated population within the United States.[45]

In sum, Foucault's general framework, especially in *History of Sexuality* (volume 1) and *Discipline and Punish*, suggests rich possibilities for analyzing the connections between sexuality and U.S. immigration control. His work also indicates three particular areas of inquiry that can be usefully pursued by immigration scholars. These areas are, first, an insistence on the centrality of sexuality as an axis of power through which immigration admission and exclusion have been organized. Second, a healthy skepticism toward all claims about immigrants' "real" identities, sexual or otherwise, and a demand that scholars examine the operations of power that both produce and naturalize such identities. Finally, Foucault draws attention to the ways that writing, including the creation of official immigration records and the books that scholars write based on these records, is centrally implicated in disciplining and subjecting immigrants. These three lines of inquiry are described in more detail below.

Immigration Control and Official Heterosexuality

Foucault was correct to insist on the centrality of sexuality as an axis of power, as shown by this book's upcoming chapters. Sexual regulation at the border matters, not just on its own terms but also because it draws on and reinforces systems of sexual regulation that are directed at populations living within the United States. Robert Chang has eloquently described the mutually constitutive nature of regulation at and within the border, by suggesting that historically subordinated groups within the United States "carry a figurative border with us."[46] According to Chang, heightened anxieties about policing the territorial border quickly translate into heightened anxieties about policing those *within* the territory, especially those who carry these bodily "figurative borders."[47]

To understand how these mutually reinforcing processes work, we must first grasp how immigration control in general constructs and naturalizes the idea of the United States as a distinct nation, people, and territory. Benedict Anderson has convincingly argued that nations and nationalisms are "cultural artifacts of a particular kind" that came into relatively recent being through historical processes that he traces.[48] The border and immigration control, which are "extremely powerful symbols of national identity and national autonomy," are central to nation-making.[49] The border "separates[s] the inside from the outside" and delineates not just the territory of the nation but also the people who supposedly belong in the territory.[50] In the late nineteenth century the Supreme Court granted Congress plenary power over immigration because "a sovereign nation must be able to exercise control over its borders. That's what it means to be a sovereign entity."[51] The doctrine gave Congress broad powers over immigration, including the ability to bar immigrants for discriminatory and arbitrary reasons, and it significantly shielded these powers from judicial review.[52]

Immigration control is not just a powerful symbol of nationhood and people but also a means to *literally* construct the nation and the people in particular ways. This fact has been compellingly documented through analyses of how immigration exclusions have produced particular racial, ethnic, and class compositions in the United States.[53] Yet immigration control has been equally integral to the reproduction of patriarchal heterosexuality as the nation's official sexual and gender order. Feminist

analyses have shown that women's bodies often demarcate the boundaries between groups that are defined in fundamentally patriarchal
terms.[54] Floya Anthias and Nira Yuval Davis further explain that "often
the distinction between one ethnic [or national] group and another is
constituted centrally by the sexual behaviour of women."[55] Under these
circumstances, "the nation becomes gendered, and women's sexuality becomes nationalized. Nation is equated with the male subject position,
and women's sexuality is reified as the property of the male nation."[56] As
a result, "heterosexuality [becomes] at once necessary to the state's ability
to constitute and imagine itself, while simultaneously marking the site of
its own instability."[57] The lesbian and the prostitute, who fail to conform
to the heterosexual imperative, emerge as figures that particularly threat-
en the nation and have to be disciplined.[58]

The immigration-control system has historically disciplined lesbians
and prostitutes by refusing them entry. Even after the ban on lesbians (but
not prostitutes) was lifted in 1990, lesbian immigrants still faced distinct
difficulties, including the fact that their intimate relationships with U.S.
citizens can never enable them to become legal residents. By contrast, intimate relationships enable heterosexuals to legalize. These discriminatory immigration policies were reaffirmed by the 1996 Defense of Marriage
Act (DOMA), which defined marriage as a male/female union. Importantly, DOMA's provisions applied not just to immigrants but also to U.S.
residents and citizens. The provisions reinforced a constellation of discriminatory laws and social practices directed at U.S. lesbians and gays,
including the refusal of the federal government to prohibit discrimination in housing and employment on the basis of sexual orientation.
DOMA, then, provides an example of how sexual regulation at the border
connects to sexual regulation within, and how such regulation punishes
anyone who does not conform to the nation's heterosexual imperative.

Race and class distinctions have further determined whose heterosexualities become valued, and here again exclusions at the border articulate exclusions within. In the mid-1990s Pete Wilson campaigned for re-
election as governor of California by portraying immigrant Mexican
women's sexuality and childbearing as a threat to the state's systems for
delivery of social, educational, health, and welfare services. Wilson's tactic drew on a long history of politicians who have risen to power by de-
monizing the childbearing of poor, minority, and immigrant women,
and immigration laws that have systematically barred the entry of poor
and minority mothers (see chapter 1). As part of his campaign, Wilson
published an "Open Letter to the President of the United States on Behalf

of the People of California" in the *New York Times,* which included the following:

> Why does the U.S. government reward illegal immigrants who successfully violate the law and manage to have a child born on U.S. soil? Rather than penalizing it, we reward their illegal act: we pay for delivery and confer U.S. citizenship on the baby. Why does the U.S. reward illegal immigrants by requiring states to pay for the exploding costs of their health care, education, and other benefits? . . . In Los Angeles alone, there is an illegal community who, with their *250,000* citizen children, number *just under a million*—or one and a half times the population of Washington, D.C.[59]

Wilson's claims legitimated heightened immigration-control efforts that particularly targeted Mexican women and men (see chapter 5). It also reinforced a long-standing provision of immigration law that denies entry to anyone deemed "liable to become a public charge," which has been used particularly against poor and minority women of childbearing age for more than a century.

Lawmakers seeking to reform welfare quickly took up Wilson's strategy by attributing a host of social ills to the allegedly irresponsible sexual behavior of poor and minority women within the United States. Welfare reform rhetoric became largely organized around the idea of controlling the "unbridled sexuality of usually racialized welfare mothers" rather than responding to such issues as low wages in the service sector, the shortage of subsidized childcare, and institutionalized discrimination.[60] Gwendolyn Mink summarizes the outcome of welfare reform, as codified by the Personal Responsibility and Work Opportunity Reconciliation Act (PRA) of 1996:

> [The Act] hardens legal differences among women [in the United States] based on their marital, maternal, class, and racial statuses. It segregates poor single mothers into a separate caste, subject to a separate system of laws. While middle-class women may choose to participate in the labor market, poor single mothers are forced by law to do so (work requirements and time limits). While middle-class women may choose to bear children, poor single mothers may be punished by the government for making that choice (the family cap and illegitimacy ratios). While middle-class women enjoy still-strong rights to sexual and reproductive privacy, poor single mothers are compelled by the government to reveal the details of intimate relationships in exchange

for survival (mandatory maternal cooperation in establishing paternity). And while middle-class mothers may choose their children's fathers by marrying them or permitting them to develop relationships with children—or not—poor mothers are required by law to make room for biological fathers in their families (mandatory cooperation in establishing and enforcing child support orders).[61]

These gender- and class-differentiated effects intersected with long-standing racial inequalities, too. Mink explains:

> Although work requirements [mandating that women on welfare work] apply indiscriminately to all poor single mothers, it is poor mothers of color who bear their heaviest weight. African American and Latina mothers are disproportionately poor and, accordingly, are disproportionately enrolled on welfare. . . . So when welfare rules indenture poor mothers as unpaid servants of local governments (in workfare programs), it is mothers of color who are disproportionately harmed. And when time limits require mothers to forsake their children for the labor market, it is mothers of color who are disproportionately deprived of their right to manage their family's lives and it is children of color who are disproportionately deprived of their mothers' care.[62]

Welfare reform, which substantially ended much public assistance rather than poverty, thus multiplied inequalities within the United States by once again targeting poor and minority women's heterosexualities for surveillance, control, and punishment.[63]

These examples make clear that although patriarchal heterosexuality has been elevated as a national imperative, race and class dimensions further determine whose heterosexualities are valued and whose are subject to surveillance and punishment. Welfare and immigration laws work in tandem to control poor and minority women's heterosexualities, making it more difficult for them to legally enter the United States and ensuring that such women within the United States are subject to punitive regimes and negative stereotyping.[64] Sexual regulation at the border articulates sexual regulation within.

Cramped Conceptions of Domination

But to grasp how struggles at the border connect to struggles within the United States, prevailing accounts of immigration exclusion need to be challenged. These accounts suggest that because explicitly discriminatory provisions based on race, ethnicity, and sexual orientation have been stricken from immigration law, immigration control is now implemented fairly. The editors of *Critical Race Theory* note that such arguments "treat the exercise of racial [and other] power as rare and aberrational rather than as systemic and ingrained."[65] They further comment that "within this cramped conception of racial domination, the evil of racism exists when—and only when—one can point to specific, discrete acts of racial discrimination, which is in turn narrowly defined as decision-making based on the irrational and irrelevant attribute of race."[66] Such a cramped conception "place[s] virtually the entire range of everyday social practices in America—social practices developed and maintained throughout the period of formal American apartheid—beyond the scope of critical examination or legal remediation."[67] Gender, class, and sexuality discrimination are conceived in equally narrow terms.

Historically, sexuality, gender, race, and class were explicitly considered when U.S. officials made decisions about whom to admit and exclude. But contrary to both conservative and liberal critics, I suggest that these were never self-evident attributes that people already "had." Rather, Foucault's framework suggests that immigration-control practices, down to their most mundane procedural details, produced and naturalized these identities. Therefore, sexuality—and by extension, race, gender, and class—have been central to immigration control since its inception not because these are essential or biological identities that can be discovered within individual bodies, but because sexualization, racialization, and so on are larger social processes whose presence is made evident by the classification of bodies into hierarchical schemes. Such classification schemes, which were rooted in histories of imperialism and modern state formation, ensured that those granted admission were incorporated into relations of surveillance and discipline within the United States.

Although immigration officials no longer explicitly categorize bodies within racial taxonomies or automatically exclude lesbians and gay men, that does not mean that racialization, sexualization, and other similar processes have been abolished. Nor does it mean that there are no longer disparities in immigration access on the basis of sexuality, race, and other categories. On the contrary, David Reimers's research compellingly suggests that even when racial criteria were excised from immigration law in 1965, lawmakers nonetheless intended for neutral admission criteria to have distinctly racial effects. By replacing the discriminatory national origins quota system with preferences that were based mainly on family ties, lawmakers expected that "the great bulk of immigrants henceforth will not merely hail from the same parent countries as our present citizens, but will be their closer relatives."[68] In other words, although openly racist provisions were removed, the law was nonetheless intended to uphold the virtual exclusion of immigrants of color. Reimer's argument echoes the decades of research on equal access to education and employment, which shows that seemingly neutral bureaucratic requirements often generate racist, (hetero)sexist, and classist effects. Various architects of the 1965 Immigration and Nationality Act (INA) apparently understood and tried to manipulate this fact. But even if they had not intended to discriminate, the 1965 INA might still have had discriminatory consequences. As Naomi Zack explains, "much institutional [discrimination] in the United States at this time is not intentional" but is nonetheless evident when one examines the outcomes, rather than intentions, of particular policies.[69]

Thus, to suggest that the seemingly neutral provisions of immigration law mark the "end" of immigration discrimination ignores both Reimers's specific research on the 1965 INA and the voluminous general scholarship on institutional discrimination. Foucault's work particularly contributes to our understanding of how immigration inequalities are institutionally reproduced by drawing attention to supposedly neutral, mundane practices of inspection and regimes of knowledge that actually discipline and subject immigrants in racializing, sexualizing, and other ways.[70] Consequently, rather than proclaiming the demise of discrimination in immigration access, we would be better served by developing more complex and nuanced accounts of how sexualization, racialization, and other processes continue to be imposed and contested at multiple levels in the immigration system today, including through inspection procedures and knowledge regimes. The importance of such analyses inheres not only in the scale and impact of contemporary immigration, but also in the fact that relations of power and inequality at the border cannot be separated from inequitable global relations that structure migration patterns or from social hierarchies within the United States.

Finally, Foucault draws attention to the ways that inspection procedures and decision-making at the border are tied to record-keeping and writing practices that comprise "a means of control and a method of domination."[71] As he explains, inspection is accompanied by "a system of intense registration and of documentary accumulation."[72] These writing practices at once constitute each individual as a "describable, analysable object" and as part of a larger corpus of knowledge that involves "the measurement of overall phenomena, the characterization of collective facts, the calculation of gaps between individuals, of their distribution in a given 'population.'"[73] This knowledge is used for distinctly disciplinary ends. Foucault's analysis of how official immigration records function as essential elements of a larger disciplinary system has important implications for immigration scholarship. At the very least, it suggests that scholars need to critically evaluate how the written materials on which we draw are part of, and therefore help to reproduce, the disciplinary apparatus that subjectifies immigrants. Equally, methods for reading official documents against the grain, utilized by scholars such as those engaged in subaltern studies, may prove to have great relevance for immigration scholarship too.

These were the lines of inquiry that emerged when I read Foucault's work in conjunction with U.S. immigration history. The chapters that follow are intended to extend these lines of inquiry, while also generating useful dialogue between immigration, sexuality, gender, and racial scholars.

"Identities beyond the Inscriptions of the State"

A book that focuses largely on immigration-control procedures may easily be understood to reinforce the common assumption that people seek legal status in order to move permanently to the United States and integrate into society. This assumption is in line with the state's view of the immigration process but has been challenged by recent scholarship that shows people seek legal status for other reasons as well. For instance, Jacqueline Hagan's ethnography of Maya immigrants in Houston shows that many applied for legalization under the Immigration Reform and Control Act of 1986, even though they expected to be denied, as a way to acquire short-term work authorization. As Hagan explains, "increasingly, immigrants began to define the program in terms of their immediate needs, paying little heed to the long-term implications of permanent residence or citizenship."[74]

Scholarship on transnationalism indicates other reasons why people seek legal status even when they do not expect to become progressively incorporated into society. Glick Schiller and her colleagues define transnationals as those who "take actions, make decisions, and feel concerns, and develop identities within social networks that connect them to two or more societies simultaneously."[75] Increasing numbers of contemporary U.S. migrants have transnational lives, for important reasons that Patricia Pessar describes. First, changes in the structure of global capitalism "contribute to deteriorating social and economic conditions in both home and host societies with no locale being, necessarily, a secure site of permanent settlement."[76] Second, institutional racial discrimination discourages "immigrants of color" from "pursuing long-term or permanent settlement in the United States."[77] Finally, nation-building projects in both host and home societies solicit migrants' loyalties. President Aristide's efforts to draw on the resources of overseas Haitian migrants, whom he characterized as Haiti's "Tenth Department" and integral to Haiti's future, is just one among many examples of how "sending" countries continue to solicit migrants' loyalties.[78]

Under these conditions, many contemporary immigrants live "chronically astride borders."[79] They seek to maximize their possibilities by "continuously translat[ing] the economic and social position gained in one political setting into political, social, and economic capital in another."[80] Sexuality is one dimension of symbolic, social, cultural, and economic capital that some migrants seek to transform through transnational migration. Acquisition of U.S. legal residence may be desired not so that migrants can settle, but so that they can more easily translate various forms of capital from one setting to another. Underscoring transnational migrants' complex reasons for seeking legal status, Nonini and Ong characterize them as people who "cast identities beyond the inscriptions and identifications made by the state" and whose search for legal status cannot be captured by statist accounts of immigration.[81] Given these circumstances, this book focuses on the connections between sexuality and immigrant women's efforts to legally cross the border but does not assume that such efforts are necessarily directed toward unilateral settlement in the United States.[82]

This book focuses primarily on how the immigration service tried to determine if an applicant was eligible for admission or not. Since relations of power and knowledge varied depending on time of entry, place of entry, and the people involved, each chapter is built around specific immigration case histories, which are then situated in relation to larger histories. Court documents and decisions, congressional hearings, immigration-service manuals, exclusionist writings, and newspaper accounts provide other valuable sources on which the analysis depends. I do not attempt to theorize immigrant women's multiple forms of agency, except to the extent that it is visibly inscribed in official documents—which in some cases it is. However, there are important realms of agency that cannot be traced unless official documents are supplemented with some other kinds of inquiry, which is a task for future research.[83]

In order to provide necessary contextual information for the chapters

that follow, chapter 1 offers an overview of the major immigration laws
through which women's sexualities have been regulated since the federal
government took charge of immigration control in the late nineteenth
century. It shows that while federal control promoted sexual activity
within marriage, concern about the "dangers" presented by the birth of
children to poor or racial minority families further shaped how immigrant women's cases were adjudicated. At the same time, efforts were
made to delineate and exclude a series of "peripheral" sexual figures, including prostitutes and lesbians, because they were deemed a threat to
the nation.

Since Chinese prostitutes were the first of the peripheral sexual figures
to be delineated and targeted for exclusion, chapter 2 describes how officials tried to differentiate Chinese prostitutes from wives after the passage of the Page Law of 1875. The chapter argues that these efforts transformed immigration control into a system of sexual regulation, which
came to encompass any immigrant who sought entry to the United States.

Chapter 3 draws on the history of Japanese picture brides in California from 1908 to 1920 to show how racial distinctions were formally introduced into immigration laws that promoted conjugal sexuality. Using
anti-immigrant writings, the chapter traces how exclusionist sentiment
coalesced around the pregnant body of the married Japanese immigrant
wife. The Immigration Act of 1924 codified the reservation of heteropatriarchal privileges for Europeans, predominantly of Western or Northern origin, and revealed how pregnancy and childbearing remain ar-
rogated to remaking the nation within strict racial, gender, and class
parameters.

Chapter 4, built from the court documents generated by Mexican-
born Sara Harb Quiroz's battle with the immigration service in 1960 and
1961, describes the only documented case (so far) of a woman deported
from the United States on charges of lesbianism. The chapter uses Quiroz's
case as a means to renarrate the history of lesbian and gay immigration
exclusion in ways that center, rather than subsume, women's experiences.
It also details how lesbians and gays might come to the attention of the
immigration service at multiple points, the mechanisms used to exclude
or deport them, and how the demand for sexual confession structures
immigration monitoring.

Chapter 5 turns its attention to two other bureaucracies that police
U.S. borders: the Border Patrol and the Refugee/Asylum system. Since
routine sexual violence has come to shape who can and cannot legally
cross the border, the chapter examines how the Border Patrol and refugee/

asylum system conceptualize and respond to women's experiences of rape, and how their responses shape women's possibilities for admission into the United States. Focusing on the 1980s and 1990s, the chapter argues that although each system's different response to rape shows disjunctures within the apparatus for managing immigration into the United States, they nonetheless each contribute to the reproduction of exclusionary forms of dominant nationalism that ensure the continued marginalization of women once they have crossed into U.S. territory.

Taken together, the chapters make clear that the immigration apparatus has been a major site for the construction and regulation of immigrant women's sexual identities and activities. Such regulation was integrally related to racial, gender, class, and national concerns. Yet although sexuality has been central to immigration control, the book argues that immigration officials never simply discovered pre-given sexualities that already existed within immigrant women. Rather, multiple processes and discourses that varied by time, location, and the individuals involved were brought to bear upon immigrant women in ways that contributed to producing the sexualities around which immigration monitoring was organized. As a result of these procedures, some women became barred from entering the United States on the ground that their sexualities presented a threat to the nation. Even when women were admitted to the United States, immigration procedures ensured that they became incorporated into webs of surveillance that disciplined them and produced them as "good" citizens, in gendered, sexualized, racial, and class terms.

1. Entry Denied

A History of U.S. Immigration Control

This chapter overviews major laws and policies and describes how they produced and regulated women's sexuality, under the federal immigration control system. However, federal immigration control was fully institutionalized only in 1891. Between 1875 and 1890, the federal government operated in partnership with individual states to manage the flow of immigration. In this time period, changes not only led to full federal control but also gave rise to strategies for regulating women's sexuality that became incorporated into the federal system. Therefore, the chapter first describes major changes that occurred in immigration control between 1875 and 1890. Second, it analyzes how these changes generated methods for regulating women's sexuality that were institutionalized in the federal system. Third, it summarizes the Act of 1891, which consolidated complete federal control over immigration, and then reviews subsequent major legislation, with particular focus on how this legislation expanded the codification of sexual regulation. The review makes clear that the regulation of sexuality has to be analyzed in terms of its constitutive interconnections with gender, racial, ethnic, class, and national concerns. At times, the narrative focuses more on these concerns than on sexuality. Thus, the narrative necessarily challenges "the status of [sexuality] itself as the authentic and centrally governing category" through which sexual histories must always be appraised.[1]

Pre-1891 Immigration Control

Until the last quarter of the nineteenth century, immigration control was largely managed by individual states. New York, Pennsylvania, and other states with major ports of entry developed systems for processing new arrivals and passed laws to control costs and exclude the ill, destitute, or criminal. Many less-populated states created programs to recruit immigrants, primarily from Europe, as a labor supply. "Their pamphlets extolled the virtue of the American frontier and its allegedly salubrious climate. An Iowa pamphlet of 1870 described the beauty of an Iowan Indian summer; Minnesota pointed out that its death rates were only a fourth or a third of that in Europe. The theme most emphasized, however, was the contrast between American opportunity and European stagnation."[2]

In 1875 the federal government started to assume a more central role in immigration control. Concomitantly, it made "'selective' immigration the official United States policy."[3] Legal and administrative developments between 1875 and 1890 fueled these twin processes. In 1875 Congress passed the Page Law, which banned the entry of contract laborers, felons, and Asian women brought to the United States for "lewd and immoral purposes." The first two provisions had little effect at the time, but the third provision greatly hampered Chinese women's ability to enter the United States. In 1876 the U.S. Supreme Court ruled that the immigration laws of California, New York, and Louisiana were unconstitutional.[4] The decision "dealt the death blow to efforts by states to regulate immigration."[5] Consequently, the Act of 1882 transferred exclusive authority over immigration to the Secretary of the Treasury, who awarded contracts to individual states to manage immigration on a day-to-day basis.[6] The law also expanded the list of those banned from immigrating, adding convicts, idiots, lunatics, and those likely to become public charges. That same year, the Chinese Exclusion Act barred the entry of all Chinese immigrants except for a select group (students, teachers, merchants, and those "proceeding to the United States from curiosity"). Restrictions further multiplied under the Contract Labor Law of 1885, which forbade the entry of immigrants who were contracted in advance to perform labor or service of any kind. However, Congress added a proviso that "nothing in this act shall be construed as prohibiting any individual from assisting any member of his family or any relative or personal friend to migrate from any foreign country to the United States for purposes of settlement here."[7] E. P. Hutchinson argues that this provision was intended to ensure that increasingly restrictive laws did not separate families.[8]

These developments between 1875 and 1890 accomplished three things. First, they laid the groundwork for complete federal control of immigration in 1891. Second, they established "selective" immigration as federal policy. Third, they institutionalized an approach to regulating women's sexuality that was taken up by the federal immigration-control system after 1891. The next section describes what their approach to regulating women's sexuality involved.

Sexuality and Immigration Control

E. P. Hutchinson claims that federal immigration control "consistently followed a policy of facilitating the coming of families as a unit and the reuniting of families whose members did not all immigrate at the same time."[9] The seeds of family reunification policy were evident in the period 1875–1890, as evinced by the Contract Labor Law's proviso to protect families. Hutchinson's claim demands fuller analysis, however. I argue here that family reunification policies in immigration produced an exclusionary sexual order that was integrally tied to gender, race, and class inequalities.

The exclusionary sexual order derived from the fact that the model of family codified in immigration law involved a husband, a wife, and children born to the couple. As anthropologist David Schneider explains, "family" has historically been defined in the United States as "a cultural unit which contains a husband and a wife who are the father and mother of their child or children."[10] Kath Weston points out that "sexuality is embedded [in this model] in ways that everybody knows but many hesitate to speak about."[11] In the model, sexuality is coded as heterosexual and organized around biological reproduction. The fact that this order is rarely characterized as sexual attests more to the hegemony of heterosexuality than to its inevitability or naturalness. Hegemonic status is not surprising, given that heterosexuality is "necessary to the state's ability to constitute and imagine itself."[12]

Family reunification provisions constructed women's sexuality not just as heterosexual but also as procreative within a patriarchal framework. Consequently, they reified women's sexuality as a form of property that men owned, controlled, and competed over, and that was most appropriately channeled into marriage and reproduction. Women also became subjected to a double standard that made them, but not men, liable to sanction for deviations from sexual norms.[13] The incorporation of these aspects of heterosexual patriarchy (or heteropatriarchy) into immigration control was evident in the case of Catherine Dolan, a pregnant, unmarried Irish woman who decided to immigrate to the United States in 1890. To her misfortune, upon arrival she ended up in an exclusion hearing:

By Commissioner Stephenson:

Q: Why did you come to this country?
A: To work, sir.
Q: Who paid your passage out here?
A: My father.
Q: Your father did?
A: Yes, sir.
Q: Did your father know of your condition before you left Ireland?
A: I don't know.
Q: You have no relatives or friends in this country?
A: No, sir.
Q: How much money have you?
A: Fourteen dollars.

By Commissioner Ridgeway:

Q: How long are you pregnant?
A: I don't know.
Q: When do you expect this child to be born?
A: I don't know.
Q: You don't know?
A: No, sir.

By Commissioner Starr:

Q: Have you ever had a child?
A: No, sir.
Q: Never?
A: Never.

By Commissioner Ridgeway:

Q: You knew the man was a married man, didn't you?
A: I did, sir.

On the motion of Mr. Stephenson, it was voted that the immigrant be not permitted to land, on the ground that she had no relatives or friends in the United States, and was unable to take care of herself.[14]

Dolan may have engineered her immigration as a way to resolve the consequences of her pregnancy outside of marriage. But she framed her immigration primarily as a labor issue—she came to support herself and the child when it was born. The commissioners reframed her immigration within a familial discourse that reduced her to her reproductive functions. They also freely condemned her for being pregnant outside of marriage, although they did not express similar censure of the married man who impregnated her. The double standard made Dolan subject not only to moral condemnation but also to exclusion under the 1882 law that barred entry by anyone liable to become a public charge (LPC). The use of the LPC provision to exclude women who were pregnant outside of marriage had become standard practice, as Dr. John Hamilton, Acting Surgeon General at the U.S. Marine Hospital Services, explained:

> The rule that was adopted within the last few days is that an unmarried woman, arriving in a state of pregnancy which could be discovered by ordinary examination, it was to be considered as presumptive evidence that she would be a public charge, and therefore be returned, be barred from landing because nobody would wish to employ a person in that condition, and it was considered that the chances were that she would have to be cared for by the Government, and therefore she was directed to be returned [sic].[15]

Thus, the pregnant, unmarried Dolan was deemed excludable. But it was highly unlikely that the man who impregnated her would have been similarly excluded.[16] Dolan's story painfully illustrates how the incorporation of patriarchal heterosexual imperatives into immigration policy resulted in the exclusion of women who violated its order.

Family reunification policies also generated a class of women who were excluded because they were deemed to directly threaten heteropatriarchy's dominance. The Page Law of 1875, which barred the arrival of Asian prostitutes, exemplifies this aspect of immigration control. As chapter 2 shows, the Page Law was primarily motivated not by concern for the Asian women involved but by fears that they threatened white heteropatriarchy. Historically, prostitutes occupy an ambiguous relationship to normative constructions of the heteropatriarchal family; they have been viewed both as direct threats to family and as women who enabled "respectable" men to satisfy their sexual appetites while keeping their families intact. However, in immigration law, the construction of the prostitute as a threat has predominated since 1875. The fact that Asian prostitutes, specifically, were targeted by the Page Law underscores the salience of intersecting racial, gender, class, and sexual categories in constructing alleged "threats" to white patriarchy. After the federal government assumed full control of immigration, not just Asian prostitutes but also other categories of women deemed threatening to white heteropatriarchy became targeted for exclusion.

Family reunification provisions also produced racial, ethnic, and class exclusions that intersected with heteropatriarchy, as illustrated by the experience of early Chinese immigrants. Most early Chinese immigrants to the United States were male. Although many were married, their wives remained in China. According to George Peffer, after these pioneering migrants got settled, most would likely have sent for their families.[17] But the Page Law made family reunification particularly hard for the Chinese, because the law's provisions to exclude Asian prostitutes were so vigorously enforced that all Chinese women experienced great difficulty gaining admission. The Chinese Exclusion Act of 1882 compounded their difficulties. Chinese men who were in the United States used the court system to press for their wives' entry. While the courts ruled that the wives of Chinese merchants were eligible to join their spouses, wives of Chinese laborers were not, thus introducing a class distinction around eligibility for family reunification. Wives of U.S. citizens of Chinese ancestry were treated in an inconsistent manner, sometimes being allowed entry and at other times facing debarment.[18]

The experiences of these early Chinese immigrant families foreshadowed what would happen to other Asian families. The fact that Europeans generally did not face these difficulties was a means through which they became implicitly constructed as white. Certainly, many European immigrants were hardly considered "white" on their arrival in the United States in the late nineteenth and early twentieth centuries. But whiteness as a racial category was undergoing reconstruction. As Michael Omi and Howard Winant explain:

> Particularly during the nineteenth century, the category of "white" was subject to challenges brought about the influx of diverse groups who were not of the same Anglo-Saxon stock as the founding immigrants. In the nineteenth century, political and ideological struggles emerged over the classification of Southern Europeans, the Irish and Jews, among other "non-white" categories. Nativism was only effectively curbed by the institutionalization of a racial order that drew the color line *around* rather than *within* Europe.[19]

Immigration control was a key institution through which the renegotiation of whiteness occurred. By privileging family reunification but then preventing nationalities like the Chinese, Japanese, Koreans, Filipinos, and Asian Indians from utilizing these provisions without great struggle, the immigration system ultimately helped to constitute European couples and their children as "white" and reaffirmed that white families were desirable and consonant with the interests in the nation. At the same time, Asians' routine exemption from family reunification affirmed Lisa Lowe's contention that

> the concept of the "immigrant" in American sociology and public policy has historically signified "European immigrants," seeking to universalize the temporality of assimilation attributed to Irish Americans and Italian Americans to ethnic minority groups from the "Third World." . . . This use erases the heterogeneities and hierarchies within the "immigrant" category and obscures the process of racialization that the immigration process instantiates.[20]

Racialization occurred not just through the Page Law and Chinese Exclusion but also through vigorous debates about polygamous families that shaped immigration legislation. Reports of the supposed horrors of plural marriages by the followers of Brigham Young and his Mormon Church in Utah were staples in the press, and in 1875 *Reynolds v. the United States* became a test case over the issue of polygamy.[21] George Reynolds, a prominent Mormon and former secretary to Brigham Young, was tried and convicted of being married to two women. In 1878 the Supreme Court rejected Reynold's argument that antibigamy laws infringed on his free exercise of religion and observed that "polygamy has always been odious among the Northern and Western nations of Europe and, until the establishment of the Mormon Church, almost exclusively a feature of the life of Asiatic and African people."[22] The court's characterization of the dangers of polygamy reflected anti-Chinese discourses of the time, which racialized the Chinese by claiming that they lacked recognizable, respectable family forms. The characterization also articulated continuing cultural anxiety, which had its roots in the pre–Civil War era, about the maintenance of whiteness. For, during slavery, many slaveholding men in effect engaged in polygamy; they had both legal wives and access to slave women who were forced to sexually submit to them and often bore them children.[23] Debates on polygamy, then, entailed complex questions about the connections between sexual, gender, and racial ordering in the making of family, and these debates would also shape federal immigration legislation.[24]

Finally, the multiple and interlocking nature of the exclusions generated by family reunification policies was demonstrated by the fact that even when racial-, ethnic-minority, and/or poor immigrant women channeled their sexuality into marriage and childbearing, their child-bearing was nonetheless singled out as a problem to be addressed by immigration policy. Scholars have shown that eugenicists and others became alarmed by falling native white birth rates in the late nineteenth century and argued that "the stock that founded this nation and nurtured it through the grave perils and trials of the formative period will soon have vanished from the face of the earth."[25] Edward A. Ross described the declining white birthrates as "race suicide," and Dr. Francis Walker, the president of the Massachusetts Institute of Technology, suggested that race suicide was occurring because the native white middle class "shrank from bringing children into the world to compete with the lower standards of immigrants."[26] Fears about the consequences of married immigrant women's childbearing also came to shape immigration control after 1891, as we will see.

In sum, in the period immediately preceding full federal control, immigration policies and laws regulated women's sexuality in a complex and sometimes contradictory manner. Family reunification policies codified a heteropatriarchal sexual and gender order and facilitated the exclusion of women who violated or threatened it. At the same time, heteropatriarchal policies also produced racial, ethnic, and class exclusions. These features became incorporated into the federal immigration system after 1891, where they were further elaborated.

The next section describes the Immigration Act of 1891, which enabled the federal government to assume full control of immigration, as well as all subsequent major legislation, with particular attention to the codification of sexual regulation. As will become evident, sexual regulation under the federal system cannot be accommodated within a linear narrative of movement from repression to liberation but instead demands attention to processes of rearticulation, which Omi and Winant define as "practice[s] of discursive reorganization" that give new meanings or coherence to existing elements.[27] As we will see, the rearticulation of sexual regulation under federal immigration control centrally involved gender, racial, class, and national concerns.

Federal Immigration Control

The Immigration Act of 1891 placed immigration control firmly in the hands of the federal government.[28] The federal government faced the challenge of developing an administrative structure capable of processing large numbers of immigrants. On 12 July 1891 the Bureau of Immigration began operation in the Department of the Treasury, twenty-four border inspection stations were set up, and a system of medical inspection was implemented. "It is from this early structure that the present Federal immigration organization has evolved"[29]

Continuing the tradition of "selective immigration" that began in 1875, the Act of 1891 excluded those deemed likely to become public charges, felons, immigrants whose passage was paid by another ("assisted aliens"), and those with "loathsome and contagious diseases." It forbade the encouragement of immigration by means of advertising. It also introduced the principle of deportation (i.e., expulsion) after entry, which represented a significant expansion in techniques for policing immigrants.

In regard to sexuality, the Act included provisions to exclude those guilty of crimes of moral turpitude. These crimes were tricky to define and encompassed—but extended beyond—the sexual.[30] At different times they included convictions on such charges as adultery, bigamy, rape, statutory rape, and sodomy.[31] The Act also included a provision to exclude polygamists. Since sexuality was becoming medicalized, physicians were instructed to watch for signs of sexually "abnormal" appetites and behavior and for venereal disease.

In 1903, in response to organizational and administrative problems that had become evident, Congress transferred the Bureau of Immigration to the newly created Department of Commerce and Labor and further revised the immigration laws. The revisions mandated the deportation of all immigrants who became public charges within two years of entering the United States. They also required the exclusion of anarchists, epileptics, "persons who have been insane within five years previously," and "persons who have had two or more attacks of insanity at any time previously."[32]

In terms of sexuality, the Act of 1903 reiterated the ban on entry by polygamists. It also excluded prostitutes, procurers, and anyone who tried to bring a woman to the United States for purposes of prostitution.[33] *The Book of Instructions for the Medical Inspection of Immigrants* listed syphilis and gonorrhea as grounds for exclusion. Pregnancy, regardless of marital status, was also listed, because it was believed to render women likely to become public charges.[34]

Identifying which women were pregnant was not always easy. One Ellis Island physician described his personal trick for identifying possibly pregnant women: "on the left side of any immigrant woman's head was a strand of hair which under normal conditions, was more or less lustrous. If it hung dull and lifeless over her ear, it marked her at once as possibly pregnant."[35] Such methods were defensible not just because of limitations in diagnostic technology and the sheer numbers that had to be processed but also because physicians' jobs were not to determine *what* medical condition immigrants had, but only that they *might* have one. Once an immigrant was singled out as possibly having a medical condition, doctors took time to more thoroughly verify his or her diagnosis. Some immigrants were aware that pregnancy could be used as a basis for exclusion and responded accordingly. Vera Gauditsa, a married woman from Czechoslovakia, described her experiences being processed at Ellis Island in this way:

> This Czech lady was talking to me about am I going to have a baby. I said yes, I was pregnant five months. At that time I was afraid I was going to mix everything up and say eight months. Maybe they would ship me back or something like that! It was against the law in those days to immigrate more than five months pregnant. But I was a pretty good liar, so all of the time I did not get myself confused and was telling them "five months!"[36]

The costs associated with pregnancy and childbearing also became the ground for the deportation of some poor women after they had been admitted. For example, while recovering from giving birth at City Hospital on Blackwell's Island in New York, twenty-year-old Maria Gambacurta from Italy was served with a warrant ordering her deportation. She was judged to have become a public charge because the hospital was supported by public funds. She and her newborn were deported to Italy, and the immigration service paid the $33 bill for her hospital stay.[37]

In 1907 another act expanded the list of exclusions to include "imbeciles," the "feeble-minded," persons with physical or mental defects that might affect their ability to earn a living, persons with tuberculosis, children unaccompanied by their parents, and persons who admitted the commission of a crime involving moral turpitude (described above).

Sexuality provisions of the Act of 1907 included a reiteration of the ban on the entry of polygamists and new exclusions directed at persons who admitted their belief in the practice of polygamy.[38] The law further provided for the exclusion of prostitutes, procurers, and any woman or girl who came to the United States for "any other immoral purpose."[39] Under the law, anyone who "shall keep, maintain, control, support, or harbor" a woman or girl for purposes of prostitution or any other immoral purpose within three years of her entry could be charged with a felony.[40] The ways that immorality was defined, and how it was differentiated from other grounds for exclusion, were complex and fluid. Deportation cases show that this provision was used, for example, against immigrant girls and women who became sexually involved with men outside of marriage. A man who paid for his female lover to join him in the United States was technically importing a woman for immoral purposes, while the woman herself was designated as immoral. (Whether the man should be considered immoral in such circumstances was subject to debate among immigration service personnel.)[41] Subsequent acts reaffirmed the exclusion of "immoral" women. The Act of 1907 also introduced a significant new policy: the deportation of any woman who began practicing prostitution within three years after entering the United States (even if she had not practiced prostitution before entry).

In 1908 the United States signed the Gentlemen's Agreement with Japan, ending the immigration of Japanese laborers to the United States. Since Korea was under Japanese rule, Korean laborers faced similar restrictions. However, the Agreement also made provisions for Japanese men living in the United States to send for wives (see chapter 3), thus reflecting the complex weave of racism, class concerns, and heteropatriarchal assumptions that shaped immigration legislation.

By this time, where race and class did not exclude them altogether, norms of domesticity and presumed dependency increasingly circumscribed women's opportunities for migration.[42] Donna Gabaccia and Doris Weatherford describe immigration practices that included holding women on dock until their husbands called for them; marrying off fiancées on dock to ensure that the woman's sexual respectability was secured; and closely inspecting the homes to which single women were bound.[43] As Weatherford relates, "a man's abode could be anything from a park bench to a freight car—the officials did not bother to ask—but a woman's intended residence could be inspected. One nineteen-year-old Russian woman who gave her uncle's address as an intended residence was refused entrance largely because there were empty beer bottles in the apartment when it was inspected."[44]

The immigration service's focus on domesticity and dependency was intended to ensure not just a woman's sexual "respectability" but also her conformity to gender norms. This becomes clear from an account provided by Edward Corsi, an Italian immigrant who eventually became the Commissioner of Immigration and Naturalization for the District of New York. Corsi described the "queer and hard to handle" case of Alejandra Veles, who arrived on a steamship from Vera Cruz. Dressed in men's clothes, "boyish in appearance, with black hair and an attractive face, she proved to be, upon examination, despite her earlier insistence to the

contrary, a young woman." Veles was "threatened with arrest for her defi-
ance of the rules" but was eventually released by immigration officials
after they extracted a promise that she would leave the country at once.[45]

Women such as Veles who "passed" by dressing, living, and acting as
men were not unknown to officials. According to Lillian Faderman,
women passed as a way to gain mobility, increased pay, and political opportunities.[46] Not all passing women were lesbians or transgendered, but,
certainly, passing enabled some to publicly take female lovers or marry
women. At least one passing immigrant woman attracted the attention of
the famous sexologist Havelock Ellis. Ellis's writings include a description of "Nicholai de Raylan," the confidential secretary to the Russian
Consul, who was found to be a woman after her death at age thirty-three
of tuberculosis. Born in Russia, de Raylan married twice. The first marriage ended after ten years on the grounds of "cruelty and misconduct
with chorus girls"; the second marriage was to a chorus "girl."[47] According to Ellis, "both wives were firmly convinced that their husband was a
man and ridiculed the idea that 'he' could be a woman. I am informed
that de Raylan wore a very elaborately constructed artificial penis. In her
will she made careful arrangements to prevent detection of sex after
death, but these were frustrated as she died in a hospital."[48]

Widespread fears about "white slavery" undoubtedly helped to fuel
the immigration service's sexuality and gender practices in this time
period. The fear underwent several transformations, but at its core it
focused attention on the problem of women and girls being coerced,
tricked, or seduced into practicing prostitution. The United States had
been represented at the first International Conference on White Slavery,
held in London in 1899, but did not send a representative to the 1902
Conference. In 1908 the United States ratified the international Treaty to
Suppress Traffic in White Women.[49] Frederick Grittner suggests that the
panic over white slavery reflected the fact that a variety of fears were con-
densed within it.[50] These fears concerned the impact of the formal abolition of slavery, industrialization, immigration, alterations in gender and
racial and class relations, and the growth of cities. Furthermore, the term
"white slavery" had a complex resonance in the United States, drawing a
parallel with recently abolished African slavery but implying that white
women's slavery was somehow worse than the slavery and sexual abuse
endured by African and African American women and men for two and a
half centuries. Thus, the term reflected the fetishization of middle-class
native white women as symbols of the nation whom white men had to

"protect." It also functioned as a warning to white women who were involved in feminism and other efforts to alter the gender balance of power. And it marginalized the experiences and issues of Asian, Latina, and African American women caught within intersecting systems of patriarchy and racialization.

Though there was unquestionably some trafficking, Grittner argues that the pervasive representation of white slavery was out of proportion to the actual dangers. "Out of 6,309 prostitutes interviewed during the Progressive Era, only 7.5 percent listed white slavery or extreme coercion as the cause for entering the life."[51] Nonetheless, immigrants became associated in the public mind with white slavery after 1909, when George Kibbe Turner published his anti-Semitic essay "Daughters of the Poor," which particularly linked Jewish immigrants to organizing the traffic in women.[52] In the same year, the Dillingham Commission presented a preliminary report to Congress, *Importation and Harboring of Women For Immoral Purposes,* which examined the trafficking in women through the immigration system. Based on these alarmist associations of immigrants with trafficking, the Act of 1910 expanded the ban on entry by prostitutes and procurers and prohibited the importation of aliens for prostitution or any other immoral purpose. It also added "persons who are supported by or receive in whole or in part the proceeds of prostitution" to the list of excluded immigrants.[53] As had happened to Asian women earlier, entry became even more difficult for European immigrant women, as inspectors sought to determine whether they were being imported (knowingly or through trickery) for prostitution.

In addition to the Act of 1910, Congress also passed the Mann Act, which prohibited the importation and interstate transportation of women for immoral purposes. Drawing selectively on the Dillingham Commission's Report, advocates of the Mann Act "raised the fear that immigration was the cause of America's urban unrest and alien pimps and procurers were the cause of white slavery."[54] Through this process, the lurid image of evil immigrant men tricking innocent white U.S.-born women into prostitution became the dominant public image.

After 1910 various immigrants were deported for violating the Mann Act. At the same time, the law sustained other forms of sexual policing, such as the ban on miscegenation. Thus, Jack Johnson, an African American world heavyweight boxing champion, was prosecuted and eventually jailed for Mann Act violations after he transported his white woman lover across state lines. "The Mann Act became a convenient tool to put a

Black man in his place."[55] Other such tools included lynching in the South.[56] D'Emilio and Freedman suggest that "the simultaneity of lynching in the South and the attack on immigrants by some Progressive reformers place in bold relief the ways sexuality figured in the maintenance of social hierarchies."[57]

Between 1910 and 1916 at least thirty-two cities and states established vice commissions to investigate prostitution and other moral concerns.[58] Some of the commissions blamed immigrants for the introduction of sexual practices that they considered objectionable and "un-American." The propensity to attribute sexual vice and corruption to immigrants had a long history. Dr. Charles H. Hughes's "Note on the Feature of Sexual Psychopathy," published in 1907 in the medical journal *The Alienist and Neurologist,* noted:

> It scarcely needs to be mentioned that Americans frequently blame one or the other ethnic group for homosexuality. For example, a criminologist from the Southern states recently stated that male prostitution first spread into his area of the country with the immigration of the Italian "Vergazzi"; and one often hears Americans claim that the yellow-skinned population is strongly given to homosexuality. This may well be true, but there is no reason to imagine that homosexuality is any less wide-spread amongst the white and black populations.[59]

However, vice commissions in the second decade of the century heavily focused on immigrants' association with sexual "vice."

In 1917, in the context of World War I, a "red" scare, continued imperial expansion, and the rise of eugenic thinking, Congress passed the Espionage and Sedition Acts, which gave the government wide powers to crack down on critics, including immigrants who were considered "undesirable" in some way. The government also passed the Immigration Act of 1917. This Act included a literacy requirement, which restrictionists had been advocating since the 1890s as a means to reduce Southern and Eastern European immigration. To the restrictionists' regret, however, the literacy requirement did not substantially reduce immigration. Mexicans, whose labor was desired while the United States was at war, were exempted from the literacy requirement.[60] The 1917 Act also created the "Asiatic Barred Zone," whose people were now barred from the United States. According to Salyer, the Barred Zone included "India, Burma, Siam, the Malay States, Arabia, Afghanistan, part of Russia, and most of the Polynesian Islands."[61] The law also expanded the list of aliens who were to be excluded on various grounds and broadened the grounds on which aliens could be deported after entry to the United States to include vagrancy, chronic alcoholism, and tuberculosis in any form.[62]

In regard to sexuality, the 1917 Act excluded "polygamists or persons who practice polygamy or believe in or advocate the practice of polygamy."[63] The Act also reiterated the ban on women and girls coming to the United States for immoral purposes and allowed for the deportation of women who acted in immoral ways after arrival. Pregnancy became downgraded to a Class C medical condition, which was defined as "defective or diseased conditions of a less serious character, but [that] must be certified for the information of the immigration officers and the boards of special inquiry under provisions of law."[64] New medical exclusions were also added, including a ban on people who were constitutional psychopathic inferiors. "Constitutional psychopathic inferior" was a medical classification that encompassed persons who were considered to "show a lifelong and constitutional tendency not to conform to the tendencies of the group."[65] The Public Health Service (PHS) *Manual for the Mental Examination of Aliens* grouped "moral imbeciles, pathological liars and swindlers . . . and persons with abnormal sexual instincts" under that category.[66] Robert Podnanski reminds us that although no court officially decided that the term encompassed lesbians and gay men, it was nonetheless a precursor of the terms "psychopathic personality" and "sexual deviant" that were later used to exclude lesbian and gay immigrants.[67]

Provisions regarding prostitution were especially strict under the Act of 1917. Fines and imprisonment were imposed on both citizens and immigrants who imported or attempted to import, or employed or attempted to employ, immigrants for purposes of prostitution. Convicted immigrants also faced deportation after they had paid fines and served time. Also deportable was "any alien receiving any share in, or deriving any benefits from the earning of a prostitute; or managing or employed by, or in connection with, a house of prostitution, music or dance hall, or place of amusement or resort habitually frequented by prostitutes or where other prostitutes gather."[68] These provisions had the potential to affect a significant number of people, including relatives and friends of women who were found guilty of prostitution and even shopkeepers who sold goods to them. Furthermore, for the penalties to be imposed, conviction was not necessary; "if prostitution can be shown to have been *practiced* [even without a legal conviction], deportation follows."[69] The Act also introduced "the principle of deportation any time after entry" for those found to be involved in prostitution. Consequently, "a small baby girl brought to this country by her parents, and some twenty years later becoming a prostitute would be deportable to the country whence she had come twenty years before, regardless of the social conditions in this country which may be responsible for her occupation."[70] The Act also prevented "sexually immoral women," including prostitutes, from acquiring citizenship through marriage as a means to avoid exclusion or deportation.[71] Finally, the Act provided that if anyone deported in connection with prostitution attempted to return to the United States at a later date, she or he would be imprisoned for up to two years and then deported again.[72]

After World War I the economic boom began to collapse, labor and race riots broke out, immigration from Europe resumed, and restrictionist sentiment grew even stronger. Japanese women became direct targets of the restrictionists, who claimed that their childbearing threatened to bring about a Japanese conquest of the United States. Japan bowed to restrictionist pressures and, in 1920, signed the "Ladies Agreement" that ended the brides' immigration. At the same time, the Bureau of Immigration concentrated on identifying and expelling immigrants whom they deemed to be Communist or anarchist.[73]

In 1921 the first National Origins Quota law established a cap on the total number of immigrants who could enter the United States in any year and established a system of preferences through which the quotas should be allocated. The law "limited the number of aliens of any nationality entering the United States to three percent of the foreign-born persons of that nationality who lived in the United States in 1910" but exempted the Western Hemisphere from these limits.[74] (The Western Hemisphere comprised Canada, Mexico, Central and South America, and much of the Caribbean.)[75] Within the quota limits, preference was given to wives, parents, brothers, sisters, children under eighteen, and fiancées of U.S. citizens; immigrants who had applied for citizenship; and immigrants eligible for citizenship who served in the military or naval forces within a certain time period.[76] In other words, a particular version of heteropatriarchal family was prioritized, one within ever-narrowing racial, ethnic, and class terms. The preference given to wives and female fiancées reflected the patriarchal assumption that women immigrants were passive and dependent followers of pioneering male immigrants.

Under the Immigration Act of 1924 even more restrictive national origins quotas became the law. The quotas were to become implemented in two stages. In the first stage, the "quotas were [to be] limited to 2 percent of the numbers of foreign born residents of each nationality [in the United States] in 1890."[77] In this way, the number of Southern and Eastern

European immigrants could be sharply cut, since the peak of their arrival occurred after the 1890 census. In the second stage, which was scheduled for implementation in 1927 but became delayed until 1929, "a total quota of 150,000 [annually was to be] parceled out in ratio to the distribution of the national origins of the white population of the United States in 1920."[78] Under this formula, approximately 85 percent of immigration slots became reserved for immigrants from Northern and Western Europe. The immigration of all Asians—except Filipinos who were under the rule of the United States—was completely ended.[79] The Western Hemisphere was again exempted from all limits, in order to ensure that the United States had access to cheap, convenient labor that could be driven out again when it was no longer needed.[80] To enhance the United States' capacity to keep or drive out unwanted labor, Congress authorized the creation of the Border Patrol.

Within the quota limits, the Act gave equal preference to immigrants skilled in agriculture who were accompanied by their families and "the unmarried child under 21 years of age, the father, the mother, the husband, or the wife of a citizen of the United States who is 21 years or older."[81] Nonquota status (that is, the right to enter regardless of numerical limits) was granted to wives and unmarried children under eighteen of citizens who were living in the United States, as well as to qualifying ministers and professors with their families.

In 1925 immigration control underwent another major revision, as a system for inspecting intending immigrants and issuing visas through U.S. consulates abroad became widely implemented.[82] Not only did U.S. consuls keep track of quotas and distribute visas accordingly but also "various other qualifications—including police checks, medical inspections, financial responsibility determinations, and political interviews—could be established long before the intending immigrant reached the country."[83] John Torpey, quoting Aristide Zolberg, describes the system as "a form of 'remote border control,' a major innovation in immigration policy."[84]

In 1933 the Bureau of Immigration and the Bureau of Naturalization were consolidated into one organization, the Immigration and Naturalization Service (INS), located within the Department of Labor. As war got underway in Europe, the INS was transferred to the Department of Justice as a "national security" measure.[85] In 1940 the Alien Registration Act required all immigrants in the United States to register with the government, and immigrants over fourteen to submit to being fingerprinted. In 1941 the United States entered World War II. One of the government's first acts was to intern Japanese Americans in camps, claiming that they threatened U.S. security.

Even during the height of the massacre of the Jews in Europe, U.S. "bureaucrats applied [immigration] rules so strictly—requiring legal documents that fleeing Jews could not possibly provide—that otherwise qualified refugees were kept out of the country."[86] Zucker and Zucker graphically illustrate how onerous immigration rules had become: "by 1943, the visa application was more than four feet long and had to be filled out on both sides and submitted in sextuplicate."[87] Even when persons faced immediate danger of death, their applications were not expedited. According to Norton et al., "the American Federation of Labor argued that new immigrants would compete with American workers for scarce jobs, and public opinion polls supported their position. This fear of economic competition was fed by anti-Semitism."[88]

The United States emerged from World War II as a superpower. "It alone had the atomic bomb. The U.S. airforce and navy were the largest anywhere. What is more, only the United States had the capital and economic resources to spur international recovery. America, Truman gloated, was 'a giant.'"[89] The INS's role changed, too. The Congressional Research Service explains that "functions that stemmed from war—departure control, alien enemy detention and parole, the seaman program, naturalization of the armed forces—all these decreased in volume and some in importance."[90] As travel restrictions eased, the INS was able to resume deporting immigrants. Meanwhile, immigration to the United States picked up, and new laws began to alter how it was controlled.

For one, racially based immigration restrictions lifted a little. The Chinese Exclusion Act was repealed in 1943, and Chinese immigrants were given a token quota of 105 immigration slots a year. In 1946 naturalization rights were extended to people from the Philippines and India, and these countries were given annual immigration quotas of 100 slots each. In 1952 the McCarran-Walter Act made everyone technically eligible to immigrate or naturalize. The largely symbolic nature of these changes, in the case of Asian countries, was underscored by the fact that the 1952 Act created the so-called Asia Pacific Triangle, encompassing 19 countries, whose combined entries to the United States could not exceed 2,000 in any given year. These modest revisions were due to a combination of factors, including military alliances, pressures from U.S. communities of color, and the United States' battle with the Soviet Union. "As the Soviet Union was quick to point out, the United States could hardly pose as the leader of the free world or condemn the denial of human rights behind the iron curtain if it condoned racism at home."[91]

The slight thawing of racial exclusion also resulted in provisions that allowed U.S. servicemen to bring their Asian brides to the United States. Back in 1945 the War Brides Act had passed but, on racial grounds, Japanese women married to GIs remained unable to enter the United States. According to Paul Spickard, the military also presented barriers to GIs who wanted to intermarry: "the total effect of U.S. policy and practice . . . was to prevent intermarriage wherever possible and encourage GIs to opt for informal, unstable relationships—even prostitution—instead of marriage."[92] But amendments to immigration law in 1947 and 1948 finally enabled Japanese brides to enter, and in 1952 the McCarran-Walter Act removed the overt racial restrictions that had affected these binational marriages.

Another significant postwar change was the start of the Cold War, which inspired profound fears of Communist subversion. Immigration laws quickly incorporated these fears. The list of excludables was expanded in 1948 to include immigrants who were suspected of coming to engage in activities that endangered U.S. public safety. The Internal Security Act of 1950 expanded the provisions for the exclusion, deportation, denial of naturalization, and denaturalization of immigrants on security grounds. The McCarran-Walter Act of 1952 buttressed the Internal Security Act by strengthening provisions to exclude immigrant "subversives." The Act also required immigrants to report their addresses to the INS on an annual basis; the addresses were kept in a central index that was available for use by security and enforcement agencies.

Cold War policies also shaped legislation that facilitated the admission of refugees. The legislation included the Displaced Persons Act of 1948, the Refugee Relief Act of 1953, the Refugee-Escapee Act of 1957, and the Fair Share Refugee Act of 1960. While humanitarian concern certainly played a part in the refugee legislation, the legislation also became "an important tool in anti-Communist foreign policy."[93] Refugee policies came to heavily favor those fleeing Communist countries, because the presence of these refugees seemed to validate the United States' claims about the evils of Communism and the desirability of capitalism. The Refugee-Escapee Act of 1957 particularly exemplified this bias by defining refugees as "victims of racial, religious, or political persecution fleeing Communist or Communist-occupied or -dominated countries, or a country in the Middle East."[94]

The Bracero Program, too, reflected the influence of the Cold War. This program "provided over 219,500 Mexican workers to farm employers in twenty-four states" during the war.[95] At the war's end, employers successfully clamored for the program's extension. It ultimately supplied a cheap, exploitable workforce who filled some five million employment slots, and it gave rise to a vast migration network that continued channeling workers to the United States even after the program officially ended in 1964. As claims circulated that Communist spies were posing as farm workers and crossing the Southwestern border to infiltrate the United States, any Bracero worker who protested poor working conditions became vulnerable to deportation as a Communist subversive.[96]

Fears of Communism also became linked to a new "moral panic" over sexuality. World War II had transformed gender and sexual relations by drawing millions of young men and women into paid employment, weakening the ties of family and community, and providing more opportunities for premarital sex. World War II also marked a turning point in lesbian and gay community formation, as a visible gay subculture took root in cities. At the end of the war, there was a concerted effort to reassert "traditional" gender and sexual roles. Women were encouraged to leave the workforce or were openly forced out. An ethos of family and consumption prevailed.[97] At the same time, fears grew that the sexual order needed reform. The Kinsey Report, issued in 1948, "pointed to a vast hidden world of sexual experience sharply at odds with publicly espoused norms" and shocked traditionalists.[98] The belief that dangerous criminals menaced the postwar family gained credence as a dozen states convened commissions to find ways to contain sexual psychopaths, and more than half the states eventually passed sexual psychopathy laws. In 1952 a congressional investigation examined obscenity and immorality in magazines, comics, and newspapers, and fourteen states tightened their obscenity laws in response.

Concerns about homosexuality became particularly linked to fears of Communist subversion. John D'Emilio explains how the analogy between Communism and homosexuality was constructed:

> The incorporation of gay women and men into the demonology of the McCarthy era required little effort. According to right-wing ideologues, leftist teachers poisoned the minds of their students; lesbians and homosexuals corrupted the bodies of the young. Since Communists bore no identifying physical characteristics, they were able to infiltrate the government and commit treason against the country. . . .

Homosexuals, too, could escape detection and thus insinuate themselves into every branch of the government. The slaves of their sexual
passions, they would stop at nothing to gratify their desires until the
satisfaction of animal needs finally destroyed their moral sense. Communists taught their children to betray their parents; "mannish"
women mocked the ideals of marriage and motherhood. Lacking
toughness, the effete men of the eastern establishment lost China and
Eastern Europe to the enemy, while weak-willed, pleasure-obsessed
homosexuals—half-men—feminized everything they touched and
sapped the masculine vigor that tamed a continent. The congruence
between the stereotypes of Communists and homosexuals made the
scapegoating of gay men and women a simple matter.[99]

Suspected lesbians and gays became targeted for investigation, expelled
from the military, fired from their jobs, and subjected to police harassment. Congress also decided to amend immigration law to exclude them,
as evinced by the Senate Committee of the Judiciary's recommendation
that the "classes of mental defectives should be enlarged to encompass
homosexuals and other sex perverts."[100] However, the Public Health
Service persuaded lawmakers that provisions for the exclusion of immigrants afflicted with psychopathic personality also applied to lesbians
and gay men. Consequently, under the Act of 1952, immigrants who were
judged to be lesbian or gay were issued Class A medical exclusion certificates by the PHS on the grounds of psychopathic personality and were
summarily excluded or deported.[101]

In 1957 legislation passed that allowed the Attorney General to grant
waivers to people seeking to immigrate who were technically excludable
but were the close relatives of citizens or legal residents.[102] This waiver
provision, which has remained a feature of immigration law, was particularly helpful for women who had been associated with prostitution but
wanted to enter the United States as wives of servicemen. It was not surprising that some brides had been involved in prostitution; in times of
war, military invasion, social and economic disruption, and massive displacement, women have often had to resort to prostitution to survive.
Furthermore, a significant number of women had been forced into sexually servicing the occupying troops during World War II.[103] These women
were ineligible to enter the United States. During the 1950s literally thousands of private bills were filed in Congress, seeking waivers to immigration exclusions. A 1957 Senate report noted that "private immigration bills
in recent years accounted for more than one third of all enactments, both

public and private," and that in the 84th Congress alone, 1,239 private relief bills, affecting 1,488 immigrants, were passed.[104] Rather than continue this onerous system, the Attorney General was granted the power to grant waivers to technically excludable people if they were close relatives of citizens or residents. The result of the waiver system was that through heterosexual marriage to a patriotic American man, a woman's past association with prostitution could become reconciled with the narrative of the nation as moral and respectable. The waiver system also enabled women who had criminal records for having abortions to gain admission, if they had close ties to U.S. citizens or residents.

In 1965 Congress passed a major revision of immigration law. Under the 1965 Immigration and Nationality Act (INA), 74 percent of all immigration slots was allocated to heteropatriarchal family reunification, 20 percent to workers with skills in demand by U.S. employers, and 6 percent to refugees.[105] No country could receive more than 20,000 slots per year. However, the Western Hemisphere was exempted from the 20,000 per country ceiling, which was helpful for Mexico, which already sent more than that number of legal immigrants to the United States each year. Total immigration from the Western Hemisphere was capped at 120,000 per year, while Eastern Hemisphere immigrants were allocated 170,000 slots.

The law was generally hailed as a landmark because it finally eliminated the explicitly racist immigration standards that had been in place since the National Origins Act of 1924. But David Reimers provides an important alternative reading of the 1965 INA. Drawing on congressional documents, he argues that the changes were intended to be cosmetic rather than substantive. Although explicit racism was stricken from the law, the preferences through which immigrants were to be granted admission were written in such a way that Southern and Eastern Europeans were expected to be the main beneficiaries of the revision (their admission had been sharply curtailed after 1924). Since immigrants of color had been substantially excluded from the United States until then, lawmakers calculated that few would be able to take advantage of the family reunification provisions. As a representative of the Foreign Legion explained, "Asiatics [sic], having far fewer immediate families now in the United States than southern Europeans, will automatically arrive in far fewer numbers than Italians, Greeks, and other southern European stock. Yet there is no sting in the law to offend the Asian nations."[106] This kind of racial calculation prompted the Japanese American Citizens League to criticize the proposed revisions: "it would seem that, although the immigration bill eliminated race as a matter of principle, in actual operation immigration would still be controlled by the now discredited national origins system and the general pattern of immigration which exists today will continue for many years yet to come."[107] Reimers's analysis suggests, then, that the law was intended to have racially discriminatory effects, while seeming to be race neutral.[108] Significantly, racism was to be perpetuated through further enshrining the heteropatriarchal family at the center of immigration policy.[109]

By the 1970s, immigration rates were beginning to climb, in part because continued U.S. investment and military involvement were creating what Saskia Sassen calls "bridges for migration" between selected countries in Asia, Latin America, and the Caribbean, and the United States.[110] U.S. manufacturers increasingly moved production offshore, which laid the groundwork for further immigration. The end of the Vietnam War in 1975 also increased immigration to the United States, with the arrival of Southeast Asian refugees and the passage of the Indochina Refugee and Assistance Act.

In 1976 the 20,000 immigrants per country per annum limit and the preference system were extended to the Western Hemisphere. The vast migration networks that had been established between Mexico and the United States during the Bracero Program could not be accommodated by the 20,000 annual limit, so the effect of the law was to render a significant portion of Mexicans as undocumented.[111]

In 1980 Congress passed the Refugee Act, which established a separate system for the admission and resettlement of the refugees and asylum seekers. The Act also incorporated the United Nations' definition of a refugee as anyone who was fleeing persecution on the grounds of race, religion, nationality, political opinion, or membership in a particular social group. Also in 1980, the INS announced its new policy on lesbian and gay exclusion. In 1979 the Surgeon General had directed the PHS to stop issuing automatic Class A medical exclusion certificates to lesbian and gay immigrants, since the American Psychiatric Association no longer deemed homosexuality to be a mental illness. But the Surgeon General's directive incurred the INS's wrath, and in 1980 the INS announced their own new policy. This was that if an immigrant made an "unsolicited, unambiguous admission of homosexuality" to an INS inspector or was identified as lesbian or gay by a third party who arrived at the same time, the person would be taken to secondary inspection and asked if she or he was a homosexual. A person answering yes would be excluded; a person answering no would be admitted.

In 1986 Congress passed the Immigration Reform and Control Act (IRCA). Under IRCA, people who had lived continuously in the United States since 1 January 1982, or for a shorter period if they were agricultural workers, and met certain requirements could apply for legalization. As a result, 3.6 million people became legal U.S. residents. The law also institutionalized a requirement that all workers had to prove their eligibility to work in the United States, and employers who failed to check eligibility or knowingly hired undocumented workers could be fined. Finally, the law increased enforcement at the U.S./Mexico border. In contradictory ways, these provisions attempted to respond to the presence of undocumented immigrants who were drawn to the United States through the disruptive effects of globalization and business's demand for cheap labor, and U.S. citizens' fears about the impact of immigration on dominant cultural institutions and norms. Pierette Hondagneu Sotelo has suggested that U.S. citizens were particularly concerned about the impact of undocumented immigrant settlement and family formation. Perhaps as a result, IRCA was implemented in ways that made the legalization of mothers with small children particularly difficult. As Grace Chang explains, the INS interpreted IRCA's provisions in ways that allowed them to deny legalization to undocumented women whose U.S. citizen children had received public assistance—even though aid to the children was perfectly legal.[112] As a result, legalization extended the historic practice of penalizing childbearing and rearing by poor and immigrant women.[113]

Days after IRCA became law, Congress also passed the Immigration Marriage Fraud Amendments (IMFA). Precisely because heterosexual marriage remained so highly privileged within the law, officials were haunted by fears that substantial numbers of immigrants were gaining legal status through marriage fraud (that is, entering into marriage simply as a means to gain legal residency).[114] Participants at a congressional hearing were regaled with details about how such fraud was carried out: "Brokers and documenters supply everything from happy-looking witnesses at bogus marriage ceremonies to reusable cardboard and paste wedding cakes that appear in wedding photo after wedding photo."[115] Getting into the swing of the hearing, Senator Simpson inquired: "what was the full 'blue plate special' rate . . . what was the cost" for a package consisting of a citizen willing to marry a foreigner, a lawyer willing to process the paperwork, and a minister to perform the ceremony?[116]

Under the terms of the IMFA, immigrant spouses receive two years conditional residence, after which time they may file for permanent residence. But the filing has to be carried out by both spouses. These provisions have had a gender-disparate effect, binding immigrant wives to U.S. resident or citizen husbands who batter. The problem has been so serious that Congress amended the law several times to enable battered wives to self-petition. The amendments notwithstanding, IMFA has presented a serious problem for immigrant women in abusive relationships.[117]

The IMFA further sanctioned immigration officials' investigation of couples who were suspected of marriage fraud. The investigation employed tactics that were borrowed from the interrogation of Chinese applicants at the turn of the century, including making surprise investigations of couple's homes and separating couples for questioning about one another.[118] The questions often include eliciting details about sexual practices; in this way, immigrant heterosexuality finds itself being inspected by the state.[119]

Even while the IMFA recodified marriage as a heteropatriarchal institution that was central to immigration and the nation, lesbian, gay, and other kinds of relationships remained invalidated. For instance:

> In *Adams v. Howerton* [1982], the United States Court of Appeals for the Ninth Circuit [had] considered whether marriage between two members of the same sex conferred preferential immigration status on the alien partner of the marriage. The court held that no immediate relative status would be granted under the Immigration and Nationality Act for partners in a homosexual marriage. The court further determined that a construction of the statute denying the petitioners the relief they sought would not violate their equal protection guarantee . . . To support its conclusion that a homosexual marriage is not valid under the Immigration and Nationality Act, the court relied on the fact that another provision of the Act allows for total exclusion of homosexuals from the United States.[120]

Other kinds of long-term relationships that were not based on state-sanctioned marriage, with its implied interest in regulating blood and property, also remained marginalized. For example, A. Lynn Bolles noted that the structure of working-class Jamaican and Afro-Caribbean families was often not understood by U.S. consular officers and generated difficulties for women when they tried to secure visas. These families included people who were not related by legal or kin ties but who were family members nonetheless.[121]

In 1990 immigration law was again recodified. Heteropatriarchal family remained the primary basis for receiving a green card, but the number of employment-based green cards expanded in ways that greatly favored professionals and technicians. Lesbians and gays won a victory, though, when their exclusion was finally removed from the law. Nonetheless, they continued to face barriers to immigration, including the fact that their relationships were still not acknowledged as a basis for gaining legal permanent residency. Lesbians and gays also remained vulnerable to arrest for their sexuality in many countries of origin and states in the United States, which resulted in an increased risk of being excluded or deported on criminal grounds. They were also liable to be considered as lacking in good moral character, which remains a requirement for legal residency. For these reasons, many lesbian and gay immigrants still try to ensure that the INS remains unaware of their sexuality. However, this sharply limits their ability to engage in activism or participate in queer communities. South Asian writer Grace Poore offers one revealing description of constraints on lesbian and gay immigrants' participation: "We understand why some of us never march on the outside of the gay pride contingent in case of cameras. Why many of us fear going to bars in case of a raid. Why we only do radio interviews, never have our photographs taken. Why I—hard line, separatist, feminist, lesbian—talk about needing to fight homophobia while using a [pseudonym]."[122]

HIV exclusion also emerged as an issue. In 1987 the government began screening applicants for legal residence for the HIV virus. In 1991 the Secretary for Health and Human Services proposed that HIV should be removed from the list of medical exclusions, on the ground that it was not contagious but rather transmitted through particular behaviors. Instead, in November of that year, thousands of Haitians fleeing their country by boat after an illegal coup toppled democratically elected President Aristide were intercepted at sea by the U.S. Coast Guard and transported to the U.S. Naval Station at Guantanamo Bay in Cuba. Those who were judged to have no credible fear of persecution were sent back to Haiti. Those who were found to have a credible fear were tested for HIV, and those who tested negative were sent to the United States. However, those who tested positive found themselves incarcerated in "the world's first HIV detention camp" at Guantanamo Bay.[123] The incarceration of HIV-positive Haitians who appeared to have valid asylum claims generated protests from a coalition of gay/HIV/civil/racial/immigrants rights advocates, and a court ruling eventually forced the government to bring the refugees to the United States.[124] In 1993 Congress passed legislation that allowed for the exclusion of anyone who was HIV-positive, including nonimmigrants such as tourists and short-term workers and also legal permanent residents. All applicants for legal permanent residence are currently required to take an HIV test from an INS-approved doctor; if they test positive, they are denied residency. Waivers are available under certain limited circumstances.

Contradictorily, since 1994 a small number of people have been granted asylum in the United States on the grounds that they have been persecuted for being HIV-positive or having AIDS. Sexuality in general also emerged as a major area of contestation in the refugee/asylum system during the 1990s (see appendix A).

New forms of eugenic discourse about the dangers presented by poor and minority women's childbearing also gained ascendance, most visibly in California's Proposition 187 campaign. This campaign attributed economic difficulties to the presence of the undocumented,[125] and represented childbearing by undocumented women as a particular threat. Reflecting these fears, one of Pete Wilson's first steps to enforce Proposition 187 was "to issue an executive order directing health care workers to discontinue providing prenatal services to undocumented immigrants."[126] Not only the undocumented but any woman who "seemed" foreign experienced difficulties obtaining prenatal care, not to mention being publicly vilified. Proposals were also introduced in the California legislature and U.S. Congress to deny citizenship to children born on U.S. soil to undocumented parents, but these did not become law.

The attack on pregnancy were part of wider assaults on poor, immigrant, and minority people's access to jobs, schooling, and public representation. The assaults were partly driven by white fears about threats to their cultural, political, and economic hegemony in the face of changing demographics. As John Taunton, founder and former chairman of the disingenuously named Federation for American Immigration Reform (FAIR), crudely summarized the issue: "will the present majority peaceably hand over its political power to a group that is simply more fertile?"[127] Scapegoating was also driven by changes in the economy, decreases in real wages, a diminishing social safety net, and new strategies for disciplining labor.[128]

Conservative Charles Murray revived the "race suicide" thesis and especially advocated "the elimination of welfare because it fostered what he called 'dysgenesis,' the reproduction of the genetically inferior in numbers larger than those with more intelligence."[129] His arguments shaped Welfare Reform in 1996, which extended the attack that began with poor undocumented women's pregnancy to also include childbearing and rearing by poor and/or minority U.S. women. Welfare-reform measures included "'family cap' legislation that denie[d] additional benefits for children born to women already on welfare and proposed cash bonuses to encourage these women to use Norplant, a long-acting contraceptive."[130] Legal immigrants were also barred from receiving a range of public benefits to which they had been previously entitled. The Defense of Marriage Act, also passed in 1996, defined marriage as involving male-female couples exclusively, for purposes of both domestic and immigration policy.[131] Finally, the Illegal Immigration Reform and Immigrant Responsibility Act (IIRIRA), passed the same year, increased income requirements for those hoping to sponsor relatives for immigration, thus ensuring that poorer families could not reunite. Taken together, Welfare Reform, DOMA, and IIRIRA mandated middle-class marital heterosexuality as the official norm and penalized anyone who was unable or unwilling to conform.

Other terms of IIRIRA included requiring people to file for asylum within one year of entering the United States; expanding the militarization of the border; implementing criminalization standards that made even legal residents deportable for minor crimes that had been committed long in the past; and restricting courts' ability to review immigration decisions. The Anti-Terrorism and Effective Death Penalty Act of 1996 reinforced the two latter provisions.

After the incidents of September 11, 2001, immigration control was significantly altered by the USA PATRIOT Act. Other immigration legislation is pending. How these legislative changes will further transform regimes of sexual normalization remains to be seen.[132]

Over the past century and a quarter, women's ability to enter the United States has been regulated on the basis of sexuality. Immigration laws and policies attempted to channel women's sexuality into heteropatriarchal marriage and penalized other arrangements. Yet marital sexual activity that resulted in the birth of significant numbers of children of color or poor children was considered a threat to the United States. Consequently, heteropatriarchal marriage policies became steadily modified to benefit primarily Europeans with some economic stability, while other couples availed of the policies only with great difficulty or not at all. The privileging of economically stable European couples went hand-in-hand with immigration policies that mandated the exclusion and deportation of immigrant women whose sexuality was deemed threatening to, or uncontained within, heteropatriarchal marriage. Discourses including scientific racism, gender, economics, public health and criminology provided tools to describe the threat represented by these "undesirable" women and to craft techniques for identifying and expelling them. As the chapter makes clear, various immigrant women's "undesirability" was constructed not only through sexual histories and proclivities that were attributed to them but also through the intersection of these ascribed sexualities with their gender, racial, ethnic, and class positions. Immigration exclusions based on sexuality were regularly challenged and reworked. But they continue to mark immigration law and policy in the present.

In the chapters that follow, I concentrate on four major aspects of the sexual regulation of immigrant women: efforts to identify and exclude prostitutes; ways that childbearing by immigrant women of color became constructed as such a threat that immigration laws became altered; efforts to exclude lesbians; and how enduring rape enables women to cross national borders.

2. A Blueprint for Exclusion

The Page Law, Prostitution, and Discrimination

against Chinese Women

The Page Law of 1875 established "the policy of direct federal regulation of immigration by prohibiting for the first time the entry of undesirable immigrants."[1] Immigrants designated as undesirable were those who could be classified as convicts, contract laborers, and Asian women coming to work in prostitution. The provisions regarding convicts and contract laborers had little effect at the time.[2] But the vigorously enforced bar on Asian women coming to work in prostitution had a noticeable effect on the ability of Chinese women to immigrate and served as a harbinger of multiple forms of sexuality based immigration exclusions.[3] The fact that the Page Law targeted Asian women, even when women of other nationalities were significantly involved in prostitution work too, highlights how the sexual monitoring of immigrants intersects with other systems of social hierarchy. As John D'Emilio and Estelle Freedman explain, "systems of sexual regulation . . . have correlated strongly with other forms of social regulation, especially those related to race, class, and gender."[4] Indeed, as chapter 1 showed, the Page Law was a harbinger not only of sexual, but also of racial, ethnic, gender, and class exclusions that were codified by subsequent immigration laws.

To explain the origins of the Page Law and its profound effects on U.S. immigration control, this chapter first describes how fears about the future of white lives, cultural forms, and nation became channeled into concerns about prostitution among Chinese immigrants. It then maps out how such concerns became concretely incorporated into the immigration control process through the strategies that officials devised to try to identify and exclude Chinese prostitutes. Although these strategies remained incapable of generating reliable information about which Chinese women were prostitutes, they had important effects. The strategies transformed the immigration control apparatus into a system that constructed and regulated sexuality and, moreover, constituted Chinese women, individually and collectively, as subjectified in gender, racial, sexual, and class terms. These effects suggest that immigration control reproduces inequalities not only through individual officials' prejudices but also through the routine monitoring strategies on which immigration control depends. These strategies, which were pioneered on Chinese women because of fears about their sexuality, gradually became extended to every immigrant who sought to enter America.

"Coolie Labor, Immoral and Diseased Heathens, and Unassimilable Aliens"

In order to understand the restrictions that were imposed on Chinese women by the Page Law, the law needs to be situated in relation to the larger, conflicted history of Chinese immigration to the United States. The first Chinese immigrants were overwhelmingly male, and San Francisco was the main port of entry. A majority came from the province of Guangdong and began arriving as part of the California gold rush of 1848. Like many other immigrants, they initially intended to make money and return to China. Thus, "although more than half of them were married, most did not bring their wives and families."[5] Despite the migrants' hopes, anti-Chinese sentiment and discrimination became institutionalized as early as 1852, blocking their possibilities. In that year, the Foreign Miner's Tax, supposedly targeting all immigrants but levied mainly against the Chinese, was passed. In steady succession, other anti-Chinese laws proliferated. Judy Yung writes:

> Special taxes were also levied on Chinese fishermen, laundrymen, and brothel owners. Other local ordinances, which did not specifically name the Chinese but which obviously were passed to harass and deprive them of a livelihood, included the cubic-air law, which prohibited residence in rooms with less than 500 cubic feet of air per person; the sidewalk ordinance, which made it a misdemeanor for any person to carry baskets across the shoulders; and the queue ordinance, which required that the hair of every male prisoner in the city jails be cut to within one inch of the scalp. Laws were also passed by the California legislature that denied Chinese basic civil rights, such as the right to immigrate, give testimony in court, be employed in public works, intermarry with whites, and own land. Negatively stereotyped as coolie

labor, immoral and diseased heathens, and unassimilable aliens, the Chinese were driven out of the better-paying jobs in the mines, factories, fishing areas, and farmlands. They were generally not allowed to live outside Chinatown, and their children were barred from attending white school.[6]

Among this predominantly male Chinese immigrant community, a prostitution industry developed. Chinese prostitution quickly emerged as a contentious issue in San Francisco. Yet prostitution was fairly common in the American West at that time:

> For the first few years of the 1850s, the arrival of Chinese female prostitutes accompanied that of European and Anglo-American *filles de joie*. The latter, and a few of the former, were primarily entrepreneurs or aspiring entrepreneurs who flocked to San Francisco to take advantage of the dramatic demand for their services. The temporary and migratory nature of the population, a critical shortage of women for companionship, and the lack of conjugal life stood out as the main features of this male-dominated society. . . . As a consequence, opportunities existed for prostitutes to move both upward in the profession and outward in the wider society.[7]

Despite the widespread existence of prostitution by many nationalities, Chinese prostitution attracted particular public attention, giving rise to negative images and discriminatory institutional structures. According to Judy Yung, "discrimination against Chinese prostitutes, as well as prostitutes from Latin American countries, was most apparent at the institutional level. Both groups of women were ghettoized and, in accordance with the racial prejudice of the day, consistently singled out for moral condemnation and legal suppression, even though white prostitution was more prevalent."[8] Laws explicitly directed at Chinese, rather than all, prostitutes began to develop. For instance, in 1854 municipal authorities in San Francisco passed an ordinance "To Suppress Houses of Ill-Fame Within City Limits" and enforced it mainly against Chinese and Mexican brothels. In 1865 municipal authorities passed an "Order to Remove Chinese Women of Ill Fame from Certain Limits in the City." A year later the state legislature passed "An Act for the Suppression of Chinese Houses of Ill-Fame," which resulted in the geographical confinement of Chinese prostitution, but not its elimination.[9] In 1867 "fourteen owners of houses of ill-fame were arrested—all of them Chinese. In 1869, there were twenty-nine arrests for importing prostitutes—all of them Chinese."[10] In March 1870 the state passed "An Act to Prevent the Kidnapping and Importation of Mongolian, Chinese, and Japanese Females for Criminal or Demoralizing Purposes." The Act stipulated that no Asian woman could land without proof that she had migrated voluntarily and was of good character. However, in 1874 the U.S. Circuit Court ruled that this Act was unconstitutional. The ruling judge added that while he was aware of anti-Chinese sentiment in California, "if their future immigration is to be stopped, recourse must be had to the federal government, where the sole power over this subject lies."[11]

Advocates for Chinese exclusion had already started looking to their representatives in Washington for assistance. They looked particularly to Horace Page, a Republican who "maintained his seat in the House for ten years, largely at the expense of the Chinese."[12] Although Page was initially unable to convince legislators of the need for full Chinese exclusion, he successfully argued for the passage of a bill that excluded Chinese women who were entering the United States for prostitution. This was the Page Law of 1875.

"An Injury and a Curse to Us"

Why target Chinese prostitution, in particular? Exclusionists' concerns centered not on the experiences and needs of poor Chinese girls and women who had been sold or tricked into prostitution, but on the fate of white men, white families, and a nation constructed as white. Transcripts of public hearings in San Francisco on Chinese immigration make this clear.[13] Mr. Pixley testified for the city that their concern was for white male laborers. "The true American hero is the man who takes his dinner out in his tin plate, works all day, six days in the week, and brings his wages home for his wife to expend in the maintenance and education of the family, in their clothing and their protection."[14] These American heroes were defined as coterminous with civilization and the U.S. nation in part because of their adherence to particular gender and sexual arrangements:

> Our white laborers are, as a rule, married, and fathers and heads of families, and according to our mode of civilization the poorest laborer with the poorest wife must occupy a room by himself for his bed and must have at least another room to cook and eat in. If he has a boy and a girl, growing to the ages of puberty, the boy must have a room for himself and the girl must have a room for herself, and both must be separate from the parents' bed. It is the ingrained decency of our civilization. It is as impossible to change it as to change us from the worship of the Christian God to the heathen tablet.[15]

Chinese immigrants were characterized not only as lacking these gender and sexual arrangements but also as threatening white families' ability to maintain them. For instance, Pixley related that Chinese men undercut white men's ability to earn, while Chinese women caused disease and immorality among white men. Testimony also attributed nine tenths of venereal disease in the city to Chinese prostitutes and accused prostitutes of spreading leprosy and incurable forms of syphilis. According to Dr. Charles C. O'Donnell, "the virus of the cooly [sic], in my opinion, is almost sure death to the white man. That is my opinion because I have seen it. There are cases of syphilis among the whites that originated from these Chinese prostitutes that are incurable."[16] Chinese women were also blamed for encouraging immorality, even among young boys:

> I am satisfied, from my experience, that nearly all the boys who have venereal disease contracted it in Chinatown. They have no difficulty there for the prices are so low that they can go whenever they please. The women do not care how old the boys are, whether five years old or more, so long as they have money.[17]

Even those who testified in support of Chinese prostitution were not concerned about the women involved but about how to ensure that Chinese men remained useful laborers who did not threaten white men, white families, and the white nation. Thus, Senator Sargent suggested that since many domestic servants were Chinese men, the fact they could have sex with Chinese prostitutes helped to "protect our own families."[18] On those grounds, "it would be better for the Chinamen if they had more of them."[19] Dr. Stout also believed that Chinese men should have access to more, not fewer, Chinese prostitutes:

> That physiological necessity of man must be satisfied or crime must ensue. It is amazing, it is astonishing that such a population of Chinese being in our country, and there being so few women to satisfy that necessity of nature, that so little crime results from it. . . . That number [of Chinese prostitutes in San Francisco] is too little. There should be more. . . . It is irrepressible; it is a necessity. If there is a certain supply of women of that character, the family is much more sacred and much more pure.[20]

Such views remained the minority, however. The majority consensus was that Chinese prostitutes represented a distinct threat to the lives of white families.

The association of Chinese prostitutes with danger to the life of white families had been constructed through multiple social and material processes. According to Stuart Creighton Miller, the writings and testimonies of missionaries, traders, and diplomats greatly shaped popular U.S. images of the Chinese. The growth of the popular press and the negative coverage of China during the Opium War "populariz[ed] the anti-Chinese themes developed and polished by diplomats, traders, and missionaries over several decades."[21] Domestic experiences with the Chinese further shaped perceptions. Chinese arrival coincided with debate among race theorists about the monogenetic versus polygenetic origin of humans and the increasing demarcation of racial hierarchies that stamped the Chinese as inferior. Some racial theorists also articulated the belief that biological racial differences could not be changed through exposure to the supposedly ameliorative effects of American institutions and ways of life; instead, racial differences corresponded to an inability to understand the very notion of democracy. Thus, the presence of the "racially distinct" Chinese presented a threat to democratic institutions.[22] Miller also notes that the Chinese arrived in the United States during serious controversy over the forced enslavement of African peoples. Because many of the Chinese were contracted laborers who seemed racially and culturally distinct from the white majority, fears of a new form of racial slavery were commonly expressed. In 1874 President Grant described Chinese women as doubly unfree: "the great proportion of the Chinese immigrants who come to our shores do not come voluntarily . . . but come under contracts with headmen who own them almost absolutely. In worse form does this apply to Chinese women."[23]

The common perception that all Chinese women were likely to be enslaved prostitutes had direct connections to scientific racism, because some scientific racists held that the status of women within various groups mirrored larger racial hierarchies. Thus, H. Hotz, whose "copious historical notes" are included in Count A. de Gobineau's tract on *The Moral and Intellectual Diversity of the Races*,[24] argued that the varied treatment of women proves that different races exist and are unequal:

> It is said that all barbarians treat their women as slaves; but, as they progress in civilization, woman gradually rises to her legitimate rank. . . .
>
> But I totally disagree that all races, in their first state of development, treated women equally. There is not only no historical testimony to prove that *any* of the white races were ever in such a state of barbarity and moral debasement as most of the dark races are to this day, and have always been, but there is positive evidence to show that our

barbarous ancestors assigned to woman the same position that we as-
sign to her now: she was the companion, and not the slave of man. . . .
it is possible to demonstrate not only that all races did not treat their
women equally in their first stage of development, but also, that no
race which assigned to woman in the beginning an inferior position
ever raised her from it in any subsequent stage of development. *I select
the Chinese for illustration.*[25]

Clearly, women in China were perceived to be treated particularly poorly,
but rather than inspiring efforts on their behalf, the perception served
mainly to support racist condemnation of all Chinese people. As Chandra
Talpade Mohanty indicates, this perception served to erase any consideration of how racism and imperialism contributed to Chinese women's
status, and to racially differentiate and elevate white women.[26]

   Chinese arrival also coincided with the development of germ theory,
which made North Americans conscious of the connection between
germs and disease. Filtered through the lens of racism, germ theory suggested that different racial groups carried distinct germs to which they
were immune but others were not. Commentators from the penny press to
the American Medical Association (AMA) took seriously the notion that
Chinese immigrants carried distinct germs to which they were immune,
but from which whites would die if exposed. "The germ theory of disease
provided an explanation of the manner in which an obviously inferior
group might best a superior one, contrary to the natural law of the social
Darwinists."[27] Many of the fears became concentrated in a particularly
dense form around the bodies of Chinese women who worked in prostitution. The sexual labor of Chinese prostitutes was believed to be the
nexus through which germs and disease could most easily be transmitted
to white men (prompting the AMA to study whether Chinese prostitutes
were poisoning the nation's bloodstream).[28] Sex with Chinese prostitutes
seemed to be the vector through which white supremacy and the perpe-
tuity of "the white race" was directly threatened. Havelock Ellis, one of the
most prominent sexologists of the nineteenth century, captured the ways
that sexual concerns were inevitably also racial, when he wrote that "the
question of sex—with the racial questions that rest on it—stands before
the coming generations as the chief problem for solution."[29]

   Thus, the Page Law, which mandated the exclusion of Asian women
coming to the United States to work as prostitutes, responded to a constellation of what were believed to be serious threats to "white" values,
lives, and futures.

Differentiating "Real" Wives from Prostitutes

By examining how the Page Law was implemented, we discover the micro-physics of power through which sexuality entered U.S. immigration control. The task, as it was presented to officials, was to differentiate "real" wives from women posing as wives but bound for sex work. According to historians, officials found such a differentiation difficult to make and, driven by racism, they implemented the law so harshly that almost all Chinese women ended up being barred from the United States. Such analyses suggest that the problem with the Page Law was officials' racist manner of implementation—but not the law's demand to differentiate among women on the basis of sexuality.

I want to suggest an alternative formulation, which is that officials had difficulty differentiating "real" wives from women bound for sex work because there is no absolute differentiation that can be made. Yet the law's demand for differentiation introduced new techniques of immigration control that were profoundly racist, sexist, and classist in their effects, as the experience of Chinese women after the Page Law shows. Formulating the problem with reference not to a question of truth but the exercise of power underscores that discrimination in immigration stems not simply from officials' individual prejudices but also from the mundane techniques through which immigration control is operationalized. Moreover, the formulation refuses to replicate the wife/prostitute distinction that legitimized the pioneering of these techniques on Chinese women's bodies in the first place.

To develop this argument, let us briefly review the scholarship that suggests that no absolute distinction can be drawn between prostitutes and other women and then explore how techniques that officials nonetheless used to *try* to make these distinctions had racial, gender, and class effects. Scholarship suggests that distinctions between women who get labeled as prostitutes and other women derive not from any inherent characteristics within the women themselves but from social relations of power. In an article about the history of prostitution in the United States, Miller, Romenesko, and Wondolkowski suggest that there are a myriad of difficulties in trying to define who is a prostitute and "whether or not [women] are so labeled depends more on the political stance of the potential moral entrepreneur who would seek to label them than on the degree to which their actual behavior deviates from some norm of correct conduct."[30] Illustrating their argument, Judith Walkowitz has documented that in Victorian England prostitutes emerged as a distinct social group, separate from regular working-class communities, not because of anything inherent in the women or distinctive about their behavior but because of strategies that officials used to enforce the Contagious Diseases Act, which aimed to control the spread of venereal disease.[31] Gayle Rubin described a similar process that occurred in the nineteenth-century United States. She explains, "prostitution began to change from a temporary job to a more permanent occupation [and distinct social group] as a result of 19th century agitation, legal reform, and police persecution. Prostitutes, who had been part of the general working class population, became increasingly isolated as members of an outcast group."[32]

Yet even as a class of marginalized women who were stigmatized as prostitutes took shape, not all women who sold or bartered sex were labeled as prostitutes. Deborah Rhode highlights the unevenness of the process whereby certain women get labeled and penalized as prostitutes:

> streetwalkers, who tend to come from the lowest socioeconomic group, account for 10 to 15 percent of all prostitutes, and 80 to 90 percent of all arrests. Women of color account for 40 percent of streetwalkers, 55 percent of those arrested, and 85 percent of those receiving jail sentences.[33]

Rhode's analysis makes clear how the label "prostitute" becomes attached to particular groups of women (but not others) through social relations that are racist, classist, and gendered rather than because of any distinguishing behavioral or moral traits of the women involved.

Rhode's argument also indicates the utility of defining prostitution "as a form of labor, even if it is not always one freely chosen, rather than (as many reformers believed) a state of degradation or moral failing."[34] The sex industry is multitiered and continually changing, but public crackdowns focus disproportionately on streetwalkers rather than on women in other tiers.[35] Thus, streetwalkers remain the paradigmatic image of "the prostitute," while other women are much less likely to be arrested, labeled, or stigmatized, even when they sell sex too.

Streetwalkers are particularly likely to become stigmatized and subjected to efforts at control in times of social transformation. At such times, prostitution becomes "a metaphor, a medium of articulation, in which . . . changing elites and emerging middle classes discuss their problems, fears, agendas, and visions."[36] According to Ruth Rosen, discourses about prostitution in the United States have provided a means for people to express concerns about "unrestricted immigration, the rate of venereal disease, the anonymity of the city, the evils of liquor, the growth of working class urban culture, and, most important of all, the changing role of women in society."[37] As definitions of these problems, as well as agendas and visions of those in power, changed, so too did the strategies through which certain groups of women (but not others) become labeled as prostitutes and controlled accordingly.

In short, women certainly sell or trade sex for money or other goods. But which women become labeled and treated as "prostitutes" as a result depends greatly on what tier of the sex industry they work in, prevailing anxieties of the time, and how these anxieties become directed at some class and racial or ethnic groups but not others. The labels also reflect culture-specific beliefs about how sex and gender systems should operate. For instance, during hard times in China, women and girls were commonly sold into domestic service, concubinage, or prostitution, and one form of sale could lead to another.[38] Yet not all domestic servants, called *mui tsai*, were resold; some continued providing domestic service until freed through marriage. But the practice of selling women, and the difficulties of differentiating between various kinds of sales, led immigration officials to assume that all girls traveling in groups were surely prostitutes, rather than, for example, *mui tsai*.[39] A further source of confusion to officials was the fact that some Chinese men had concubines, in addition to first wives. Concubines, who were usually of lower social status and acquired through purchase, were legal members of the family, and their children were their fathers' legal heirs. But concubinage, which reflected a sex and gender system that was different from the dominant U.S. culture, contributed to officials' beliefs that virtually all immigrant Chinese women were enslaved prostitutes.[40]

The variety of sex/gender arrangements evident among Chinese immigrants actually underscores a more general point, which is that there is no necessary opposition between women who sell or trade sex while occupying various social statuses, and wives.[41] William Sanger's pioneering study of prostitution in New York City in the 1850s showed that among the 2,000 women he identified as prostitutes, 490 (or 25 percent) were also married, and 71 lived with their husbands while working in prostitution.[42] Historians of Chinese women in America have also documented that marriage was one of the routes through which sex workers left the industry. Based on census figures, Benson Tong estimates that "during the 1870s, a large number of Chinese prostitutes left the trade and very likely entered into matrimony."[43] Peggy Pascoe affirms that "the highly skewed sex ratio in immigrant Chinatowns . . . and the absence of established in-laws, created unusual opportunities for immigrant prostitutes to marry and leave prostitution behind."[44] Indeed, Pascoe further suggests that many Chinese immigrant women "regarded prostitution as a means of finding a husband or making a financial start in the United States, an opportunity that would enable them to lead a better life or support a poverty-stricken family at home."[45] While marriage provided a way out of sex work for some early immigrant Chinese women, a small number of women were both married and engaged in sex work. Sucheng Chan notes that "the 1900 census manuscript showed that some brothels in San Francisco were run by couples, among whom a few wives were apparently continuing their profession [as prostitutes]."[46] Women in other racial and ethnic groups also combined marriage and sex work, too.

Implementing the Page Law

The notion that prostitutes are inherently distinct in some way from other women is a ruse of power, which upholds literal and symbolic policing strategies that have markedly racist, sexist, and classist effects.[47] The fact that the Page Law was implemented with such severity that, as historians put it, "real" wives were turned away along with prostitutes actually confirms this argument. Racism and sexism ensured that "real" wives became labeled and treated administratively as prostitutes—because that category designates women who occupy positions of social vulnerability, rather than a distinct "type" of woman.

To understand more precisely how efforts to differentiate "real" wives from prostitutes produced racist, sexist, and classist effects (without actually yielding any reliable distinctions), let us examine exactly how officials tried to differentiate among Chinese women. During the first years after passage of the Page Law, the American Consul in Hong Kong played a pivotal role in its enforcement. Prior to emigration, each Chinese woman had to submit "an official declaration of purpose in emigration and personal morality" statement, accompanied by an application for clearance and a fee, to the American Consul.[48] The declaration was sent to an association of the most prominent businessmen in Hong Kong, the Tung Wah Hospital Committee, for investigation. A list of intending emigrants was also sent to the British colonial government in Hong Kong for investigation. The day before the ship sailed, each woman had to answer questions before the consul. These included such inquiries as:

> Have you entered into contract or agreement with any person or persons whomsoever, for a term of service within the United States for

lewd and immoral purposes? Do you wish of your own free and voluntary will to go to the United States? Do you go to the United States for the purposes of prostitution? Are you married or single? What are you going to the United States for? What is to be your occupation there? Have you lived in a house of prostitution in Hong Kong, Macao, or China? Have you engaged in prostitution in either *[sic]* of the above places? Are you a virtuous woman? Do you intend to live a virtuous life in the United States? Do you know that you are at liberty now to go to the United States, or remain in your own country, and that you cannot be forced to go away from your home?[49]

On the day of sailing, each woman had to answer similar questions about morality and reasons for emigration, this time put by the Harbor Master. Once on board the ship, she was questioned again. Women who passed this rigorous series of interrogations were given a certificate of good moral character, which they had to present on arrival in San Francisco if they wanted to land. While the ship sailed, the Consul sent a photograph of each woman who had been approved, along with a letter testifying to her character, to the ship's destination. Sometimes he also sent a letter urging further investigation of a particular woman.[50]

Information about how women were processed on arrival in San Francisco after passage of the Page Law is somewhat sketchy. But transcripts of a habeas corpus hearing involving several Chinese women, held in San Francisco just prior to the passage of the Chinese Exclusion Act in 1882, provide some indication. According to testimony by Colonel Bee, the American Consul for the Chinese, he met all arriving ships from Hong Kong. Accompanied by his Vice Consul and interpreter and by the Deputy Surveyor of the Port of San Francisco, he boarded the ship, and "[got] access to the women before anyone else."[51] He gathered copies of their paperwork with the photographs attached and, using the interpreter, he asked each woman the same questions that she had been asked in Hong Kong. The replies given in Hong Kong were included in each woman's paperwork, and these replies were cross-checked against what she said on arrival in San Francisco.[52] According to Bee's testimony, the questions asked of the women had changed somewhat since Consul Bailey's tenure. For the court, Bee listed the questions that women were asked:

Native residence in Hong Kong; number of the storeys to the house; name of the people in the house; when and from what place I came to Hong Kong; person or persons with whom I came; name, country, and occupation of my father; name, country, and occupation of my husband; names and addresses of sureties; relatives or friends from whom inquiries can be made; the person or persons with whom I am going; the object of my going; the place to which I am going; the street and number of the house where I can be seen.[53]

If the women answered the questions with the same information that was included in their paperwork, and if they matched the photographs, "we have no authority whatever to detain them."[54] But if women did not answer the questions the same way, or did not match the photographs, or carried paperwork that was incompletely filled out, they were liable to be detained. George Peffer estimates that between 1875 and 1882 at least one hundred and perhaps several hundred women were sent back as a result of these procedures.

These procedures, which involved elicitation of biographical data, photography, and the creation of case files, transformed the relationship between the immigrant Chinese woman and the immigration-control bureaucracy into one of discipline and subjection within sexualized, racialized, gendered, and classist parameters. Beginning with biographical data, we see that any Chinese woman wanting to enter the United States after 1875 was compelled to provide details of her life to a degree that was unprecedented in immigration control. Furthermore, she had to provide details specifically related to her sexual "virtue," which were minutely scrutinized and analyzed. Foucault has suggested that the drive to elicit biographical details from ordinary people marked an important shift in relations of power. Traditionally, powerful and important people were the ones from whom biographical details were elicited, recorded, and scrutinized. But in disciplinary societies, it was society's "Others"— the poor, colored, female, and criminal—who were required to provide biographical details. This change did not, by any means, reflect a leveling of the social field. On the contrary, such detailed "description [became] a means of control and a method of domination."[55] For instance, if Chinese women refused to provide details of their lives for official scrutiny, they were denied the possibility of immigrating.

Foucault draws attention to the ways that the calculated manipulation of spatial relations is integral to disciplinary societies, writing poetically, "stones can make people docile and knowable."[56] In the case of Chinese women seeking to immigrate to the United States, biographical details were elicited only after they had been corralled into carefully controlled spaces. The first two interrogations were carried out in the Consul's and Harbor Master's offices, and on their terms. The third interrogation took place immediately before the ship sailed, in a manner designed to ensure that the woman who answered the officials' questions "correctly" was also the one who sailed for San Francisco (rather than a substitute being sent in her place). On arrival in San Francisco, the women were confined on the ship to ensure that Colonel Bee "[got] access to them before anyone else." Only after answering questions to Bee's satisfaction were the women permitted to join relatives and friends waiting on the dock. The strategic control of space that Chinese women endured was intended by officials to generate the "truth" of their sexual pasts and likely sexual futures. Spatial control was designed to minimize opportunities for the women to be "coached" about what to say to officials, to avoid substitutions, and most likely to provide women who had been kidnapped with an opportunity to speak openly outside the hearing of their procurers. Yet, as Benson Tong suggests, the likelihood of kidnapped women speaking openly to an unknown official was small (though it did sometimes happen).[57] Furthermore, the whole process was shaped by the larger, explicitly racist assumption that "a Chinaman prefers a lie to the truth" and that Chinese women were equally dishonest.[58] As Stuart Creighton Miller describes, a founding image among Western traders, diplomats, and missionaries was that the Chinese were dishonest, tricky, and sneaky, and this image led to the development of exhaustive regimes of questioning, conducted through strictly controlling space and minimizing contact with other Chinese people, which were believed to be the best way to elicit "truth" from Chinese immigrants.[59] Judy Yung underscores that this process was "different not only in degree but in kind" from that endured by other immigrants.[60] The process was not just racist but also racializing, in the sense of helping to literally construct the Chinese as a distinct and racialized group. After passage of the Page Law, Chinese women became subjected to an early form of this racializing process.[61]

The questioning to which Chinese women were subjected involved gender and class dimensions, too. For instance, although the women's individual histories mattered, their fathers' and husbands' mattered more. Officials assumed that women's likelihood of becoming sex workers in the United States depended on their family background and husbands' occupations. Therefore, they wanted to be sure that women came from "respectable" families and were joining husbands who were demonstrably able to support them. To some extent, the officials' approach was cognizant of the realities of limited economic possibilities for immigrant women of color in the U.S. economy at that time. It also took into account the fact that Chinese women did often enter the United States believing that they were joining husbands, only to find that they had been tricked and sold into prostitution. But rather than challenging these conditions, officials simply accepted that male intentions and actions were more likely to determine a woman's sexual future than her own actions and intentions, and processed her case accordingly. Thus, ironically, officials further institutionalized the structures of patriarchy for which they condemned Chinese men. Their processes also institutionalized a distinct class bias regarding Chinese women's possibilities for immigration.[62]

The information that Chinese women produced under these regimes of questioning was not deemed sufficiently reliable on its own terms. Instead, it became subject to verification by external groups, including the Tung Wah Hospital Committee, the British colonial government, and sometimes the U.S. Consul in Hong Kong. In the United States, the consular and port authorities also attempted to independently verify the information that women provided. Through these processes, as Foucault describes, discourses related to sexuality proliferated, emanated from ever more centers, and provided the means to chart new relations of power.[63] Individual Chinese women's testimonies never enabled a reliable differentation between "real" wives and prostitutes. But the testimonies' circulation structurally changed the organization of immigration control.

Biographical data, however, was made fully subjectifying only when it was attached to a photograph. Photographs provided one of the earliest methods for officially recording the body's distinctiveness and using the record to control an individual's mobility. This system was used on Chinese women before any other group of immigrants, because of the "threat" of their sexuality to the United States. A photograph was attached to each woman's consular clearance, and another photograph was sent in advance of the ship, so that when the ship arrived, officials already had in their possession photographs of the women who had been approved for migration. Women who arrived without photographs, or who did not match the photographs that had been sent in advance, were detained and returned to Hong Kong. Through these very simple techniques, officials tried to ensure that if a particular woman was cleared for immigration on the basis of biographical data provided, another woman was not sent in her place.[64]

By contrast, officials did not attempt to link together specific biographies and bodies in the case of Chinese men or anyone else who immigrated at the same time. In testimony before Congress in 1877, the collector of the port related that if one thousand Chinese men were authorized to land and twelve hundred arrived, officials let any thousand land, without trying to determine exactly which thousand were cleared.[65] Some five years later, Colonel Bee testified in court that immigrating Chinese men were still treated less rigorously than women. "We go through the steerage and ask them if they are free laborers, if they come under contract to anybody or under bond to any one and if any one says he is not free we send him back."[66] Mr. Quint, the attorney representing several Chinese women who had been denied landing because they were suspected of coming to the United States for prostitution, asked, "are not each one of these [men] required to have papers the same as females?" But Bee affirmed, "No, I believe not, sir."[67] Men were also not required to carry photographs, nor to match photographs that had been sent in advance to San Francisco port authorities.

Thus, Chinese women were the first group of immigrants whose mobility was regulated by the exchange of photographs between officials. Photographs tied a specific body to biographical data that had been approved by officials for migration. Only as of the second decade of the twentieth century, according to John Torpey, would such a system become broadly implemented in the United States through passport controls.[68] Until then, racialized, gendered, and sexualized Others disproportionately bore the burden of such techniques, as the experience of Chinese women shows.

Other techniques also supplemented (and in some cases supplanted) the use of photography as a means to anchor a body to a specific biography in ways that ensured official control. For instance, Bertillionage, a system of taking nine measurements of different parts of the body and recording these measurements in file cards, was certainly used on Chinese immigrants by the turn of the century.[69] Immigrants who left and wanted to reenter had to submit to being remeasured; if their measurements matched those recorded in the file cards, they were let in. Fingerprinting also came to provide an unchangeable physical mark that officials used to tie individuals to specific biographies in ways that controlled them.[70] More recently, the INS has pioneered a biometric data system called INPASS. As Daniel Sutherland describes:

An INPASS is available to U.S. citizens and resident aliens who fly internationally on a regular basis. The [person] provided the INS with biographical data—home address, date of birth, office address, position in his company, and number of international trips he anticipates making—so the agency could verify that he is authorized by the government to travel. The INS then took an image of his hand geometry (a type of "biometric" data—physical characteristics that are unique to each person, such as a person's voice or retina pattern) and electronically recorded it on a plastic card. The agency also stored the biographical and biometric data in a central computer. Although INPASS is currently a voluntary program, it is designed to demonstrate the feasibility of including machinereadable biographical and biometric data on U.S. passports.[71]

The *New York Times* also reports that the INS has begun to rely on dental and bone X rays when trying to determine how to process people who arrive at airports without documents, or with questionable documents.[72] The X rays are intended to determine whether the person is under eighteen, because adults and minors are processed differently. At some large U.S. airports, arrivals with problematic or missing documents are brought directly to the airport dentist, where the dental drill and row of medicine bottles is their first glimpse of America, and where they are X-rayed. The use of X rays as a means to definitively determine age has been disputed, but nonetheless continues. Through these and other techniques, which were initially used against Chinese women after passage of the Page Law, official techniques for recording the body's distinctiveness and anchoring it to specific biographical data became the locus for new forms of subjection.

That photography enabled new forms of subjection through the body is hardly surprising. As Alan Sekula describes, many official uses of photography developed from and further extended a philosophical paradigm that held that "the surface of the body, and especially the face and head, bore the outward signs of inner character."[73] This paradigm found expression in the various strands of "scientific" studies of "race," as well as in sexology and criminology, in which bodies were photographed, divided into zones, and classified into taxonomic schemes. Thus, the photograph also served as an index of other processes that shaped Chinese women's immigration possibilities. These processes, which have largely remained below the level of description and analysis, involved official scrutiny of the women's appearance and efforts by officials to interpret what they saw by drawing on popular forms of sociological, economic, sexological, racial, and other knowledge. Sucheng Chan indicates the importance of appearance in shaping Chinese women's immigration by describing a court case in which "several missionaries, half a dozen Chinese merchants, and two Chinese male passengers gave contradictory opinions about whether it was possible to tell Chinese prostitutes apart from 'moral' women *by their looks and clothing.*[74] Twenty-two Chinese women's admission hinged on the case's outcome. The U.S. government's 1911 report, *Importation and Harboring of Women for Immoral Purposes,* also acknowledges that in attempting to differentiate prostitutes from other women, "the inspector has to judge *mainly by their appearance* and the stories they tell."[75]

I noted above that scientific racism and popular prejudice facilitated the assumption that bodies that "looked" Chinese were likely to be involved in prostitution. Of course, the idea that Chinese bodies "look" a particular way had to be constructed by scientific racism and then disseminated into popular wisdom.[76] At the risk of stating the obvious, these bodies also had to "look" female, in order to be presumed to be prostitutes. Little has been written about the significance of seeming to have a female, rather than a male, body when being processed for immigration, but there can be no doubt that gender appearance mattered.[77] The salience of gender is suggested by Lucie Cheng's description of how some Chinese tongs smuggled women into the United States for work in prostitution by dressing them as boys.[78] The strategy would be effective only if females and males were subjected to different regimes of processing, regardless of their common "Chineseness." Therefore, "looking" both Chinese and female was what triggered official suspicions that the immigrant was likely a prostitute.

Yet the conflation of Chinese women's bodies with prostitute bodies was never absolute, or officials would not have needed to try to differentiate prostitutes from "real" wives. Accordingly, other signs were also sought. A series of "scientific" discourses, which predated the Page Law, suggested that prostitute bodies carried distinct marks, in addition to features that we are accustomed to thinking of as racial or gendered, which set them apart. For instance, Dr. Alexandre Parent-Duchatelet published an 1836 book about Parisian prostitutes, describing his efforts to delineate a distinct prostitute physiognomy.[79] Subsequent work by the St. Petersburg physician Pauline Tarnowsky claimed that over the course of their lives, the faces of prostitutes looked more degenerate and more mannish, and their genitalia became visibly altered.[80] In 1893 Cesare Lombroso published a study that suggested that prostitutes had distinct genitalia and prehensile feet.[81] By the early twentieth century, eugenicists argued that prostitutes suffered from feeblemindedness and that this condition might be discerned from looking at the face, but could also be objectively diagnosed through use of the Binet intelligence test.[82] In these and other ways, prostitute bodies were believed to be visibly distinct, though no one could agree on what was a reliable differentiating mark.

But testimonies before Congress and reports in immigrant case files show that one of the physical marks that officials often seized upon when inspecting Chinese women was bound feet. At an 1877 hearing before the Joint Special Committee to Investigate Chinese Immigration, dissenting opinions were expressed about the extent to which bound feet were a reliable indicator of "respectability." But Judy Yung suggests that at least some inspectors relied heavily on bound feet when determining whether a Chinese woman was likely to be a prostitute:

> Only women such as my great grandmother who had bound feet and a modest demeanor were considered upper class women with "moral integrity." As one immigration officer wrote in his report, "There has never come to this port, I believe, a bound footed woman who was found to be of immoral character, this condition of affairs being due, it is stated, to the fact that such women, and especially those in the interior, are necessarily confined to their home and seldom frequent the city districts."[83]

This interpretation of the significance of bound feet was not necessarily accurate.[84] But for some officials, bound feet came to serve as a physical mark on which to rely when trying to differentiate prostitutes from "real" wives, as is evident from the extent to which immigration records regularly contain questions and notes about Chinese women's feet.

No doubt, questions of "prettiness," youth, demeanor, and how she walked, were among other bodily "clues" that shaped officials' responses to a Chinese woman seeking to immigrate. As Yung relates, the inspector who processed her great grandmother also wrote, "the present applicant No. 14418 is a very modest appearing woman whose evident sincerity, frankness of expression, and generally favorable demeanor is very convincing."[85]

Officials looked not only at the body but also at the woman's clothes when making judgments about her. Prostitutes have a history of dressing distinctively,[86] sometimes because they were required to, or as a means to advertise their services, display subcultural solidarity, or express class aspirations.[87] It is not entirely surprising, then, that immigration officials carefully examined the clothing of women seeking entry to the United States. At a hearing on Chinese immigration, one official asked, "I have heard there is a difference in the coloring of the lining of the sleeves of the gown [of prostitutes], and that they are distinguished by different costumes?"[88] Though differences in dress were not substantiated, dress remained another aspect of appearance that inspectors carefully examined.

In sum, the appearance of the body and clothing supposedly offered a range of possible clues about "inner character," on which some officials drew when trying to differentiate prostitutes from "real" wives. Though this approach, too, failed to yield any reliable differentiations, it ensured that the dominant philosophical paradigm of the time and the "scientific" studies it generated were centrally though informally incorporated into immigration control. The photographs that were employed to constrain Chinese women's mobility serve as traces of the incorporation of these other processes into immigration control.

"A Vast, Meticulous Documentary Apparatus"

Photographs and biographical information, which combined to sharply restrict Chinese women's immigration possibilities, were joined together in the form of the official case file. According to Foucault, the case file was integral to the functioning of disciplinary societies, because it:

> opened up two correlative possibilities: firstly, the constitution of the individual as a describable, analyzable object, not in order to reduce her to specific features, as did the naturalists in relation to living beings, but in order to maintain her in her individual features, in her particular evolution, in her own aptitudes and abilities, under the gaze of a permanent corpus of knowledge; and secondly, the constitution of a comparative system that made possible the measurement of overall phenomena, the description of groups, the characterization of collective facts, the calculation of the gaps between individuals, their distribution in a given "population" [pronouns transposed].[89]

Chinese women seeking to enter the United States after passage of the Page Law had their photographs and biographical data elicited in ways that constituted them as "describable, analyzable object(s)." Combined together in case files, photographs and biographical data served less to endow women with "personal identities" than to enable ongoing relations of power to be brought to bear upon them. For instance, when the U.S. police investigated prostitution, the women's case files could be pulled, and the photographs and information used to track them down and investigate them further. If they left and reentered the country, their case files served as instruments to govern that process too.

Chinese women's files were also used to locate them within larger collectivities, through which relations of power were also operationalized.[90] One of these collectives was familial. As one inspector explained:

> Suppose the ship came into New York with the newcomer Chinese. The New York office, then Ellis Island, would send out here [to San Francisco] for any records we might have on that person's relatives. My job would be to go through the San Francisco records and pick out the person's father, brother, or sister's files, bundle them up, and send them to New York. It was the same way with Boston, Philadelphia, Seattle, and Los Angeles.[91]

The place of an individual file within a larger familial circuit of cases was marked in many Chinese immigrant case files by the first sheet in the file, titled "Cases Used in Connection With Above Case." The sheet listed the numbers of all case files to which a woman's case could be connected, the relationships between her and these other "cases," the dates of her and their arrival, and the steamers on which they each came. As an organizing device, the sheet ensured that the case files from earlier arrivals were used to police new arrivals, and that their cases, in turn, became instruments for interrogating relatives and friends who arrived later.[92]

Cases undoubtedly also became part of the "calculation of the gaps between individuals, their distribution within a given population,"[93] from which writing and policy recommendations about Chinese women, Chinese immigration, and immigration in general developed. For instance, by the 1890s, individual cases were aggregated into the *Annual Report of the Commissioner General of Immigration,* and today into the *Statistical Yearbook of the Immigration and Naturalization Service.* Over the years there have been significant changes in the numbers and kinds of tables included in these reports, and these shifts suggest changes in how the "calculated management of life" became organized. As Foucault reminds us, "in the form of disciplinary distribution . . . the table has the function of treating multiplicity itself, distributing it and deriving from it as many effects as possible."[94] From these reports and their tables, other kinds of writing about immigration proliferated. Silvia Pedraza notes that "the study of immigrants was closely wedded with the beginnings of social science in America."[95] Data on immigrants also underpinned economic analyses, population and fertility studies, labor market projections, and evaluation of resources, among other forms of official writing through which the state and nation were literally produced.[96]

The photographs that Chinese women were forced to provide for their case files also contributed to the nineteenth-century development of a photographic archive that "encompassed an entire social terrain while positioning individuals within that terrain."[97] The archive included photographs not just of society's Others, such as Chinese women immigrants, but also the U.S.-born white middle class, who reconstructed their race and class identities in part through their perceived difference from these photographed Others. As Sekula explains, "it was only on the basis of mutual comparison, on the basis of the construction of a larger, universal archive, that zones of deviance and respectability could be established."[98] These photographic archives built on, extended, and offered instruction in visual approaches to reading (and at the same time, of course, constructing) race, gender, and class distinctions in ways that "produce[d] subjectivities."[99] They also provided new strategies for constructing a national community that was imagined as white, patriarchal, and bourgeois. For, while looking at photographs, the white middle class "imagine[d] themselves linked to others, similarly represented," while at the same time they were encouraged to engage in "constant surveillance of the social body for 'deviant' outsiders."[100] Visual practices thus ensured that the imagined community of the nation was "not simply a referent of photographic images but also the product."[101]

The circulation of photographs in ways that constrained mobility helped to produce contemporary state structures as well. According to John Torpey, there was a mutually constitutive interplay between emergence of governmental systems for controlling people's mobility across national borders, the consolidation of industrial capitalism, and the emergence of "modern" state structures over the last several centuries.[102] Systems for controlling mobility depended on the creation of documents that uniquely and unambiguously identified each individual, of which the passport is the paradigmatic contemporary example.[103] The passport system, which combines a photograph with biographical and other identifying data, began to take shape only in the nineteenth century and was not widely used in the United States until after 1915. Although Torpey draws connections between the development of the passport system and the procedures adopted to control Chinese immigration after the 1882 Exclusion Act, I suggest that his chronology should be back-dated to acknowledge that Chinese women after the Page Law were actually the first immigrant group in the United States on whom passportlike controls were tried out. In this respect, Chinese women's experiences both illuminated and facilitated key aspects of "modern" state formation in the United States.

The Page Law, which particularly targeted working-class Chinese immigrant women, required officials to differentiate "real" wives from women bound for sex work and to deny entry to the latter. It was an impossible task. The idea that such a differentiation could be made was, as Foucault puts it, a "ruse" that both marked and facilitated particular arrangements of power. But these arrangements were sanctioned because Chinese prostitutes had become popularly identified with multiple dangers to white lives, institutions, and nation. As a result, officials developed techniques for trying to differentiate "real" wives from prostitutes through the elicitation of biographical details, photography, and the creation of case files. Although these techniques never enabled officials to reliably differentiate among women, they had several important effects. For one, the techniques concretely introduced concerns about sexuality into U.S. immigration control processes. They compelled the production of discourses about sexuality and gave rise to varied circuits for exchanging and evaluating these discourses. The circuits linked together bureaucrats, experts, politicians, and the public in new ways, around preoccupations with sexuality, immigration, and nation. The techniques also enabled officials to constitute Chinese women as subjectified and disciplined in racial, gendered, class, and sexual terms. Over time, the policing of immigrants around sexuality, which the Page Law inaugurated, became extended to all newcomers. It remains a central feature of immigration control today.

A focus on the problematic effects of techniques for trying to differentiate prostitutes from other women suggests the need to revise traditional analyses about how immigration control reproduces social inequalities. Certainly, discriminatory laws and officials' prejudices have substantially ensured that U.S. immigration control functioned to sustain racial, gender, sexual, and class hierarchies. But even if the laws were overturned and prejudiced officials let go, immigration control would still reproduce social hierarchies. This is because the techniques and systems of knowledge on which its daily operations depend are deeply rooted in histories of racism, sexism, imperialism, and exploitation, as the history of restrictions on Chinese immigrant women shows. To create real transformation, these techniques and systems of knowledge must also be analyzed and changed.

The traces of these subjectifying technologies and systems of knowledge are contained in immigrant case files, on which immigration scholars often rely. Indeed, I spent time at the National Archives, looking through immigrant case files while formulating this chapter. Yet as the chapter makes clear, the case file is never just evidence of an individual's history. It is also evidence of larger processes through which individuals have been produced *as individuals* in racializing, sexualizing, gendering, and class ways. As Foucault puts it, the case file "at one and the same time constitutes a branch of knowledge and a hold for a branch of power."[104] Thus, immigration scholarship that builds from case files and other official documents needs to critically interrogate the grounds of its own possibility.[105] A reflexive approach toward analyzing case files can contribute to challenging, rather than consolidating, the disciplinary relations that were imposed on Chinese women and are extended to all immigrants today.[106]

3. Birthing a Nation

Race, Ethnicity, and Childbearing

Between 1907 and 1908 Japan and the United States negotiated the Gentlemen's Agreement, which regulated Japanese immigration to the United States for the years to come. In response to anti-Japanese agitation, the agreement terminated the migration of all Japanese laborers to the United States. But it allowed Japanese men who were already resident in the United States to send for wives. Consequently, from 1908 to 1920, wives comprised a substantial proportion of Japanese migration to the United States. Most of the wives were picture brides, a term that referred to the practice whereby men sent photographs of themselves to Japan, accompanied by information about their lives and backgrounds, and asked relatives or friends to find them suitable wives. If families mutually consented, marriage ensued. Picture marriages were in line with customary marriage arrangements in Japan,[1] and also had additional advantages for migrant men. As Yuji Ichioka explains, "few [men] could afford the time and expense of [returning to Japan to find a wife . . . and] some returnees faced the possibility of being inducted into the military."[2] Picture marriages offered a way around these difficulties. Although bridegrooms were not physically present in Japan when the marriage was finalized, the marriage was fully legal and also socially acceptable. The brides then traveled to the United States.

This chapter analyzes the history of Japanese picture brides' immigration to California between 1908 and 1920 in order to illustrate two key, interrelated aspects of how sexuality has historically been regulated through U.S. immigration control.[3] First, immigration laws and practices have privileged conjugal relationships and their attendant sexual forms. As a result, spouses have been exempted from many exclusion and deportation laws, granted preference when numerical quota limits were imposed, and even exempted altogether from quota limitations. Such spousal privilege is consonant with the fact that dominant cultural standards suggest that "sexuality that is 'good,' 'normal,' and 'natural' should ideally be heterosexual, marital, monogamous, reproductive, and non-commercial."[4] Picture brides were admitted despite powerful anti-Japanese prejudice in part because those who crafted the Gentlemen's Agreement were guided by these heteropatriarchal standards.

But racial, ethnic, and class biases have regularly counterbalanced, if not completely overridden, heteropatriarchal standards. Thus, after picture brides began entering the United States in growing numbers, exclusionists constructed their childbearing within marriage—which is supposedly the most respectable end to which female sexuality can be directed within a heteropatriarchal order—as a racial and economic threat to the nation. These exclusionist charges contributed to a distinct shift in immigration law and policy, as evinced by the Immigration Act of 1924, which combined complete Asian exclusion with a preference for European families of "good" stock that were unlikely to become public financial burdens.

This chapter explores the experiences of Japanese picture brides in order to illustrate these two intersecting dimensions of sexual regulation: heteropatriarchal sexual ideals, crosscut by racial and class criteria.[5] Additionally, Japanese picture brides' experiences draw attention to the more general history of how exclusionist movements have regularly gained credibility and followers by attacking immigrants' childbearing. Before the Japanese picture brides arrived, Southern and Eastern European immigrant women's childbearing created a public furor; more recently, Mexican women's childbearing was used to generate support for Proposition 187 in California, which denied services to undocumented immigrants and implicitly legitimized discrimination against all Latinos and Asians.

Japanese Immigration in Context

The arrival of Japanese picture brides in California occurred within the larger context of significant social, political, and economic transformations in Japan. In 1853 United States Commodore Matthew Perry sailed into Tokyo Bay and forcibly opened the country to navigation, trade, and diplomatic relations with the West. The resulting political crisis ushered in the Meiji Restoration, whose leaders pursued a vigorous program of industrialization and Westernization, in part to protect Japan from fur-

ther invasions. Industrialization was substantially financed through bur-
densome new taxes that were levied on farmers, which resulted in literally hundreds of thousands losing their lands. The displaced farmers became internal migrants, seeking new ways to earn a living. Women were
among the displaced. Ronald Takaki relates, "women in rural areas were
leaving home for work almost as commonly as men, and this pattern became increasingly widespread as the Meiji government accelerated modern capitalistic development."[6] Young women became the backbone of
the emerging textile industry and were employed as construction laborers and in the coal mines, among other occupations.[7] Displaced women
and men were ready recruits for overseas migration, through which they
hoped to earn money to pay off family debts or establish themselves back
in Japan. Men had an additional incentive for migration: emigrants and
students studying abroad became exempted from the new conscription
laws. Labor recruiters from Hawaiian plantations vigorously lobbied the
Japanese government to permit labor immigration, and in 1885 the Japanese government agreed, but only on condition that the process was
strictly supervised. Since Japan was eager to be recognized as a world
power, officials wanted to send abroad only those who reflected well on
the nation. When Japanese workers began immigrating not just to Hawaii but also to the U.S. West Coast, Japanese officials screened them particularly carefully and kept close watch over their activities even after
they arrived in the United States.[8]

Most early migrants to the West Coast were men, who were employed
as agricultural laborers or in industries such as the railroads, mining, and
lumber. Evelyn Nakano Glenn writes that "those who managed to accumulate a little capital and know-how launched small enterprises, usually
laundries or shops catering to other Japanese."[9] A small number of women
also immigrated. Census data for 1900 records that 24,326 Japanese
people lived in the continental United States at that time, of whom 985
were women.[10] The majority of these women was unmarried and working in prostitution.[11]

Despite the Japanese government's efforts, the immigrants quickly
came under great pressure from U.S. nativists who demanded their exclusion. It was charged that the Japanese were unfair economic competitors who were bankrupting whites, and that they were racially and culturally unassimilable. Roger Daniels summarizes the major phases of the
anti-Japanese movement in California, where a majority of Japanese immigrants to the mainland settled. According to Daniels, Japanese immigrants were the subject of negative newspaper coverage in 1892 and of an

exclusionist harangue by the anti-Chinese zealot Dennis Kearney. In 1900 an anti-Japanese rally was held in San Francisco, and the major political parties discussed Japanese exclusion at the national level. Between 1901 and 1902, with Chinese exclusion up for renewal, there was ominous discussion of including the Japanese under its provisions. In 1905, the year that the Japanese defeated Russia in Manchuria, anti-Japanese prejudice and discrimination became virtually permanent. Newspapers published anti-Japanese features, anti-Japanese laws were introduced into the California legislature, and anti-Japanese organizations—including the Asiatic Exclusion League, the anti-Jap [sic] Laundry League, and the anti-Japanese League of Alameda County—were founded.[12] In 1906 efforts to segregate Japanese school children in San Francisco generated a national furor and a diplomatic crisis.

Between 1907 and 1908, in response to growing exclusionist sentiments, the United States and Japan negotiated the Gentlemen's Agreement. According to Daniels, this agreement, which involved the exchange of diplomatic notes but not a formal treaty, was presented by President Roosevelt to California agitators as a form of exclusion, albeit one that avoided deliberate affront to Japan. The provisions of the Gentlemen's Agreement provided that (1) no more passports would be issued to skilled or unskilled Japanese laborers, but (2) passports would be issued to Japanese laborers who had previously been in the United States, as well as to the parents, wives, and children of Japanese laborers who were resident in the United States.[13] The first of these provisions was unquestionably racist and classist. European laborers were still permitted to enter the United States, provided they had not secured jobs in advance of their arrival and, paradoxically, that they could prove that they were not "liable to become public charges" despite arriving without jobs. The second provision fit within the historic heteropatriarchal imperatives of the immigration system and became the means for facilitating immigration by Japanese brides to the United States. Their arrival brought about a substantial transformation in the gender composition of the Japanese community. According to Glenn, women comprised a third of the Japanese community by 1924—a substantial increase from the ratio of one woman to every twenty-four men that existed in 1900.[14]

Binational Patriarchy: Constructing Proper Wives through Immigration Control

Japanese and U.S. officials worked together to ensure that the women who wanted to migrate under the Gentlemen's Agreement's provision for brides were indeed legitimately married. Through the verification of women's marriages, officials reinforced patriarchal sexual and gender structures in their own countries and binationally.

In Japan, for instance, the Meiji Civil Code of 1898 had newly "enshrined a conservative, patriarchal form of samurai family as the law of the land, a tradition quite alien to the more fluid and egalitarian family lives of most Japanese."[15] The Code mandated female subordination and male-centered households, to the great dismay of Japanese feminists who had been lobbying for greater equality.[16] It also tied women's subordinate roles more firmly to the state's industrialization and development policies.[17] As Dorinne Kondo observes, the Meiji Civil Code's emphasis on female domesticity was "especially ironic in light of women's prominent role in the industrialization of Japan. . . . Between 1894 and 1912, women formed an average of 60 percent of the industrial workforce in Japan."[18]

The terms of the Gentlemen's Agreement offered Japanese officials new opportunities to enforce the Civil Code's gender norms. For instance, to become eligible to migrate, brides had to show that their names had been entered in their husbands' family registries for at least six months. This requirement was intended to prevent procurers from bringing women to the United States as picture brides and then turning them over to prostitution. Thus, it was supposed to ensure women's sexual "respectability." But the requirement also provided an opportunity for Japanese officials to further their control over systems of marriage, with their attendant sexual and gender roles. As Kondo explains, "general agreement seems to exist that marriage and divorce were easy to obtain before the institution of the Meiji Civil Code. Afterwards, people had to register both marriages and divorces, making the process more cumbersome."[19] Yoshizumi asserts that "only those marriages that had been reported to the person in charge of one's register were officially recognized."[20] Women who did not comply with registration were not eligible to migrate to the United States as brides.

The fact that the Gentlemen's Agreement gave rise to a substantial migration of women yet mandated that they had to be married also reinforced U.S. patriarchal norms. Independent migration by women was increasingly viewed with concern, in part because of widespread public fears, expressed in the debates about "white slavery," that such women would become recruited into prostitution.[21] Married women were considered much more desirable as immigrants, because their sexuality was not deemed threatening and they fit into U.S. state- and nation-building strategies. Thus, the Gentlemen's Agreement also reinforced the centrality of conjugal unions and heteropatriarchal sexuality in the United States.

In order to prove that they met marital and other criteria, Japanese women underwent encounters with Japanese and U.S. bureaucracies that contributed to materializing and reinforcing heteropatriarchal sexual and gender orders. For example, eighteen-year-old Sen Iseno from Fukushima arrived in San Francisco on the *Tenyo Maru* on 26 July 1915. Her case file, number 14533/21-20, includes a standard "primary inspection" form.[22] The form frames Iseno's immigration within a patriarchal trajectory with a distinct class inflection. It records that she was arriving to join a husband. Indeed, the officials even had a special stamp for "photograph marriage," which they used on her documents. Several items on the form, which refer to standard grounds for exclusion, are left blank because her status as a wife joining a husband overrode them. For instance, "whether under contract" and "condition of health" are blank. All contract laborers had been barred since 1885, and those with dangerous contagious diseases were barred as of 1891. Yet wives joining husbands were sometimes exempted from stringent health requirements. Tanioka Take, who also traveled as a picture bride on the *Tenyo Maru,* was certified as having "trachoma—a dangerous contagious disease." But she was "retained in hospital" rather than denied entry, because she was joining a husband.[23] The heteropatriarchal prerogative is also evident in the question "who paid passage?" listed on the primary inspection document. Immigrants whose passage had been paid by another were barred from the United States after 1891. But a husband paying for a wife's passage was exempted. And indeed, Iseno's husband is recorded as paying her passage. Occupationally, Iseno is described as "helping housework *[sic]*." Presumably, housework was a sign of respectability for a married woman. But were she not joining a husband, her occupation would likely be grounds to exclude her as "liable to become a public charge," another class of "undesirables" that was delineated in 1891. The form also asks, "able to read? write?" and the inspector recorded "yes." These questions reflect the fact that literacy requirements for immigrants had been acrimoniously debated; in 1917, illiterates would be mandatorily excluded (though again, norms of female domesticity exempted married women).[24] Iseno's primary inspection form thus makes clear that immigration policy upheld a heteropatriarchal order that gave women joining husbands privileged access to entering the United States.

Iseno was constructed not just in heteropatriarchal terms but also racially. The primary inspection form asks her nationality and race, and officials conflate the two into a single rubber-stamped mark as "Japanese."[25] The form also asks for physical information: height in feet and inches, complexion, color of hair, color of eyes, and marks of identification. But these are left blank, perhaps because the photographs of Iseno and her husband are considered sufficient.

Other documents in Iseno's file extend the patriarchal framing of her immigration within the implicit context of racial conflict. These documents largely concern her husband rather than Iseno herself: a letter from the Japanese Consulate in San Francisco attesting to her husband's occupation as a farmer and that "he is a man of good character and has means to support his family"; a letter from the Bethlehem Japanese Congregational Church in Los Angeles, stating that "Mr. Iseno became a member of our Church in [sic] November 6th, 1910, and during [sic] which period we found him a very faithful and honest man"; a letter from the Dendo-Dan Japanese Interdenominational Board of Missions attesting that "Mr. Iseno is loved and respected by all who know him."[26] The files of other brides who arrived on the *Tenyo Maru* also include letters from banks, public officials, and employers. These letters reveal the ways that acceptable husbands' identities were institutionally constructed. In addition to having to prove social respectability and financial solvency and being certified by the Japanese Consulate, several other standards for husbands prevailed. Until 1915 only businessmen and farmers could send for wives, and only if they met income guidelines. After 1915 occupationally based differentiations were replaced by a single cash standard: any Japanese man residing in the United States could send for a bride if he had $800 in savings. Each man had to submit a bankbook, showing this sum in his bank account for a minimum of five months prior to applying to bring a bride to the United States.[27]

To unite with their brides, husbands presented themselves and their documents at the immigration station. If officials found them acceptable, the brides were released from detention.[28] The fact that husbands sometimes had difficulty persuading officials to release the brides is suggested by Kazu Ito, who relates, "there were many strategies to get the brides out of the Immigration Department's House of Detention as quickly as possible. One method was to put a $50 or $100 bill in a box of cigars or chocolates and send it to an official's house."[29] Women sometimes had to undergo marriage on dock before officials would release them. Alternatively, a husband could present evidence that he planned to hold a marriage ceremony in accordance with U.S. law. Thus Iseno's file includes a form certifying that her husband has applied for a marriage license and another certifying that the minister of the Japanese M.E. Church has "united said persons in marriage." Only in 1917 did the U.S. government make a determination that picture marriage was "legal," thus ending the necessity of marriage on dock for the Japanese brides.

Through these requirements, the U.S. and Japanese governments together brought women and men more firmly under state control, mandating their submission to bourgeois patriarchal marriage forms. Japanese participation in promoting "respectable" marriage was also intended, to some extent, to symbolize the respectability, assimilability, and equality of their immigrants.

Japanese immigrants were also aware that marriages provided leverage through which to try to renegotiate their negative image and subordinated social status. Thus, women who had been released by the immigration service often went directly to clothing stores that were built by the dock, where they were outfitted in "American" clothing. Yuji Ichioka characterized the donning of American clothing as a strategic move intended to symbolize willingness to assimilate, contrary to the exclusionist charges.[30] One new arrival described her visit to the clothing store:

> There was a store set up especially for these new arrivals. There was a hotel run by a Japanese and also Japanese food available. The Japanese couldn't go into the stores run by whites, so there were stores run by the Japanese to deal with Japanese customers. We did all our shopping there. The lady there would show us how to use a corset, since we had never used one in Japan. And how to wear stockings and shoes.[31]

Clearly, clothes shopping materially introduced newly arrived Japanese brides to the reality of U.S. racial segregation and at the same time suggested how recrafting gender and sexual norms in conformity with aspects of the dominant U.S. standards offered possibilities for contesting racism and exclusionist agitation.[32]

It is tragic and ironic that despite their efforts to use bourgeois, patriarchal marriage forms as a means to symbolize assimilability, Japanese immigrants became the focus of renewed exclusionist agitation after the Gentlemen's Agreement was signed. This time, however, the long-standing claims of racial unassimilability and economic competition became routed through charges that Japanese wives bore too many children and mothered them inappropriately. These charges illustrate how valorized female sexual norms, epitomized by women's submission of their sexuality to childbearing within marriage, involve racial limits. An anti-Japanese pamphlet written by V. S. McClatchy as a brief for the State

Department offers one means to analyze how such racial limits became expressed—with consequences for immigration laws.

"Securing Lands and Begetting Many Children"

V. S. McClatchy, the author of the anti-Japanese pamphlet "Japanese Immigration and Colonization,"[33] was a significant figure in the Japanese exclusion movement. Roger Daniels relates that he was one of two sons of the founder of a Sacramento newspaper, the *Bee*, and he served as the publisher of the *Bee* for some time while also using the *Bee* to circulate his anti-Japanese views. When the Japanese Exclusion League was formed in 1920, its power devolved into McClatchy's hands. In 1922, when the League ran out of funds, McClatchy and James McPhelan decided to subsidize the whole anti-Japanese movement.[34] McClatchy was the leader of a three-man delegation sent to Washington in 1924 to try to persuade senators to vote for complete Japanese exclusion. Daniels credits McClatchy, in partnership with Hiram Johnson, with "the final exclusionist victory" of 1924.[35] McClatchy was also the author of many anti-Japanese tracts, and his claims were mirrored by other anti-Japanese discourses that circulated in California at the time. His pamphlet "Japanese Immigration and Colonization" both reflected and further fueled the exclusionists' angry charges about the supposed dangers presented to California and the nation by Japanese wives' childbearing, in particular.

McClatchy's core claim was that Japan was bent on colonizing more and more territory: after colonizing Korea and Manchuria, the Japanese people "look[ed] with eager eyes for an opportunity to cultivate land abroad.... Only Hawaii and California seemed in all respects satisfactory for Japanese immigration."[36] Japan began sending labor to Hawaii, with the eventual result that "Hawaii is now lost to the white race, and in a few years a majority of its total population will be Japanese."[37] McClatchy claimed that California was the next frontier for such Japanese colonization, and once California had fallen, the Japanese would extend their efforts further eastward until the entire continental United States fell under Japanese control. Thus, McClatchy's brief was intended as a warning "of a grave and imminent danger, not only to California and the Pacific Coast States, but to the Nation itself."[38]

McClatchy's fears of colonization were undoubtedly reinforced by the fact that both the United States and Japan were actively engaged in various colonization projects and sometimes came to blows when their imperialism overlapped or clashed. For instance, the United States annexed the Philippines, Puerto Rico, Guam, and Hawaii in 1898. That same year,

U.S. troops were sent to Cuba to help roust the Spanish and to ensure as well that the United States remained in control of the island. Samoa was annexed the following year. Between 1900 and 1917 the United States intervened in Panama, Nicaragua, the Dominican Republic, Mexico, and Haiti. Japan, meanwhile, acquired Taiwan in 1895 and substantial holdings in Manchuria in 1905. In 1910 it annexed Korea.[39] After World War I, Japan and the United States clashed at the Paris Peace Conference over the issue of who would take over the German leasehold on the Shantung province of China. The province was awarded to Japan, provoking great indignation in the U.S. press. According to Benjamin Ringer, "the disposition of the North Pacific German islands, including the island of Yap, also produced a direct confrontation between Japan and the United States" in 1919.[40] The harsh Japanese suppression of a rebellion in Korea received negative coverage in the United States, further fueling images of ruthless imperialism. Japan and the United States also came to blows as a result of their joint occupation of Siberia, ostensibly intended to rescue Czech troops.[41]

In McClatchy's view, Japan had imperialist designs on the United States too, and immigration was to be the means for realizing these plans. Through immigration, the Japanese could acquire land, and through population-increase from childbirth by immigrants they could begin to crowd out white Americans. Thus, the procreative Japanese married immigrant couple, in particular, would serve as the instrument for Japanese colonization.[42]

McClatchy's fear of the procreative Japanese couple interestingly connects with Foucault's work. As I discussed in the introduction, Foucault argued that the exercise of sovereign power came to assume not the right to kill but to foster and expand life. In particular, "population came to appear above all else as the ultimate end of [that is, purpose for] government."[43] In *The History of Sexuality* Foucault identified the "Malthusian couple" as the site for a deployment of sexuality that was intended to foster population. He connected the Malthusian couple to

> a socialization of procreative behavior; an economic socialization via all the incentives that were brought to bear upon the fertility of couples; a political socialization through the "responsibilization" of couples in regard to the social body as a whole . . . and a medical socialization carried out by attributing a parthogenic value—for the individual and the species—to birth control.[44]

However, Foucault's couple was clearly figured in relation to a project of fostering and extending a homogenous population. McClatchy's writings and the eventual U.S. immigration policy of fully excluding procreative Asian couples reveal that the regulation of couples is also tied to fostering or eliminating racially and nationally distinct populations. Thus, Japanese picture brides' experiences underscore the importance of rerouting Foucault's analysis through the histories of imperialism and racialization. Equally, they reveal the need to analyze gender and sexual roles within the Malthusian couple.

In McClatchy's view, the Gentlemen's Agreement had been intended to stem the growth of the Japanese immigrant population in the continental United States, thus ending the threat of Japanese colonization. Yet the Agreement's family reunification provisions—most importantly, the provisions for wives to join husbands—subverted this intent. Indeed, according to McClatchy, the terms of the Gentlemen's Agreement actually offered Japan a more *effective* means to "increase in her population here by the importation of adult females"[45] who then gave birth at great rates. Under the heading of "The Extraordinary Birth Rate of the Japanese," McClatchy's pamphlet claimed that "no race within our borders can compare with the Japanese in rate of reproduction and vitality . . . the Japanese rate is really about three times that of whites."[46] McClatchy predicted that "in 2002—82 years hence—the Japanese population will equal, and in 2017 will double, the white population of California."[47]

Japanese women's alleged high fertility had dramatic consequences for the U.S. nation. According to white racial dogma exemplified by Lothrop Stoddard's popular book *The Rising Tide of Color Against White World Supremacy,* North America had been settled in a way that established white racial ownership and an opportunity for the "white race" to evolve to an ever more elevated plane:

> Probably few persons appreciate what magnificent racial treasures America possessed at the beginning of the nineteenth century. The colonial stock was perhaps the finest that nature had evolved since the classic Greeks. It was the very pick of the Nordics of the British Isles and adjacent regions of the European continent—picked at a time when those countries were more Nordic than now.[48]

The very process of colonial settlement had been "one continuous, drastic cycle of eugenic selection. . . . The eugenic results were magnificent."[49] But when "non-Nordic" groups entered the United States—or were forcibly incorporated—they became "a menace to our race, ideals, and institutions."[50] While Southern and Eastern Europeans—considered inferior to but nonetheless racially related to the founding stock—lowered American standards, the arrival of Asians, blacks, and others had infinitely worse consequences. "If the white immigrant can gravely disorder the national life, it is not too much to say that the colored immigrant would doom it to certain death."[51]

One possible way to prevent the "certain death" of national life was to "fuse" immigrants of color with whites. Fusion could occur through intermarriage and the bearing of children (again illustrating how women's reproduction stands at the center of social possibilities and national futures). But as Harry Laughlin, the Expert Eugenics Agent to the House Committee on Immigration, explained, "radically different races" could not be safely fused with the "white race." This was because biological theories of the day held that children born to couples of "radically different races" would be unstable and lack the "best" characteristics of either parent.[52] Thus, intermarriage and childbearing were not desirable solutions to the reality of racial difference in the United States.

McClatchy's pamphlet reiterated this racial thinking as it applied to the growing population of Japanese and Japanese Americans on the West Coast. As he explained, "perfect assimilation or amalgamation can only be had through intermarriage. [But] this is impractical" in the case of Japanese immigrants. For one thing, "intermarriage between races widely different in characteristics does not perpetuate the good qualities of either race. The differences between Japanese and American whites are claimed to be so radical as to bring them within this category."[53] Also, race pride among both Japanese and white Americans prevented intermarriage—not to mention that antimiscegenation laws made it illegal. Another barrier was "the practical deprivation of social status suffered thereby on both sides of the Pacific,"[54] as evinced by the difficult social status of "Eurasian" children.

Not only was it impossible to eliminate the Japanese presence through intermarriage but, in fact, the Japanese presence supposedly threatened to reduce white birthrates and white population, even while Japanese population expanded. As Stoddard explained, "inferior" immigrants

> tend to sterilize all strata of higher social and economic levels already in that country. . . . Put into that community a number of immigrants, inferior mentally, socially, and economically, and the natives are un-

willing to have their children associate with them in work or social life. They [natives] then limit the number of their children . . .[55]

In sum, the valorization of women's sexuality when it was channeled into marriage and childbearing clearly did not apply to Japanese immigrants. Those who crafted the Gentlemen's Agreement had included a provision for brides to join husbands, in accordance with heteropatriarchal standards. But when the brides began bearing children, in conformity with patriarchal sexual norms, exclusionists seized upon childbearing itself as evidence of a sinister plot to colonize the United States.

Disloyal Mothering

In addition to their fertility rates, Japanese picture brides' mothering practices became subject to criticism. Nazli Kibria explains that immigrants are expected to "shed their loyalties and connections with traditional immigrant culture and community and become assimilated into the 'melting pot' of America,"[56] and "proper" mothering has been identified as key to ensuring these processes.[57] For example, George Sanchez documents that social reformers in the years between 1910 and 1930 targeted Mexican immigrant mothers for special reeducation programs. They gave particular emphasis to dietary and health practices, which were supposedly "tools in a system of social control intended to construct a well-behaved citizenry."[58] Similarly, John McClymer describes how reformers targeted the "inappropriate" mothering carried out by Polish and other immigrant women in New York's Lower East Side. Among other things, they conducted a "campaign against 'foreign' vegetables, especially cabbage."[59] But even as the state and social reformers targeted mothers, mothering assumed special significance for immigrant women. As Evelyn Glenn explains, mothering was an act of resistance through which women transmitted their culture and ensured the survival and self-esteem of their children in the face of racism.[60]

There is no evidence that Japanese mothers were the targets of such Americanization campaigns. This may be because their children were considered unredeemable anyway, on the grounds of racial "difference."[61] McClatchy's writings nonetheless make clear that Japanese women's mothering was negatively seen as reinforcing the "biological" problem represented by American-born Japanese children. According to McClatchy, Japanese women's mothering practices were driven by fanatical loyalty to the emperor's imperial designs and functioned as forms of disloyalty to the U.S. nation and its future. For instance, schooling is the usual method for transforming children into loyal citizens. But McClatchy claimed that Japanese mothers educated their children in ways that served the interests of the Japanese emperor, not the U.S. state: "the child in this country is forced to attend separate Japanese schools, presided over by Buddhist priests, where he is taught the language, ideals, and duty of a Japanese,"[62] or was even sent directly to Japan for education. That segregated U.S. schools impressed the language, ideals, and duty of white America on Japanese children in a manner intended to deracinate their cultures and retrain them into racial, gender, and class subordination either escaped McClatchy's notice or else seemed perfectly acceptable to him.[63] His account also ignored the substantial debates within the Japanese immigrant community about how best to educate children so that they could avail themselves of U.S. opportunities yet adapt if the parents were forced by exclusionists to return to Japan.[64]

To McClatchy, Japanese immigrants' schooling practices reinforced rather than countered the effects on children of being raised in Japanese families and communities. One of the most significant effects of such an upbringing was that children were raised to become, in McClatchy's view, "inappropriate" laborers. Rather than being content to serve as a racialized labor force that worked on terms defined by white men (and to some extent, white women),[65] they were being socialized into labor practices that McClatchy viewed as threatening to white interests. These labor practices included working in family groups, rather than as individual units of labor.[66] McClatchy recapitulates the common argument against this kind of labor:

> The Japanese possess special advantages in economic competition, partly because of racial characteristics, thrift, industry, low standards of living, general use of women as laborers regardless of their condition as prospective mothers, and prevalence of child labor. The Japanese seem to stand that sort of life without strain on the nervous system; they have been accustomed to it through the generations. The white race as educated in American environment [sic] not only will not do it, but perhaps can not do it.[67]

McClatchy mapped out the full dimensions of the economic threat represented by Japanese laboring families of "low standards of living and high birthrate."[68] The Japanese, he says, moved into an industry, underbid white workers, and then took over the industry. More and more industries were being taken over. The Japanese refused to work for whites but instead worked for one another, sometimes employing whites to work for them. They did not confine themselves to farming but moved into trades and small business where they supplanted white workers. According to McClatchy, they also controlled "through ownership or lease, one sixth of the rich irrigated lands of the State."[69] To him, Japanese control of land seemed to be a direct implementation of Japanese plans to colonize the United States. Through the 1913 Alien Land Law, the California legislature had tried to strip Japanese immigrants of the ability to lease or own land. But the "inappropriately" bred and reared children, who were automatically entitled to U.S. citizenship by virtue of U.S. birth, enabled their Japanese parents to circumvent the ban on ownership or leasing of land. Immigrant parents simply leased or owned lands in the names of these citizen children. Given McClatchy's claim that Japanese colonization plans rested on "securing lands and begetting many children," the fact that the birth of children directly extended Japanese control of land was extremely threatening.[70] McClatchy gloomily predicted the eventual outcome of these arrangements:

> It is only a question of time when such children will come of age and be entitled to unrestricted possession and use of any land which they can purchase. If the Japanese population continues to increase in accordance with present conditions and predictions, it seems inevitable that most of our best lands will pass into the hands of a race which at present is unassimilable.[71]

To McClatchy, the ways that citizen children enabled Japanese parents to control land epitomized the larger problem posed by the birth of a second generation. He reasoned that "a Japanese born here and entitled to all the rights of American citizenship is much more valuable to Japan, in peace and in war, than is an immigrant who is ineligible to citizenship."[72] The utility of these children was reinforced by the Japanese state, which "insists that a child born of Japanese parents anywhere is always Japanese."[73] Parents who failed to petition the Japanese government for expatriation of their children compounded the problem.[74] McClatchy claimed that the parents of less than one child in a thousand petitioned the Japanese government for the child's expatriation.

In short, McClatchy believed that Japanese women's mothering practices, like their childbearing rates, were a significant threat to the U.S. nation and its future. Japanese mothering produced substantial numbers of children who were, in his view, inappropriately schooled, reared in environments that reinforced Japanese pride and identity, encouraged to become economic competitors, and taught to use their U.S. citizenship rights in the interests of the Japanese Emperor.

Fanatical Uterine Nationalists—or Merely Women "With Their Own Hopes"?

According to McClatchy, Japanese women's reasons for having children were unconnected to maternal or wifely sentiment but rather stemmed from fanatical submission to the dictates of the Japanese Emperor:

> Every girl (school girl) is thoroughly drilled in the doctrine that, should she become a "picture bride" in America, or an immigrant to other lands, her loyal duty to her Emperor is to have as many children as possible, so that the foreigners' land may become in time a possession of Japan.[75]

In his view, Japan had cynically used the Gentlemen's Agreement to "create wives" for single Japanese men.[76] Under the terms of the Agreement, brainwashed and submissive Japanese women allowed themselves to be "imported"[77] as wives for unattached Japanese men. Once in the United States, they deployed their "uterine nationalism,"[78] bearing extraordinary numbers of children so that Japan could expand her empire.[79]

Conveniently erased from McClatchy's account was the fact that the United States' own immigration agreements made marriage (and presumed motherhood) a requirement for most Japanese women seeking to enter the country. By requiring Japanese women to marry in order to migrate, these immigration agreements powerfully shaped women's gender and sexual possibilities in the United States.

When women acquiesced to these terms, it was not from blind obedience to Emperor or husband. Instead, social and economic changes in Japan had mobilized women, as well as men, for migration, and some women were actively interested in immigrating to the United States. Evelyn Glenn observes, "Issei women came with their own hopes" to the United States.[80] Mei Nakano lists reasons that motivated many women to migrate to America. Her list includes filial duty but mentions other considerations too:

> I believe we all go to America for one of the following reasons:
> 1. Hope of becoming rich.
> 2. Curiosity of this civilized country called America.
> 3. Fear of the mother-in-law in Japan.
> 4. Sexual anxiety in those who have passed marriage age.

5. Dreams of an idyllic, romantic life in the new land.

6. Lack of ability to support self.

7. Filial obedience; sacrificing self to obey parents' wishes.[81]

But restrictionist immigration laws were closing the door on further Japanese migration. One of the few ways available for a Japanese woman to legally migrate was as the wife of a man already in the United States. Therefore, when a woman consented to marry a man already in the United States, one reason may have been that marriage represented the most practical way to become eligible to immigrate.

Peter Li's work provides a useful focus for understanding how people strategically cultivate family ties that enable them to migrate. Li's ideas were developed in relation to Chinese immigration. Using interview data, he showed that Chinese immigrants, in response to harsh exclusionist laws, strategically created particular kinship ties as a means to gain entry to the United States.[82] Li's work makes clear that immigration provisions do not neutrally apply to preexisting heteropatriarchal families but instead may compel the formation of families in particular ways, or else compel the performance of being a family within parameters that are designed to satisfy immigration officials.[83] Li's analysis is clearly applicable to the situation of Japanese immigrants and helps to illuminate why some women may have been willing to become wives of immigrant men.

Confirming Li's analysis, Akemi Kikimura documented that her mother married her father in large part because she wanted to go to America. Her mother told her:

> I kept coaxing Papa, "Let's go to America." I was on the adventurous side. I wasn't afraid of anything. I wanted to see foreign countries and besides I had consented to marriage with Papa because I had a dream of seeing America. I didn't care for him much . . . he didn't have much education. I could have married a real good person in Japan, but I wanted to see America and Papa was a way to get there.[84]

This particular woman was not a picture bride. However, she married a man whose family history connected him to America, rather than a more educated and high-status man, precisely because she hoped he would offer her a means for migration. By her account, *she* was the instigator of the couple's migration to America—even if immigration rules constructed her as the passive wife following a pioneering male migrant. She was adventurous, eager to see other countries, and particularly driven by curiosity about America.

That some women used marriage as a means for migrating is also suggested by the work of Barbara Kawakami, who refers to a practice called *kari fufu*, or taking on a temporary spouse in order to gain the right to migrate. According to Kawakami:

> To come as a "temporary spouse" was one way to gain entry into the United States or its territories during the Restricted Immigration Period (1908–1924), when married couples were allowed to enter but unmarried persons were barred unless they were immediate relatives of immigrants or were themselves former residents of the United States. After the temporarily married couple entered Hawaii, each applied for a divorce and waited for a year, the required waiting period to be free to remarry. Undoubtedly some of the women who came as *kari fufu* are included in the estimate [of picture bride arrivals]. . . . There are no official records of their numbers, and because of the delicate nature of the matter, it was difficult to arrive at even a reasonable approximation. One Issei woman I interviewed said, almost in a whisper, "You ask me if I came as a picture bride. Not really. I came to Hawaii as a *kari fufu*. So actually this is my second marriage. But I hardly knew the man I came to Hawaii with. I do not even remember his name. We parted as soon as we got here."[85]

Of course, the vast majority of women did not come as *kari fufu*. But the practice makes clear that some women actively created marriage arrangements so that they would be able to immigrate under the terms of the Gentlemen's Agreement.[86]

In short, the construction of Japanese women as passive, dependent wives following pioneering migrant men at the Emperor's behest fails to account for the fact that conditions in Japan had mobilized women as much as men for migration, and Japanese women were often interested in migrating for reasons of their own.[87] Women came primarily as wives not because their racial/gender status rendered them "naturally" subordinate to either Japanese men or the Japanese Emperor, but for a simpler reason—agreements between the United States and Japan meant that marriage was one of the few avenues available to women for legal immigration. Therefore, McClatchy's contention that Japanese women came to the United States because of an imperial command to expand the Japanese empire by childbearing is not particularly plausible. Yet his views were echoed by such individuals and groups as Senator James McPhelan, the State Board of Control of California, and the Asiatic Exclusion League.[88] Even the Commissioner General of Immigration chimed in, characterizing the "prolific tendencies" of Japanese immigrants as "a menace to the peace and prosperity of our citizens" in his 1919 annual report.[89] Clearly, there existed an explicit, widely shared public narrative about how the nation's racial and economic future was threatened by Japanese women's childbearing within heteropatriarchal marriage.[90] Marriage, in turn, was attributed to sinister Japanese designs rather than to the very routine requirements of an immigration agreement.

Not surprisingly, McClatchy's brief concluded with a call to repeal the Gentlemen's Agreement. In his analysis, the Agreement's provisions for ending labor migration were a failure. But worse failure resulted from the provision that allowed entry to picture brides, because this provision was "used to evade the presumable original intent on this side of the Pacific to prevent the development here of an unassimilable Japanese population."[91] Japanese immigration, especially by picture brides of childbearing age, had to be stopped.

Japanese Exclusion

In response to the exclusionists, Japan voluntarily terminated the arrival of picture brides in 1920. But this did not stem the exclusionist tide. The year 1921 saw general restriction of immigration by means of capping entry at 3 percent of "foreign born persons of such nationality resident in the United States as determined by the 1910 census."[92] However, countries whose migration was controlled by treaty (including Japan and Western Hemisphere countries such as Mexico and Canada) were exempted. By 1924 it was clear that even more restrictive national legislation would pass. California exclusionists, bolstered by the 1922 Supreme Court decision that Japanese people were ineligible for citizenship (thus legally establishing that they were neither black nor white, but racially "other"), went to Washington to lobby for total Japanese exclusion under the 1924 bill. McClatchy led the lobbying effort.

Establishing a numerical quota for each nationality remained the favored approach. But senators were unsure what to do about immigration regulated by treaty, such as that from Japan. They initially favored keeping the Gentlemen's Agreement in place and perhaps assigning a quota to Japan, too. But according to Daniels, because the Gentlemen's Agreement was not a formal document and had not been seen by the senators (though its contents had been summarized for them), Secretary of State Hughes asked Japanese Ambassador Hanihara to explicate the terms of the Agreement in a letter. Hanihara did so, and at the same time he expressed concern about calls to fully exclude Japanese immigration. Daniels relates that Hanihara's letter, in the hands of exclusionist Senator Henry

Cabot Lodge, became reinterpreted as a "veiled threat" against the United States, which Lodge used to convince other senators to vote for full Japanese exclusion.[93] Consequently, when the 1924 Immigration Act passed, it apportioned quotas for European countries in a way that drastically reduced Southern and Eastern European immigration; it exempted the Western Hemisphere from quotas; and it denied all "aliens ineligible for citizenship" the right to immigrate. This last clause was specifically directed at Japan and terminated all Japanese migration.

The Act not only capped annual immigration by nationality in a way that ruled out Asian entry but it also extended a heteropatriarchal "preference" system for allocating the numbers of available immigration slots. "Preferences" had been first introduced in 1921, when a numerical cap was set on the total number of immigrants who could be admitted to the United States in any one year. The 1921 Act granted immigration preference to "wives [but not husbands], parents, brothers, sisters, children under 18 years of age, and fiancées" of U.S. citizens, aliens who had applied for citizenship, and aliens who were eligible for citizenship because of military service. The 1924 Act upgraded the status of wives of U.S. citizens, granting them nonquota status, which meant they were exempt from numerical limitations. Wives of residents remained designated as "preference" immigrants. It was only in 1928 that husbands were first granted nonquota status—which reflected the fact that heteropatriarchy apportioned its privileges in a gender-differentiated manner. As Candice Bredbenner explains, "spousal reunification, as understood generally within the framework of immigration policy, meant that a wife moved to rejoin her husband, not the reverse. . . . What was widely acknowledged to be one of men's basic rights—family companionship and the services of family members—seemed at best to be women's uninsured privilege."[94]

Thus, the 1924 Immigration Act institutionalized a convergence between Asian exclusion and the increased privileging of European married couples, weaving racial and heteropatriarchal inclusion/exclusion more tightly together.[95] Although childbearing by Southern and Eastern European women had also generated a significant public outcry,[96] the 1924 Act's preference system actually facilitated the migration of Southern and Eastern European wives who were joining husbands.[97] But Japanese (and Asian) wives found they could not join husbands in the United States after 1924.[98] Bredbenner summarizes, "as immigration law became more restrictive, it exhibited a pronounced partiality, not only for specific racial and ethnic groups but for particular family arrangements" and, indeed, for particular racial/ethnic heteropatriarchal families of "good" stock that were deemed unlikely to become public charges.[99]

The 1924 National Origins Quota Act, which sealed Japanese exclusion until after World War II, embodied a "wishful fantasy of exact self-replication" that was enforced through immigration laws.[100] The Act established racial and ethnic ratios, based on the 1890 census, within which the nation was to be regenerated. However, Asians were completely excluded from these ratios.[101] National regeneration, moreover, proceeded through a heteropatriarchal order that subordinated European immigrant women to the role of biological reproducers within fixed parameters, while expelling Asian immigrant women's biological reproduction as a form of extreme national danger.[102]

Dr. Harry Laughlin, the Immigration Committee's Expert Eugenics Agent, vividly summed up the significance of the 1924 Immigration Act. Conflating family, gender, sexuality, race, and nation into one astonishing metaphor of heterosexual reproduction, he explained:

> Uncle Sam is not an old bachelor; he is the pater familias par excellence, and he should, therefore, look upon every immigrant as a prospective son-in-law. If this view had always been followed, it would have worked to the great advantage of the American people. When Uncle Sam takes such a view, it ties both the old stocks and the new stocks together in the same family tree. The father-in-law will, if he is wise, select only well-endowed sires for his grandchildren. He will reject those too distant in race as well as those inferior in individual and hereditary qualities of mind, body, and spirit. The perpetuity of American institutions depends first of all upon the soundness of the American race. Several great biological advances in this direction were made by the Johnson immigration act of 1924.[103]

Heteropatriarchy after 1924

In 1948 the Asian War Brides Act lifted the ban on Asian wives immigrating to join husbands in the United States. Subsequent changes further removed explicit racial and ethnic barriers to migration.[104] Today, immigration law still promotes sex and childbearing within marriage, endlessly reproducing both heteropatriarchy and classes of immigrants who face exclusion for nonreproductive sexuality or childbearing outside marriage, or childbearing within marriage that costs the state money. Though racial and ethnic limits are no longer explicitly written into immigration law, these concerns nonetheless still shape calculations about the impact of immigrants' heterosexual reproduction on the nation's future. For example, congressional debates in the 1980s and '90s about changing family reunification provisions in immigration law, not to mention California's anti-immigrant Proposition 187 campaign, reflected deep anxieties about the national impact of heterosexual reproduction by immigrant women of color, especially when they are poor or working class.

Time magazine's (special issue) "The New Face of America" (fall 1993) exemplified how racial calculus inevitably informs the public representation of heteropatriarchal reproduction by immigrants. The cover of the issue showed a woman's face, neck, and bare shoulders. Readers were urged to "take a good look at this woman. She was created by computer from a mix of several races. What you see is a remarkable preview of . . . The New Face of America." The mixed-race woman was intended to "dramatize the impact of interethnic marriage" on American's population and likely future. Interethnic marriage, in turn, was attributed to "the latest wave of immigration."[105] Inside, in an article titled "Intermarried . . . With Children," UCLA anthropologist Karen Stephenson explained that "marriage is the main assimilator . . . if you really want to affect change, it's through marriage and childrearing."[106] The article further noted that "some critics fret that all this criss-crossing will damage society's essential 'American' core" but concluded that "those who intermarry have perhaps the strongest sense of what it will take to *return America to an unhyphenated whole.*"[107] The next two pages contained a grid of seemingly unclothed men and women. Women of seven "races" are depicted along the X-axis, and men of the same seven "races" are depicted along the Y-axis (X and Y serving as reminders of the chromosomal calculus of heterosexual biological reproduction).[108] Pictures of the children that would supposedly result from any combinations of these couples having (hetero)sex fill out the grid. Certainly, we were to understand, the children would be born to (inter)*married* couples.

The special issue makes clear that racial and ethnic difference remains at the heart of North American concerns. But now, women's childbearing within mixed marriage, spurred by recent waves of immigration, is portrayed as the instrument to resolve that difference and "return America to an unhyphenated whole."[109] Not coincidentally, that whole is posited as "tending towards whiteness or lightness"[110] through reproduction that results in continually lighter-skinned children.[111] Japanese picture brides' experiences, then, were one important episode in the larger, ongoing social struggle over the link between heteropatriarchal sexuality and racial/ethnic hierarchies in North America.

4. Looking Like a Lesbian

Sexual Monitoring at the U.S.–Mexico Border

While returning by taxicab from Juarez, Mexico, to El Paso, Texas, on 6 January 1960, Sara Harb Quiroz was stopped for questioning by an immigration-service agent. Quiroz was not a newcomer to the United States. She had acquired permanent U.S. residency in July 1954, at the age of twenty, and lived in El Paso where she worked as a domestic. We do not know why she traveled to Juarez on that particular occasion. But her parents and her nine-year-old daughter lived there. Other familial, economic, and social ties also drew the residents of El Paso to Juarez.

Documentation that explains why Quiroz was stopped no longer exists. But Albert Armendariz, the attorney who handled her case, believes she was stopped because of her appearance. "Based on looks. Based on the way she dressed. The way she acted. The way she talked."[1] In the eyes of the immigration inspector who stopped her, Quiroz seemed to be a lesbian. Until as recently as 1990, lesbian immigrants were excludable and deportable from the United States.

The case of Quiroz provides us with a window onto immigration-service efforts to identify and exclude foreign-born women who were believed to be lesbians. Some scholars date lesbian and gay exclusion from 1917, when "constitutional psychopathic inferiors," including those with "abnormal sexual instincts," became excludable.[2] However, the most extensive records about immigration-service efforts to police the border against lesbians and gay men date from after the passage of the 1952 McCarran-Walter Act. In anticipation of the Act, the Senate Committee of the Judiciary had recommended in 1950 that "classes of mental defectives [who are excludable] should be enlarged to include homosexuals and other sex perverts."[3] However, the final wording of the McCarran-Walter Act did not explicitly mention homosexuals. Instead, homosexual exclusion became rolled into the provision that barred entry by psychopathic personalities. A Senate report explained:

> The Public Health Service has advised that the provision for the exclusion of aliens afflicted with psychopathic personality or a mental defect . . . is sufficiently broad to provide for the exclusion of homosexuals and sex perverts. This change in nomenclature is not to be constructed in any way as modifying the intent to exclude all aliens who are sexual deviants.[4]

In 1965 lesbian and gay exclusion was recodified, this time under a provision barring entry by "sexual deviates."

To date, only cases involving men who were alleged by the Immigration and Naturalization Service to be gay have received substantive scholarly analysis. Little is known about the experiences of women.[5] By providing information about Quiroz's case, which is the only documented case involving a woman that has been uncovered to date, I renarrate the history of lesbian and gay immigration exclusion in a way that centers, rather than subsumes, specifically female experiences.[6] In addition, Quiroz's case raises questions about the complexities of mapping histories of immigrant, refugee, and transnational women while using sexual categories that substantially derive their meanings from metropolitan centers.[7]

That Quiroz encountered difficulties when entering at El Paso because an agent suspected that she was a lesbian clearly demonstrates that sexuality functioned as a "dense transfer point for relations of power" at the border.[8] But in analyzing her case, I resist making efforts to determine whether she was a lesbian, since such efforts participate in power relations that recirculate and naturalize dominant cultural notions of sexual "types."[9] Instead, my approach to Quiroz's case focuses on problematizing how mainstream institutions, including the INS, remain invested in constructing fixed boundaries around what homosexuality "is." Such boundary marking involves operations by which mainstream institutions empower and legitimize themselves, while producing diverse minoritized populations.

In addition to using Quiroz's case to explore U.S. immigration-service constructions of homosexuality, this chapter analyzes two related issues. First, I examine how the demand for sexual confession structures immigration monitoring. Second, I argue that immigration exclusions, including those directed at lesbians and gay men, are multiply constructed through overlapping discursive structures, and, therefore, the repeal of a particular exclusion depends on either undoing or rearticulating the various discourses and practices that sustain it.

"Her Hair Was Cut Shorter Than Some Women's": Constructing Lesbianism

According to Foucault, discourses actually construct the very sexualities around which policing is then organized. This certainly proves to be the case when we examine how immigrants came to be designated as excludable on the basis of homosexuality. Since there is no easy way to differentiate lesbians and gay men from heterosexuals, what led certain people to be singled out? On looking through case histories, it appears that immigrants came to INS attention as possible lesbians or gay men on the basis of checkpoints that were set up within the immigration process. These checkpoints served as particularly dense points where dominant institutions constructed (and individuals contested) the possible meanings of lesbian or gay identity and who should be included within these categories.

In thinking through the operation of these checkpoints, we must avoid two common and related mistakes. First, we should not imagine that coherent, predefined lesbian or gay identities always existed among immigrant applicants, and that the checkpoints simply captured these preformed "queer" subjects. To frame the issue in this way is to miss the myriad ways that these checkpoints often regulated the terms by which formation of identity occurs.[10]

Second, and conversely, we have to conceptualize lesbian and gay identities as being never reducible to these checkpoints. Though the checkpoints were dense power points in the dominant culture's production and policing of homosexuality, not all (potential) lesbian/gay subjects were equally affected. This is because lesbian and gay identities are also inflected by race, class, gender, cultural, and religious features that defy the possibility that there can be any uniform queer identity; equally, the checkpoints themselves reflected some degree of bias, such that they captured males more than females, and Latin Americans and Europeans more than Asians. Consequently, in looking at who was likely to become ensnared by these checkpoints, we should never imagine that this was the totality of the kinds of lesbian, gay, or "queer" identities that were passing into the United States.[11]

One of the richest sources of information about these immigration checkpoints comes from court records. Perhaps not surprisingly, almost all of the court cases that have been reconstructed concern men. Very striking is the number of men who ended up being targeted by the INS because of criminal convictions related to sexual activity. Writing about German-born Horst Nemetz, who had no criminal record connected to his sexual activities with men, Shannon Minter describes the extent to which male-male sexual practices remain heavily criminalized:

> his denial of public activity [for which he could have been convicted] means that he never made love on a beach, in a car, in a park, or in any of the other quasi-public places in which heterosexual couples occasionally engage in sexual relations. His denial of "recruiting" means that he never sexually propositioned a man in a bar, at a party, on the street, or anywhere outside his home. His denial of ever being arrested or questioned by the police means either that he was fortunate, or that he avoided gay bars, gay bathhouses, gay cruising areas in parks and bathrooms, and other places that gay men informally gather and socialize. It also means he never had the misfortune of expressing sexual interest to an undercover police officer posing as a gay man.[12]

Court cases confirm that significant numbers of immigrant men came to INS attention on the basis of sexual criminalization.

But given that lesbian sexual activity is not usually as heavily policed, how can we map lesbians onto this history of immigration exclusion? Less policing does not mean that lesbian sexuality is more socially acceptable than gay male sexuality. However, disbelief that women can have sex without the presence of a male penis, and the ways that gender, in conjunction with race and class, has differentially shaped the acquisition and formation of spaces where women could come together to have sex, means that lesbian sexuality has not been scrutinized and policed in the same ways as gay male sexuality. The result was that INS criminal record checks were more likely to affect men, rather than women, who engaged in same-sex activities.

Were lesbians therefore relatively unaffected by the historic practices of homosexual exclusion? That is one possibility. A second possibility is that indicators other than criminal record checks were used to identify women who might be lesbians. Given the dearth of known lesbian exclusion cases, it is difficult to know what these indicators were.[13] The Quiroz case provides one (possibly unrepresentative) example.[14]

As noted above, the lawyer who handled Quiroz's case believes she was stopped because she looked, spoke, and acted "like a lesbian." Quiroz was also unlucky enough to encounter an immigration inspector who had undertaken a personal campaign to identify and expel women who he believed were "sexual deviates":

> There was this fellow who was at the International Bridge. . . . He had a thing for people, especially women . . . who were lesbian, or in his mind were deviates, and met the requirements of the statute [for exclusion]. . . . They would go to Mexico on a visit, and on the way back he would send them to secondary [inspection] where he would determine they were ineligible to enter. This officer was very, very good at making people admit that they were sexual deviates.[15]

The importance of appearance is confirmed by testimony that was given to the INS by Quiroz's employer, to the effect that "the respondent usually wore trousers and a shirt when she came to work and that her hair was cut shorter than some women's."[16]

The use of visual appearance to monitor the border against possible entry by lesbians connects to a complex history. A 1952 Public Health Service report to Congress mentioned visual appearance as one possible index of homosexuality:

> In some instances considerable difficulty may be encountered in substantiating a diagnosis of homosexuality or sexual perversion. In other instances, where the action or behavior of the person *is more obvious, as might be noted in the manner of dress* (so called transvestism [sic] or fetishism), the condition may be more easily substantiated.[17]

This passage suggests that monitoring based on visual appearance operated around the notion of gender inversion—that is, homosexuals could be visually identified by the fact that gay men looked effeminate or lesbians looked masculine.[18] The PHS formulation connects to a broader cultural history of conceptualizing homosexuality as a problem of one gender being trapped in the other gender's body. Linked to that conceptualization was a range of endeavors to scientifically delineate, in a measurable and absolute way, the difference between homosexual and heterosexual bodies. Jennifer Terry has documented the activities of the Committee for the Study of Sex Variants, active in New York City in the 1930s and 1940s. Members of the committee included "psychiatrists, gynecologists, obstetricians, surgeons, radiologists, neurologists, as well as clinical psychologists, an urban sociologist, a criminal anthropologist, and a former Commissioner of the New York City Department of Corrections."[19] This truly impressive array of professionals, scientists, and academics, connected through their efforts to delineate how the homosexual was distinct from the heterosexual, conducted its research under the assumption that "the female sex variant would exhibit traits of the opposite sex. In other words, she would invert her proper gender role."[20] Under this guiding assumption,

> Pathologists looked at skin complexion, fat distribution, coarseness of hair, the condition of the teeth, and commented on the overall facial and bodily structure of each subject. Radiologists took x-rays to determine cranial densities of the skull and "carrying angles" of the pelvis in order to identify anomalous gender characteristics. A dense skull was presumed to be masculine. "Graceful" and "delicate" pelvic bones were feminine.
>
> Endocrinologists measured hormonal levels. . . . Sketches of genitals and breasts were drawn in order to document particular characteristics of sex variance. . . . In analyzing the thirty pages of graphic sketches of breasts and genitals, Dr. Dickinson reported on the general genital differences recognizable in the female sex variant population. He identified ten characteristics which he argued set the sex variant apart from "normal women."[21]

These and other studies were formed around, and helped to keep alive, the notion that lesbians were visibly different from heterosexuals, that lesbian difference had a biological basis, and that lesbianism and heterosexuality were opposites. Thus, it was not surprising that immigration officers tried to identify immigrants who might be lesbians by using the index of gender-inverted appearance. Gay men were similarly sought.

The notion that lesbian and gay immigrants could be identified on the basis of visible difference marks out an area where homophobia and racism share important commonalities. For example, Siobhan Somerville argues that "the structures and methodologies that drove dominant ideologies of race also fueled the pursuit of knowledge about the homosexual body." According to Somerville, comparative anatomy, which was a key methodology of nineteenth-century scientific racism, also provided sexologists with "a ready-made set of procedures and assumptions with which to scan the body visually for discrete markers of [lesbian] difference." Scientific racists particularly focused on the sexual anatomy of African females as a means to establish racial difference; equally, sexologists focused on sexual anatomy, and "one of the most consistent medical characterizations of the anatomy of both African American women and lesbians was the myth of an unusually large clitoris."[22] Finally, anxious efforts at social engineering coalesced around the bodies of the mulatto and the homosexual, who were figured as dangerously "mixed."

While these overlaps reveal significant connections between homophobia and racism, based on economies and epistemologies of visibility, there are also important differences. Nice Rodriguez has described altering her sexuality- and gender-appearance so as to pass official scrutiny during her migration from the Philippines to Canada. Her account resonates with the experiences of U.S.-bound immigrants:

> On the day of her interview [for a visa at the embassy] she wore a tailored suit but she looked like a man and knew she did not stand a chance.
>
> They did not want masculine women in that underpopulated land. They needed babymakers. . . . Her wife got mascara and lipstick and made her look like a babymaker. During her interview with the consular officer she looked ovulating and fertile so she passed it.
>
> Canada had strict immigration laws, but even bugs could sift through a fine mosquito net.[23]

This account captures the process of "straightening up" that many lesbians undertake when they expect to deal with immigration officials. Straightening up includes practices like growing one's hair and nails, buying a dress, accessorizing, and donning makeup. Clearly there is privilege involved in the fact that many visual markers of lesbianism—unlike many visual markers that are conventionally associated with race or gender[24]—can usually be altered or toned down, so as to pass homophobic border guards. But at the same time, the fact that one *has to* straighten up so as to avoid a penalty serves as a reminder that lesbianism *is* a difference. Consequently, Rodriguez suggests that her self-presentation as an ovulating and fertile woman wearing lipstick and mascara did not erase her lesbian difference but instead confirmed the "bug"-like status of lesbians within the immigration system. Monitoring the border on the basis of visual appearance does lend itself to lesbian and gay male subversion, yet at the same time it marks out an area where the identity the INS is trying to contain and expel is also reestablished and reinforced.

The experiences of women of color like Quiroz further complicate analysis of visually based border monitoring. The visual, or that which gets seen, is driven by and redeploys particular cultural knowledges and blindnesses.[25] Though the inspector who stopped Quiroz for questioning saw something different about her, there are many questions we need to ask. Was there really anything different about Quiroz to see? Was the difference he claimed to see really a lesbian difference, or was it another kind of difference that simply became named as "lesbian" through a combination of procedures and expediency? What cultural knowledges and blindnesses organized this inspector's regime of seeing, such that he picked out Quiroz for investigation? What are the connections between the inspector's suspicion that Quiroz was a "sexual deviate" and the long U.S. history of viewing and treating the bodies of women of color as sexually other? The use of visual judgment to monitor the border involves levels of complexity that have yet to be unraveled, where immigrant women of color with diverse sexualities are involved.

In the context of the El Paso–Juarez border where Quiroz was stopped, the regimes through which Mexican immigrants get visually evaluated are further complicated by the historical processes through which that border was imposed. Timothy Dunn explains that "for many decades, the [U.S.-Mexico] border was a tenuous social construct, established and maintained by force."[26] The border, which derived from the Texas Revolution of 1836, the Mexican War of 1846–48, and the Gadsden Purchase of 1853, was

> in large part either ignored or actively contested by *Mexicanos* in the region . . . because it was imposed on them and it disrupted their lives. . . . The full pacification of the region required some 70 years, and involved the prominent use of a variety of coercive measures both by the state and by Anglo groups.[27]

The Border Patrol, created by the Immigration Act of 1924, became a key state institution through which the border was maintained. Border enforcement efforts have continually legitimated the subordination of Mexican-origin peoples in the region, regardless of whether they were citizens, residents, or immigrants. The scrutiny Quiroz received from immigration-service officials derived from and further extended this history.[28] Immigration-service techniques, which involved atomizing and evaluating her appearance, documents, and speech, also echoed and extended the historical processes whereby Latina bodies became racialized and sexualized in the context of imposing the U.S.-Mexico border. As Yvonne Yarbro-Bejarano reminds us, it is not only "our attitudes about our bodies, but our very bodies themselves," that are constructed within social relations, including the relations that Mexican immigrant women negotiate at U.S. southern borders.[29]

Multiple Checkpoints

Ways that lesbians (and gay men) might come to INS attention were not restricted to the visible nor to the existence of police records. Individuals also became suspected of homosexuality during required premigration medical inspections; through the timing and location of their arrival (e.g., people coming into San Francisco just before the lesbian, gay, bisexual, transgender parade); because of information given to the INS by third parties; based on the contents of their suitcases; and as a result of information contained in the forms that all immigrants must complete. Immigration forms included questions about whether one was of good moral character or a sexual deviate or a psychopathic personality, and they also asked the applicant to list all affiliations. Anyone who participated in a lesbian or gay organization potentially had to list that fact. One could, of course, lie or omit information when completing the forms, but only at the risk of a substantial penalty if the INS found out.[30] No doubt there were other ways that lesbians and gay men came to INS attention, but these ways have yet to be uncovered. The impact of these methods for identifying women who might be lesbians was undoubtedly differentiated by race, nationality, class, and other features.[31]

Techniques of Exclusion and Deportation

Once immigrants came to INS attention as possible lesbians, the means used to officially exclude them was to issue them a Class A medical exclusion certificate.[32] This practice no doubt inspired Richard Green's observation that "American immigration policy regarding homosexuals has been a marriage of one government bureaucracy with another: the Immigration and Naturalization Service (INS) and the Public Health Service (PHS)."[33]

It is tempting to assume that use of a medical exclusion certification process signals that medical fears motivated the exclusionary treatment of lesbians and gays. But such a reading does not take into account the full complexity of how exclusion operated. Exclusion never only involved a simple "failure" of medical knowledge. And although medicine is one key discourse through which the homosexual has been constructed as a threatening type, it is not the only such discourse. Robert Poznanski's analysis notes that fears about "morality, subversion, or destitution may have motivated Congress" to enact lesbian and gay exclusion.[34] A plurality of discourses and institutional practices, not just one, underpinned exclusion. Furthermore, these discourses and practices were neither necessarily rational nor commensurate with one another.

The workings of exclusion must therefore be grasped not at the level of lack or plenitude of knowledge but rather at the level of how homophobia is strategically organized and deployed within institutional circuits of power. As David Halperin writes, "Homophobic discourses are not reducible to a set of statements with a specifiable truth-content that can be rationally tested. Rather, homophobic discourses function as part of more general and systemic strategies of delegitimation."[35] Consequently, the practice of issuing Class A medical exclusion certificates to immigrants who were judged lesbian or gay reflected not just that medicine was a key discourse through which lesbians and gay men were constructed as threatening "Others" but also that medical practices provided a means through which a larger discourse of homophobia could be mobilized, channeled, and legitimated.[36]

The medical exclusion certification process connected to the drive for rationalized efficiency. Its use required few additional resources, since the PHS already inspected the physical and mental health of aspiring immigrants and had a system whereby "unfit" people could be certified for exclusion.[37] It was easy to add one more group to the list of those already weeded out.[38] The medical exclusion certification process further fit into the rationality that stressed "scientific" management, since it enabled deployment of disparate homophobic practices under the sign of "medical" intervention.

Issuance of medical exclusion certificates to suspected lesbian and gay immigrants was also congruent with the operations of other government apparatuses. During the massive World War II troop mobilizations, the handling of homosexuality in the ranks underwent a shift from criminalization to psychiatrization. Dishonorably discharging homosexuals for mental illness, rather than charging them with a crime, was deemed preferable on various grounds. Mental illness discharges eliminated time-consuming trials and costly imprisonment; they "made it easier for the military to extend its antihomosexual apparatus to women"; and the process could be conducted in a discretionary manner, without strict evidentiary requirements.[39]

After World War II these military policies toward homosexuality "served as a model for senators who, in 1950, launched the most aggressive attack on homosexual employees that had ever taken place in the federal government."[40] Under Eisenhower, the attack widened further as lesbians and gays became constructed as threats to national security:[41]

> the government's anti-homosexual policies and procedures, which had originated in the wartime military, expanded to include every agency and department of the federal government, and every private company or corporation with a government contract, such as railroad companies and aircraft plants. This affected the job security of more than

six million government workers and armed forces personnel. By the mid-1950s, similar policies had also gone into effect in state and local governments, extending the prohibition on employment of homosexuals to over twelve million workers.... Similar policies were adopted independently by some private companies, and even by such private organizations as the American Red Cross.[42]

At the same time, the American Psychiatric Association (APA), "building on the standardized nomenclature developed by the Army in 1945," issued its first *Diagnostic and Statistical Manual of Mental Disorders* (DSM-I) in 1952. The manual "firmly established homosexuality as a sociopathic personality disorder."[43] This APA classification legitimated the PHS practice of issuing Class A medical exclusion certificates to immigrants who were thought to be lesbian or gay.[44] Class A medical exclusion certification thus shared significant connections with military and employment apparatuses.

Foucault's *The History of Sexuality* (Vol. 1) provides further specification of how the PHS certification system organized a circuit of homophobic discourses and practices. Within immigration monitoring, procedures were needed to ensure that "the will to knowledge regarding sex ... caused the ritual of confession to function within the norms of scientific regularity."[45] In other words, although foreign-born peoples' sexuality could be inquired into at various points within the process, there had to be a way to make the process seem legitimately scientific and to regularize what happened if information such as "I am a lesbian" became revealed. Five procedures, through which these aims could be accomplished, are described by Foucault:

> [first] a clinical codification of the inducement to speak.... [second] the postulate of a general and diffuse causality ... that endowed sex with an inexhaustible and polymorphous causal power. The most discrete event in one's sexual behavior ... was deemed capable of entailing the most varied consequences throughout one's existence.... [third] the principle of a latency intrinsic to sexuality ... [that] made it possible to link the forcing of a difficult confession to scientific practice.... [fourth] through methods of interpretation.... [and lastly] through the medicalization of the effects of confession.[46]

The case of Quiroz offers us an opportunity to examine how these procedures operated together, around the Class A medical exclusion certification system, to create an integrated circuit of power, knowledge, and homophobic practices.

"Scientifically" Eliciting Sexual Confessions

The first feature of this discursive circuit involves the "clinical codification of the inducement to speak." Inducement to speak conjoins neatly
with the third feature, the assumption of a "principle of latency intrinsic
to sexuality . . . [that] ma[kes] it possible to link the forcing of a difficult
confession to scientific practice."

A very basic "inducement to speak" is built into the immigration system, in that one's ability to gain entry into the United States depends on
willingness to respond to any and all questions of immigration officials.
One risks a substantial penalty for lying or omitting information that the
immigration service might consider pertinent to one's application.[47] This
substantial inducement to speak is compounded during the experience
of being held for secondary inspection, as happened to Quiroz when she
attempted to reenter at El Paso. There are variations on how secondary inspection is conducted, but Mr. Armendariz offered one description of how
intimidating the process can be:

> When you go down to the bridge, these people [immigration officials]
> are kings. And they act like kings. They put them [i.e., people detained
> for secondary inspection] in a little room. And they keep them there
> for hours and don't feed them. And one comes in and asks a few ques-
> tions and then leaves them alone. Then another comes in: "We're
> going to put you in the penitentiary for five years, and we're waiting
> for them to pick you up and take you to jail. Unless you tell us the
> truth." And then they end up transcribing what they [the detained]
> said. . . . In my 45 years, I have come across at least 1,000 people who
> insisted they did not say [what the INS statement says they said].
> Under oath.[48]

We do not know if this description reflects Quiroz's experience. But at a
hearing before a Special Inquiry Officer, she attempted to refute the statements that the INS obtained from her during questioning. The Special
Inquiry Officer's decision related that "the respondent testified in an attempt to impeach her statements (Exhibits 3 and 4). She said that the
statements were not read to her and that she cannot read or speak
English. She denied that she had ever been a lesbian and stated that she
has a 9 year old daughter. She testified that she signed the statements because she was told that everything would be all right."[49] Quiroz thus tried
to contest the speech that was attributed to her. This is important, because it was primarily on the basis of her *speech* that she was constructed

as a lesbian. If the speech could be impeached, the "evidence" of homosexuality became severely undermined.[50]

How the INS overturned Quiroz's impeachment efforts is interesting, because of the connections it reveals between inducement to speak, the forcing of a sexual confession, and the use of "scientific practice" to legitimate the whole proceedings. The INS testimony read:

> To rebut the respondent's testimony impeaching the statements, the Government had the two immigration officers who took the statements testify as witnesses. Their testimony was that the statement was read to the respondent at the conclusion, that it was made voluntarily, that she was cooperative, and that her answers were responsive to the questions. Their testimony was also to the effect that there was comprehension between them and the respondent in their speaking with her in the Spanish language during the taking of the statement. In passing it is to be noted that Dr. Coleman [the PHS surgeon who signed the Class A medical exclusion certificate issued to Quiroz] during his testimony, stated that he was present during the taking of the statement (Exhibit 3) and that the respondent replied readily, was relaxed, cooperative, not under duress and did not show hesitancy or embarrassment.
>
> The respondent's attempt to impeach her sworn statements (Exhibits 3 and 4) must fail. Each statement recites at the end thereof that it was read to her. The first statement shows a material correction was made . . . and this was initialed by the respondent . . . I shall therefore consider these two statements [signed by Quiroz] as true and correct.[51]

In essence, the INS argued that they followed proper procedures in the Quiroz case. These included correct administration of the immigration system, requisite adherence to legal doctrines concerning how evidence may be obtained, and validation by a medical authority.

But procedural propriety is not necessarily the key issue here. More significant, in light of Foucault's description of how an economy of discourses becomes organized to generate confession about sexual practices and feelings, is that there *are* procedures, and they *did* work together to ensure that Quiroz provided explicit statements about her sexuality. It was INS adherence to proper procedures that led Quiroz to "confess"

> that she has had homosexual desires for at least a year, that she had homosexual relations on numerous occasions over this period of time with two women whom she named, that she had these relations both

in El Paso, Texas, and Juarez, Mexico, and that the relations were had with weekly frequency. She described in detail the manner in which these homosexual relations were performed . . . the respondent stated that she enjoyed the sexual relations more with women than with men, and that she had entered into such relations voluntarily.[52]

The very scientific and correct nature of the INS procedures operated as relations of force that induced a certain kind of speaking, or confessing, by this woman. It is difficult to believe that Quiroz would have freely volunteered this information to the INS, without being compelled to do so by the procedures. That INS procedures were scientific and proper, however, meant that their operation as relations designed to force sexual confessions become invisible. Consequently, Quiroz's confession, but not the existence of procedures that compelled the confession, became the subject of adjudication in her case. Unfortunately for Quiroz, the alleged "perversity" of lesbians and gay men is often backed up by the claim that they "willingly" talk about their deviant sexual practices so as to "recruit" others into lives of depravity. The erasure of the induced nature of Quiroz's speech subjected her to this derogatory construction, which reconfirmed the original contention of the government about her undesirability.[53]

A third feature of the economy of discourses, referred to by Foucault and evident in the Class A medical exclusion process, was:

> the postulate of a general and diffuse causality . . . that endowed sex with an inexhaustible and polymorphous causal power. The most discrete event in one's sexual behavior . . . was deemed capable of entailing the most varied consequences throughout one's existence.[54]

In Quiroz's case, this feature is perhaps clearest in the Board of Immigration Appeals (BIA) judgment that

> her relations with several women on many occasions demonstrated a pattern of behavior which was antisocial, irresponsible, lacking in social judgment and "without any true judgment of what the results may be" (Doctor Schlenker's testimony, p.33). To use the Public Health Service parlance, she has manifested a disorder of the personality which has brought her into conflict with "the prevailing culture."[55]

The mere fact that Quiroz testified to having sexual relations with two women was deemed evidence that she was irresponsible, antisocial, and personality disordered. The principle of "diffuse causality" is an ever-present resource on which the dominant culture can draw to justify penalizing lesbian and gay existence.

The fourth and fifth features of the economy, which visibly worked through the Class A medical exclusion certificate system, were "methods of interpretation . . . [and] medicalization of the effects of confession."[56] In immigration exclusion cases, issues of interpretation play out at every stage of the process. For example, two key interpretive issues (along with many lesser ones) that emerged in the course of Quiroz's extended court battle to overturn the deportation order against her were: was she a lesbian, and, if so, did that mean she was necessarily a psychopathic personality? (After all, exclusion was based on a certificate issued to her for being a psychopathic personality, not for lesbianism.) The law became the key site within which these interpretive battles were fought—yet medical and psychiatric interpretation also had a role within this process.

As we have seen, Quiroz's first line of defense in the preliminary case was to challenge the manner in which her statements were obtained and used as proof of homosexuality. She also bluntly denied that she was a homosexual and invoked the fact that she had a daughter as clear evidence of her sexual relations with men. Invoking her daughter played into hegemonic constructions of female heterosexuality. Quiroz's second line of defense drew on medical and psychiatric testimony to suggest that being a homosexual was not necessarily equivalent to being a psychopathic personality.

However, the government found that Quiroz's statements to the INS were unimpeachable. They thus found her to be a homosexual, even if she had a daughter. Regarding the second issue, the government acknowledged that there was a possible gap between homosexuality and psychopathic personality. They even included the testimony of one of the PHS surgeons who had signed Quiroz's exclusion certificate that "there are persons who are sexual deviates who are not afflicted with psychopathic personality . . . but [the PHS doctor] is required to certify all homosexuals as psychopathic personalities regardless as to how he privately might feel."[57] Nonetheless, the INS ruled:

> The history of the enactment of Section 212(a)(4) of the Immigration and Nationality Act shows that Congress intended that homosexuals and other sex perverts were to be excluded from admission to the United States and that rather than make a separate class of homosexuals and sex perverts within the excluding provisions, these individuals are to be included within the category of individuals afflicted with psychopathic personality. . . . Notwithstanding the medical opinion of both physician witnesses that a person who is homosexual is not per se afflicted with psychopathic personality and that other character

traits must also be considered, Congress has intended that persons who are homosexuals are to be considered as being afflicted with psychopathic personality. It is on the basis of this clear intent of Congress that the United States Public Health Service, in its manual for the examination of aliens, classifies homosexuals and sexual deviates as being afflicted with psychopathic personality.[58]

Thus, within a legal framework, congressional intent to exclude lesbians and gay men—grounded in Congress's plenary power over immigration, which is not bound by common legal and procedural standards—was affirmed.[59] The order deporting Quiroz stood.

When the case was appealed to the BIA, Quiroz essentially employed the same two lines of defense. But the BIA responded even more harshly than had the Special Inquiry Officer. Regarding the question of whether the evidence established that she was a homosexual, members of the BIA affirmed that Quiroz's original statements were unimpeachable. The BIA also addressed the fact that Quiroz had a daughter. The ruling related the circumstances behind the birth of the daughter: "When she was around sixteen years of age, respondent lived for about two months with a man who then deserted her, apparently when she became pregnant."[60] The Board opinioned that "that affair of ten years ago does not establish that she is not now a homosexual" and, furthermore, reconstructed that affair as a possible reason for her (to them, confirmed) present homosexuality. "There may be a causal connection between this earlier incident and her present problems." Quiroz's efforts to reconstruct herself within a heterosexual framework, through reference to the birth of her daughter, thus backfired, since the BIA used these same facts to advance the common homophobic proposition that unfortunate experiences with a man are the reason why a woman turns to lesbianism.[61] This only strengthened their case.

Regarding the possible gap between homosexuality and psychopathic personality, the BIA tartly ruled:

Each psychiatrist or psychoanalyst may construe the term "homosexual" and "psychopathic personality" according to his own perspective, but within the Public Health Service and the Immigration Service, in order to achieve a degree of uniformity and fairness in the interpretation and administration of this law, we are bound to a more rigid system of classification.[62]

Therefore, within this interpretive struggle, the exigencies of uniform administration took precedence over psychiatric opinion. Not only did administrative need require that homosexuality be treated as equivalent to psychopathic personality; furthermore, the BIA ruled, the two categories actually came together in the person of Quiroz herself. Because Quiroz had engaged in sexual relations with women, "it is our opinion that the respondent falls within the class of [psychopathic] persons defined by the two doctors who testified in this case." Not surprisingly, the BIA concluded that "since Congress unquestionably intended to include homosexuals within the class of aliens afflicted with psychopathic personality, no finding is possible in this case except that she is subject to deportation."[63]

At the district court level, to which Quiroz next appealed, her counsel no longer tried to refute the finding that she was a homosexual. Instead, he concentrated on trying to undo the contention that a homosexual is necessarily a psychopathic personality. But the district court merely affirmed the legal overlap between the two, ruling that "since the record shows the plaintiff is a homosexual she is therefore a person of psychopathic personality."[64]

The fifth circuit brief for Quiroz again hinged on the argument that "the court erred in concluding as a matter of law that since the record shows that plaintiff is a homosexual, she is, therefore, a person of psychopathic personality."[65] Various arguments were marshaled to support this contention. The government's counterbrief acknowledged that Congress had not defined the term "psychopathic personality" and that there were no cases on which to rely for precedent. Nonetheless, Congress had (and has) the right to decide who shall be excluded from immigrating, and government documents suggested that Congress intended to exclude lesbians and gay men. Quiroz was sent yet another letter that ordered her deportation.

Ultimately, Quiroz's lawyer was unable to drive a wedge between the notion of equivalence between homosexuality and psychopathic personality, despite engaging in a prolonged interpretive battle within the courts. He was also unable to challenge the evidence that was used to construct her as homosexual.

Quiroz had one last card to play, however. On 23 June 1961 the Fifth Circuit Court ruled against her and ordered her deportation by 15 August 1961. On 2 August 1961 she married Edward Escudero and filed a motion to reopen her case. We will probably never know the circumstances surrounding this marriage. Was Quiroz a lesbian engaging in a sham marriage, with Escudero as either a willing participant or a dupe? Or did she enter into the marriage in good faith, perhaps trying to "go straight," or even from honest feelings of love, attraction, and affection? Whatever the

circumstances, the motion filed on her behalf requested the right to reopen her case so as to

> present evidence of her marriage and full rehabilitation, being new
> facts which touch upon the issue of deportability. . . . That since the
> order of deportation was entered herein, your applicant has married
> Edward Escudero, who joins this application, and that she is prepared
> to prove that she is, at this time, a normal individual and no longer a
> psychopathic personality.[66]

Given the timing of the marriage, it certainly seems to constitute an effort
to take the charges brought against her and use them to craft a response
that satisfied dominant cultural terms regarding women and sexuality.
The argument that her marriage offered evidence of "rehabilitation" and
of becoming "a normal individual" fits neatly into mainstream assumptions that homosexuality can be "cured" (and, even better, that lesbianism
can be cured by finding the right man).

It was a brave effort. But marriage, too, failed to prevent Quiroz's deportation. This is because, as the INS noted in their "Brief in Opposition,"

> According to counsel's motion the new facts to be proven at the pro-
> posed reopening will show that the respondent has married since the
> order of deportation was entered, is now a normal individual and no
> longer a psychopathic personality. Even if all this should be proven, no
> application is apparent to the matter of the respondent's deportability,
> *which is based on her condition at entry* on January 6, 1960 and not on
> circumstances which may have arisen since that time.[67]

Both sides thus tried to play on the temporal ambiguity of when one
might be said to have "become" homosexual. Quiroz initially tried to
deny her homosexuality; then she presented the birth of her daughter as
evidence that she had had sexual relations with a man sometime in the
past (which might cast doubt on present allegations of homosexuality);
then, through marriage, she tried to construct homosexuality as a prior
condition that was now "cured." The INS, for its part, refuted her initial
denials. The BIA hearing then suggested that the circumstances surrounding the birth of her daughter may have "caused" her lesbianism. Finally, they invoked their legal power by which lesbianism was defined as
significant at time of entry, regardless of any changes later. In the interpretive battle over the construction and penalizing of lesbianism, the INS
eventually won.

We will never know with absolute certainty whether Quiroz was a lesbian. After all, lesbianism has no clear, predefined content that allows us to draw a marker between it and other forms of sexuality. But her case shows how the immigration service, in conjunction with larger circuits of power and knowledge, established the boundaries of who and what counted as a lesbian and then confined Quiroz within that definition. The effects of Quiroz's battle and its resolution were indeed "medicalized" (the fifth feature mentioned by Foucault): Quiroz's Class A medical exclusion certificate stood, and she was deported. Her deportation underscored how U.S. national identity and security were produced through the symbolic and, where possible, literal expulsion of women deemed to be lesbians—especially when these women were working-class Mexicans.

Quiroz's refusal of the lesbian label was certainly intended to avoid deportation. But other reasons may also have motivated her. Perhaps she did not consider herself a lesbian, despite reporting sexual relations with women. Anthropologists such as Joseph Carrier have documented how the construction of male homosexuality in Mexico differs from dominant U.S. constructions, such that men who have sexual relations with other men are not necessarily stigmatized as homosexual.[68] Carrier's work raises questions about how lesbian identity was constructed in the late 1950s and early 1960s in Mexican and U.S. communities that were familiar to Quiroz. It also raises questions about how Quiroz, who was situated at the intersection of several cultures, communities, and traditions, negotiated her sexual identity, which may have changed over time.[69] Though she reported sexual relations with women, did this make her a lesbian? If so, according to whose definition?

Even if Quiroz considered herself a lesbian, claiming the label was undoubtedly complicated by being a Mexican immigrant woman living in a U.S. border city. Oliva Espín notes that immigrant lesbians often remain situated within the contradictory space "between the racism of the dominant society and the sexist and heterosexist expectations of [their] own community."[70] Under those circumstances female sexuality becomes a site through which cultural contestations are played out. Thus, Cherríe Moraga, among others, eloquently documents how declaring oneself a lesbian leaves Latinas vulnerable to the charge of *vendida*, or race traitor.[71] Yolanda Leyva further explains that silence, rather than public admission, enables many Latina lesbians to remain connected to family and community. "Latina lesbians have survived because of that silence, and the protection it has provided, despite the many limits and compromises it has imposed."[72] The INS charge that Quiroz was a lesbian, whether true or not, shattered the protective silence and jeopardized her access to family and community resources. The lesbian label may also have followed her to Mexico, through the gossip of other returnees, or when she was asked to explain her deportation to family and friends. Resettlement becomes very difficult under those circumstances. Quiroz's efforts to refuse the label of lesbian must be framed, therefore, within the context of multiple jeopardies and competing pressures that she faced as an immigrant woman living in a U.S. border city with an anti-Mexican history, as well as the incommensurabilities between different cultural practices of constructing and naming sexual identities.

For these reasons, and in the absence of documents other than official ones, I have resisted offering a judgment about whether Quiroz was a lesbian. My resistance is intended to foreground the dangers of reading immigrant women's sexualities within dominant U.S. frameworks—even when the reading is intended to assist in the formation of a counter-history—because unqualified use of the term "lesbian" may arrogate immigrant women's experiences to U.S.-based paradigms that do not allow for theorization of the ways that immigrant status, allied with experiences of racism, cultural difference, and class exploitation, complicate sexual identities. As Quiroz's case shows, this arrogation may occur in conjunction with systemic violence that is imposed by the state (in the form of deportation). But it is important to emphasize that lesbians do cross borders. Immigrant lesbian lives remain little documented or understood, however.[73]

"A Private Matter That Had No Relevance to Immigration": Repeal of Exclusion

In 1990 Congress repealed immigration provisions that excluded lesbians and gay men. A congressional report stated that "In order to make it clear that the U.S. does not view personal decisions about sexual orientation as a danger to other people in our society, the bill repeals the 'sexual deviation' exclusion ground [in immigration law]."[74] The "end" of exclusion based on sexual orientation has received little attention in studies of immigration. However, a congressional report demonstrates one way that this policy change has been framed and explained:

> The law also needs to be updated in its treatment of sexual orientation. The term "sexual deviation" (INA 212(a)(4)) was included with the other mental health exclusion grounds expressly for the purpose of excluding homosexuals. Not only is this provision out of step with

current notions of privacy and personal dignity, it is also inconsistent with contemporary psychiatric theories. . . . To put an end to this unfairness, Congress must repeal the "sexual deviation" ground [for immigration exclusion].[75]

Tempting as it is to attribute the repeal of exclusion as an outgrowth of "current notions of privacy and personal dignity . . . [and] contemporary psychiatric theories," this explanation is partial at best. As discussed above, exclusion never hinged solely on medical or psychiatric knowledge; rather, that knowledge was deployed as part of a larger strategic formation of homophobic discourses and practices. Alterations in the composition of that knowledge were not sufficient to generate repeal, unless alterations also occurred in the discursive economy as a whole.

One of the most significant alterations to the discursive economy that organized exclusion occurred more than a decade before the 1990 change. In 1979 the Surgeon General directed the PHS to stop automatically issuing Class A medical exclusion certificates solely on the basis of homosexuality. One factor bearing on the Surgeon General's decision was the fact that in 1973 trustees of the American Psychiatric Association "voted to remove homosexuality *per se* from the categories of mental disorder. In the next year, a referendum upholding the decision was passed by the full APA membership."[76] Until this APA action, homosexuality was listed as an illness; and even if its exact nature was disputed, the fact it was officially an illness meant that lesbians and gay men came under PHS purview. After 1974, however, in the absence of an official illness categorization, the PHS was arguably no longer responsible for lesbians or gay men (unless they had specific medical or mental conditions).[77] Other factors, too, undoubtedly had a bearing on the Surgeon General's decision.

When the Surgeon General declared that the PHS would no longer automatically issue Class A medical exclusion certificates to lesbians and gay men, he evoked a sharp response from John M. Harmon, Assistant Attorney General for the Department of Justice. In a memorandum to David M. Crosland, Acting Commissioner of the INS, Harmon excoriated the Surgeon General for his decision and suggested he had overstepped the bounds of his authority. "Congress clearly intended that homosexuality be included in the statutory phrase 'mental defect or disease' and the Surgeon General has no authority to determine that homosexuality is not a 'mental defect or disease' for the purpose of applying the [Immigration] Act," stated the memo.[78] Harmon ruled that the INS remained bound to exclude lesbians and gay men, even without PHS assistance.

In 1980 the INS announced how exclusion would operate:

> If an alien made an "unsolicited, unambiguous admission of homo-
> sexuality" to an INS inspector or was identified as homosexual by a
> "third party who arrived at the same time," the alleged homosexual
> would be subject to a secondary inspection. At that inspection, the
> person would be asked whether he or she was a homosexual. If the
> person answered "no," entry would be permitted. If the person an-
> swered "yes," a formal exclusionary hearing would follow.[79]

In some respects, this approach to exclusion was not very different
from before. Well before 1980, the INS relied on self-disclosure and identification by a third party (though not necessarily a party who arrived at
the same time) to pick out immigrants who might be lesbians or gay
men. Other identificatory practices, such as criminal record checks and
inclusion of key questions on immigration application forms, operated
both pre- and post-1980. Perhaps the main difference was simply the
elimination of one step in the exclusion process: whereas pre-1980, a suspected lesbian or gay immigrant was sent to the PHS for certification before exclusion, after 1980, the INS skipped the certification process and
excluded directly.

The growing questions and criticisms directed toward lesbian and gay
exclusion in the 1980s therefore reflect not the implementation of new,
egregious forms of border control but the loss of the certification process. Various practices were suddenly unbound from the legitimation offered by a medical exclusion certificate, in a way that made them available for further questioning and contestation. In addition, new political
and social formations, including lesbian/gay legal defense and political
advocacy groups, had also emerged, and they directly contested practices
like exclusion. During the 1980s

> the question of how to identify lesbians and gay men had become an
> increasingly vexed one. . . . The INS's stated policy of relying on volun-
> tary admission drew an openly arbitrary line between lesbians and gay
> men who, perhaps unaware of the consequences, announced their
> homosexuality to INS inspectors and those who did not. The enforce-
> ment of the procedure was, as even the State Department and some
> INS officials admitted, uneven and arbitrary . . . the legal uncertainties
> [arising from contradictory court rulings in the 1980s] and adminis-
> trative inconsistencies surrounding the exclusion had made an already
> controversial provision increasingly difficult to justify.[80]

Concerns about discrimination against lesbians and gay men was voiced. Some public officials suggested that "a person's sexual orientation should be a private matter that had no relevance to immigration."[81]

The expression of these problematizations continued unchecked, since neither the medical certification system remained nor did an equally effective new organization of homophobic discourses emerge. The diversity of problematizations meant that a wide spectrum of groups could find something to support in proposals to repeal the exclusion. "Those who supported [the exclusion's] elimination spanned a broad ideological range, including the Carter, Reagan, and Bush administrations, the Select Commission on Immigration and Refugee Policy, the American Psychiatric Association, and numerous civil rights organizations."[82] In 1990 Congress repealed immigration exclusion based on sexual deviation.

New Possibilities, New Struggles

Since 1990 lesbians and gay men have no longer been automatically debarred from emigrating to the United States. The change is significant. But the meanings of this change must be carefully evaluated. After all, although lesbians and gay men are no longer excluded, judicial interpretations of aspects of immigration law remain "heavily influenced by the categoric exclusion of lesbians and gay men under the 1952 Act" and by a heterosexual norm.[83] Lesbians and gay men are still likely to be excluded for lacking good moral character. They also remain unable to use long-term relationships with U.S. citizens or residents as a basis for gaining their own U.S. residency (a right that is available to male/female couples). Once within the United States, lesbians and gay men must continually contend with homophobia.[84]

These are some of the *effects* of homosexuality that continue to make immigration difficult, even after 1990. To assess how homosexuality is likely to remain salient in immigration in the foreseeable future, we would need to examine the operation of major discourses and practices that are critical to the current production of homosexuality. We would also need to analyze how lesbian and gay identities may be reproduced within new collectivities that are no longer delineated within clear lesbian or gay parameters. For example, HIV has become a significant issue in the administration of the immigration system. And HIV, as Katie King observes, is both altering the terrain of what counts as the gay/lesbian community and producing new collectivities that cannot be captured within a gay/straight model.[85] In addition to the reconfiguration of identities caused by HIV/AIDS exclusions, the 1990 Act also established

a new general category of exclusion based on mental or physical disorders. Although general in nature, this ground is linked carefully to
behavior and potentially harmful activities . . . two requirements must
be met if an alien is to be excluded because of a mental or physical disorder. The alien must be determined to have a mental or physical disorder and a history of behavior (or current behaviors associated with
the disorder) that may pose a threat to the property or the safety of the
alien or others . . . the standard is based on the behavior of the alien.[86]

The standard of "harmful activities" and behaviors has the potential to be
unfairly applied to lesbians and gay men in particular, as well as to produce new minoritized collectivities that include but are not limited to
lesbians and gay men.

Clearly, then, despite the 1990 changes, lesbian and gay identities continue to have various kinds of salience in immigration. Nonetheless, the
Act is a key piece of legislation that makes new social justice strategies
possible. Because the Act protects foreign-born lesbians, gay men, and
"queers" from automatic exclusion, a national movement to secure
spousal immigration privileges for same-sex couples,[87] as well as novel
ways of publicly linking struggles around homophobia, racism and anti-
immigrant sentiment, have emerged. Before 1990 these political projects
were greatly handicapped (if not virtually impossible), since foreign-
born people who identified as lesbian, gay, or queer risked exclusion by
announcing their presence, publicizing their struggles, or participating
in organizing.

Repeal of exclusion based on sexual deviation is intelligible within a
framework that is sensitive to the operations of power. Foucault writes:

> power must be understood in the first instance as the multiplicity of
> force relations immanent in the sphere in which they operate and
> which constitute their own organization; as the processes which,
> through ceaseless struggles and confrontations, transforms, strength-
> ens, or reverses them; as the support which these force relations find
> in one another, thus forming a chain or system, or on the contrary, the
> disjunctions and contradictions which isolate them from one another;
> and lastly, as the strategies in which they take effect, whose general de-
> sign or institutional crystallization is embodied in the state apparatus,
> in the formulation of the law, in the various social hegemonies.[88]

Lesbian and gay exclusion functioned until 1990 not because of its
grounding in rational thought but because of its ability to weave together

a range of disparate, sometimes contradictory, and often clearly unreasonable homophobic discourses and practices into a "chain or system." This weaving-together found institutional crystallization in the Class A medical exclusion system, which was supported by "the state apparatus, in the formulation of the law, [and] in the various social hegemonies." At the same time, this formation generated its own "disjunctions and contradictions." Contradictions included the ways that the formation contributed to production of the very sexuality against which it claimed to guard the nation. Quiroz's case offers a valuable window onto the ways that border monitoring enabled the production of official immigration-service definitions of lesbianism, around which exclusions—that potentially affected not just self-identified lesbians but any woman who did not clearly conform to current heterosexual standard—were organized. Border monitoring, in turn, crucially depended on establishing procedures whereby immigrant sexual confessions could be mandated. Quiroz's case, and her strategies of resistance, also provide information about the ways that sexual monitoring of the border was gender differentiated, even though suspected lesbians and gay men were barred from entry under a shared provision. As the case makes clear, racial and class histories integrally structure how gender and sexual identities are produced, negotiated, oppositionally deployed, and sanctioned at the border. Quiroz's case also raises critical questions about how migrant women negotiate sexual identities and communities when the threat of state-sanctioned exclusion or deportation structures their options. Though an "end" to lesbian/gay exclusion in the broadest sense has not occurred, the transformation of conditions of struggle, and of relations between affected individuals and groups, is beyond question.

5. Rape, Asylum, and the U.S. Border Patrol

Previous chapters have examined how standard immigration procedures construct female sexualities and use those constructions to police women's admission to the United States. This chapter focuses on two other major systems for managing migration into the United States: the refugee/asylum system and the Border Patrol. These two systems have undergone significant growth and transformation in the last quarter century. Not insignificantly, those years have also been marked by the emergence of mass migration and the globalization of capital, goods, technologies, information, and services on such a scale that some scholars have proclaimed the death of the nation-state. In this chapter, however, I argue that strategies for managing migration into the United States provide a means through which exclusionary forms of dominant nationalism are continually reinscribed (even though they are continually challenged, too).[1] To develop this argument, I focus on key legal cases from the 1980s and 1990s and examine how the refugee/asylum and Border Patrol systems, in very different ways, conceptualize and respond to migrant women's experiences of rape. As I show, these responses contribute to reinscribing exclusionary nationalism.

Analyzing responses to rape by institutions including the refugee/asylum system and the Border Patrol is complicated by the fact that official definitions of rape have frequently changed. Susan Brownmiller's classic *Against Our Will: Men, Women, and Rape* describes how "rape entered the law . . . as a property crime of man against man. Woman, of course, was viewed as the property."[2] In this framework, rape was an offense committed by one male against another male's property, and the seriousness ascribed to rape depended on the status of the males involved, rather than on the violence inflicted on women. The legacy of this approach is evinced by the ways that "definitions of the crime of rape itself [remain] inscribed with male visions of the sexual sphere—the focus on penetration, the definition of consent . . . the images of female provocation and spiteful false accusation, and the links between desirability, purity, chastity, and value."[3] Rapes of women of color, poor women, and "unchaste" women often did not count within official categories of rape, and these exclusions also shape contemporary institutional responses. For example, "pervasive myths and stereotypes about black women [still] not only shape the kinds of harassment that black women experience but also influence whether black women's stories are likely to be believed."[4] Today, institutional responses to instances of rape continue to both draw on and reinscribe these sorts of sexual, gender, racial, and class hierarchies. As this chapter will make clear, the refugee/asylum and Border Patrol systems' responses reinscribe nationality distinctions, too.[5]

The chapter first describes how the U.S. refugee/asylum system came to recognize that some instances of rape constitute persecution, for which women should be granted asylum. No longer relegated to the realm of the strictly personal, rape became redefined as a political issue that engaged complex social relations. Yet the testimonies about rape that asylum-seeking women provide are often evaluated by asylum officials and the public in heteropatriarchal, racist, and nationalist terms. In these ways, the refugee/asylum system participates in the reinscription of exclusionary forms of nationalism, even while it simultaneously extends new asylum opportunities to women. The Border Patrol's response to rape, however, especially when perpetrated by its own agents, greatly differs from that of the refugee/asylum system. Indeed, the general inability of undocumented women who have been raped by Border Patrol agents to demand accountability from the U.S. government makes clear that "the politics of violence [also] operate through regulating what will or will not . . . qualify under the sign of rape."[6] Thus, the following section analyzes why the rapes of undocumented women remain largely unrepresentable as crimes or problems to address, from the point of view of the government; it then shows how these rapes serve as technologies that reproduce the U.S. social body as stratified by gender, sexuality, race, class, and legal status. In this way, the lack of response to rapes of undocumented women by Border Patrol agents also reinscribes exclusionary nationalism.

By comparing how the refugee/asylum and Border Patrol systems construct the category of rape, and by theorizing the effects of these constructions, this chapter suggests that critical lessons learned from Bosnia and Rwanda about the connections between rape and nation-making have important application to the United States as well.

Rape and Asylum

How best to respond to women's experiences of rape became a pressing issue in asylum cases in the United States in the 1980s. Asylum, like refugee status, is supposedly available to people fleeing persecution on account of race, religion, nationality, membership in a particular social group, or political opinion.[7] Through passage of the 1980 Refugee Act, the United States incorporated this international standard into its own laws.[8] Although the international definition appears neutral, it has been interpreted in ways that privileged some applicants while marginalizing others. In particular, the refugee category has historically been interpreted in ways that presumed a male subject. As Jacqueline Bhabha succinctly explains, "the refugee par excellence was someone heroically seeking to assert his (typically male) individuality against an oppressive state."[9] As a result, realms of experience that usually belonged to women—including experiences of rape—were foreclosed from consideration as "political" and as possible grounds for asylum. In the 1980s feminist advocates began to suggest that in some cases women's experiences of rape amounted to persecution, for which they should be eligible for asylum.

There were good reasons to press for a reinterpretation of women's experiences of rape under refugee law.[10] Rape has been a standard weapon of war and political persecution for centuries.[11] Yet as the authors of a report on genocide in Rwanda note,

> Rape has long been mischaracterized and dismissed by military and political leaders as a private crime or the unfortunate behavior of a renegade soldier. Worse still, it has been accepted precisely because it is so commonplace. The fact that rape often functions in ways similar to other human rights abuse makes all the more striking the fact that, until recently, it has not been exposed and condemned like other violations.[12]

Women seeking asylum sometimes related brutal experiences of rape. Their accounts challenged the usual asylum-granting standards of immigration officials and the courts, which were still accustomed to thinking in terms of male subjects who politically opposed repressive regimes.[13] Two landmark asylum cases, both filed by women from El Salvador and decided in 1987, revealed the contradictory ways that the courts interpreted women's experiences of rape in light of international refugee standards.

The first case involved Sofia Campos Guardado, an undocumented Salvadoran woman who entered the United States in 1984. She applied for asylum on the grounds that she faced persecution for a political opinion that was attributed to her on the basis of her membership in a particular social group, her family.[14] To support her claim, she related the experience of visiting her uncle, who was the chairman of a local agricultural cooperative, and her cousins. While she was there

> An older woman and two young men with rifles arrived and knocked down the door. They dragged Ms. Campos, her uncle, a male cousin and three female cousins to the rim of the farm's waste pit. They tied all the victims' hands and feet and gagged the women. Forcing the women to watch, they hacked the flesh from the men's bodies with machetes, finally shooting them to death. The male attackers then raped the women, including Ms. Campos, while the woman who accompanied the attackers shouted political slogans. The attackers cut the victims loose, [and] threatened to kill them unless they fled immediately.[15]

Campos was hospitalized with a breakdown and later went to work in a factory in San Salvador. On her first visit home, her mother introduced two young men as cousins who had fled the guerillas and moved into the neighborhood. Campos recognized one of them as one of her assailants. He sought her out and threatened on several occasions to kill her if she revealed his identity to her family. Eventually, "after her workplace in San Salvador was burned down by guerillas, Ms. Campos did not want to return to live at her parents' home near her cousin-assailant. She came to this country."[16]

When she applied for asylum, the Board of Immigration Appeals (BIA) ruled that her account was insufficient to prove that the harm she feared was based on political opinion, membership in a particular social group, or a combination of the two. Furthermore, the harm she had experienced was not considered persecution. The Fifth Circuit Court agreed, and ordered Ms. Campos to be returned to El Salvador. Writing about the Campos case in 1995, the INS itself commented that "in what might appear to have been an extreme assessment of the evidence, the court affirmed the Board's determination that the attackers were not motivated by a political opinion they imputed to the victim. Reasonable minds could differ over this record. The court might reasonably have concluded that the chanting of political slogans during rape indicated not merely that the attackers were politically motivated, but more specifically that they believed the petitioner to have contrary political views and they punished her because of it."[17]

The same year that the Campos case was decided in the Fifth Circuit, the Ninth Circuit was also presented with an asylum case involving rape and sexual abuse. The plaintiff was Olimpia Lazo-Majano, also from El Salvador. She had been subjected to repeated beatings, rapes, and other forms of abuse at the hands of Sargent Rene Zuniga of the Salvadoran military, for whom she worked as a domestic. He told her that if she resisted or refused he would "have her tongue cut off, her nails removed one by one, her eyes pulled out, and she would then be killed."[18] He further claimed that he would denounce her as a subversive, which would legitimize his killing of her. According to the court record, "Olimpia believed the Armed Forces would let Zuniga carry out his threat" because she believed that the armed forces were "responsible for lawlessness, rape, torture, and murder" in general.[19]

The Board of Immigration Appeals had ruled that Zuniga's actions were "strictly personal" and therefore Lazo-Majano was ineligible for asylum. A majority of the Ninth Circuit Court disagreed, ruling that "persecution is stamped on every page of this record. Olimpia has been singled out to be bullied, beaten, injured, raped, and enslaved. Olimpia's initial acquiescence does not alter the persecutory character of her treatment."[20] In addition to recognizing rape and beating as persecution, the majority rather astonishingly analyzed Lazo-Majano's experiences in terms of patterns and histories of male domination of women that are clearly political. They wrote: "If the situation is seen in its social context, Zuniga is asserting the political opinion that a man has a right to dominate and he has persecuted Olimpia to force her to accept this opinion without rebellion. . . . When by flight she asserted [a contrary opinion], she became exposed to persecution for her assertion. Persecution threatened her because of her political opinion."[21] Based on the majority's opinion, Lazo-Majano was granted asylum. The decision was unusual but provided a valuable basis for later cases involving rape and sexual abuse.

Judge Poole dissented from the majority in this case, in part because he believed that the relationship between Lazo-Majano and Zuniga was strictly "personal." As he expressed it, Zuniga "wore a uniform, carried a gun, and used both to alternatively vent upon her his rapacious assault or his pathological display of a lover's wooing."[22] Poole's dissent reveals the more common way that rape tended to be read in asylum cases. As Anker et al. write, "Despite the apparent move forward reflected in the court's opinion in Lazo-Majano, the Board and other courts issuing decisions . . . continued to articulate a conception of rape as an act of sexual attraction that is mere 'personal harm' not amounting to persecution."[23]

Within the next decade, national and international developments intersected to cause a shift in the INS's and courts' interpretations of rape in the context of refugee and asylum claims. For one thing, the needs of refugee women began to be acknowledged and addressed at the international level. In April 1985 the United Nations High Commissioner for Refugees (UNHCR) organized a Roundtable on Refugee Women, and in October 1985 it adopted Conclusion 39, which addressed the needs of refugee women.[24] Rape and sexual violence during refugee flight received some international attention when women fleeing Vietnam by boat were raped by pirates in the Gulf of Siam and then often thrown overboard to drown.[25] In 1991 the UNHCR issued "Guidelines for the Protection of Refugee Women," which highlighted, among other issues, that sexual violence may be used as a form of persecution.[26] The use of rape as a weapon of war and a tool of genocide in the former Yugoslavia also drew international attention and condemnation. The judges and chief prosecutor of the International Criminal Tribunal for the Former Yugoslavia committed to prosecuting those who had used rape in such a brutal manner. The Tribunal's mandate was expanded in 1994, requiring that it also investigate and prosecute war crimes that occurred during the Rwandan genocide. The Tribunal was "explicitly empowered to prosecute rape as a crime against humanity and as a violation of the Geneva Conventions" in the aftermath of the Rwandan genocide.[27]

In the context of these international developments, the Women Refugees Project in Cambridge/Somerville, Massachusetts, presented draft guidelines for more gender-sensitive asylum policies to the INS in the fall of 1994.[28] These draft guidelines were widely endorsed by human rights and immigrant rights advocates. Audrey Macklin explains that such guidelines were designed to function as administrative directives, rather than as changes in the law. They did not require an alteration in or addition to the five grounds for claiming asylum that were contained in international law and adopted by the United States in the 1980 Refugee Act. Instead, the guidelines advocated a change in the INS's *interpretation* of the law. They explained how the claims and issues presented by women asylum applicants—including accounts of rape—could be more appro-priately evaluated within existing case law. They also provided "practical instructions on rendering the hearing process less intimidating and more respectful to women."[29] Since the guidelines did not require a change in the law, they ensured that the U.S. system remained consonant with international standards—with the result that useful gender and sexuality decisions from other countries or international tribunals could be drawn on to buttress claims in U.S. courts. A change in administrative proce-dures, rather than in law, was also easier to accomplish.

INS officials were favorably predisposed to consider the gender guide-lines. International developments, especially the attention to rape in the former Yugoslavia, provided an impetus. The Organization of American States, at the urging of groups including the Women Refugees Project, had also issued a report about political violence in Haiti after President Aristide was overthrown. The report documented the systemic use of rape under the illegal regime that ruled Haiti and condemned it as a form of torture.[30] The Board of Immigration Appeals had previously granted a case of asylum to a Haitian woman who had been gang-raped and beaten in retaliation for her pro-Aristide activities, and advocates were cam-paigning to have the decision elevated as a precedent.[31] Canada had pub-lished its own gender guidelines. All these developments contributed to the INS's willingness to consider the draft guidelines.

In May 1995 the INS issued its gender guidelines. The guidelines ac-knowledged that some women present asylum claims on grounds that are similar to males', but others present claims on grounds that are gen-der specific.[32] They also acknowledged that rape may constitute persecu-tion, for which the rape victim may be eligible for asylum: "serious physi-cal harm consistently has been held to constitute persecution. Rape and other forms of severe sexual violence clearly can fall within this rule."[33] Officers were cautioned that "the appearance of sexual violence in a claim should not lead adjudicators to conclude automatically that the claim is an instance of purely personal harm."[34] The guidelines offered suggestions for eliciting and evaluating testimonies in cases that involved sexual violence. For instance, they acknowledged that some women may prefer to speak with a female, rather than a male, asylum officer, and when possible this preference may be accommodated. They also recommended providing women with an opportunity to be interviewed outside the hearing of family members, because speaking about issues of sexual vio-lence in front of family is extremely difficult. The guidelines underscored that sexual violence and rape are traumatic, which "can have a significant impact on the ability to present testimony," including causing memory loss and distortion.[35] The guidelines also noted that trauma affects the demeanor that applicants present, and that "questionable demeanor can be a product of trauma rather than lack of credibility."[36] Traumatized applicants may appear numb or passive, which has at times been misinterpreted in asylum hearings as evidence that they are lying.

Because of advocates' efforts and INS willingness to adopt advocates' recommendations, there has been an important change in how women's experiences of rape and sexual violence tend to be handled within the asylum system. Rape is no longer seen as strictly "personal" harm or as "sexual attraction" clumsily expressed. Instead, rape, especially when it is inflicted because of a woman's political beliefs or actions, is increasingly likely to be analyzed as an instance of a human rights violation and as a possible ground for being admitted to the United States as a legal refugee or asylee.

Nonetheless, only in certain contexts is rape viewed by U.S. asylum officers and the courts as a form of persecution that merits asylum.

When Rape Is Not a Basis for Asylum

Not all experiences of rape are deemed to provide a basis for asylum. Nowhere are these limits more visible than in the handling of women's claims for asylum based on domestic violence. Domestic violence cases often involve instances of rape and sexual abuse, but it remains very difficult to win asylum for domestic violence victims, although a small number of such cases have been granted.[37]

Take the case of R.A., a Guatemalan woman who applied for asylum in the United States after years of severe domestic violence.[38] The violence included rape and sexual abuse:

> The respondent's husband raped her repeatedly. He would beat her before and during unwanted sex. When the respondent resisted, he would accuse her of seeing other men and threaten her with death. The rapes occurred "almost daily," and they caused her severe pain. He passed on a sexually transmitted disease to the respondent from his sexual relations outside their marriage. Once, he kicked the respondent in her genitalia, apparently for no reason, causing the respondent to bleed severely for 8 days. The respondent suffered the most severe pain when he forcefully sodomized her. When she protested, he responded, as he often did, "You're my woman, you do what I say."[39]

In addition, R.A. endured constant and frightening levels of violence, including having her head slammed against a mirror and windows until they broke, being beaten unconscious, having a machete thrown at her, being dragged down the street by her hair, and being pistol whipped. Twice she called the police, but they never came. Her husband ignored three summons to appear in court and the court took no further action. A judge told her that he would not "interfere in domestic disputes." She knew of no shelters or organizations to which she could turn. R.A. eventually fled Guatemala and learned that her husband planned to hunt her down and kill her if she ever returned.

The Board of Immigration Appeals agreed that the treatment R.A. endured had amounted to persecution. Nonetheless, the majority found her to be ineligible for asylum. Their ruling overturned an earlier decision by an immigration judge that had granted asylum to R.A.[40] In deciding to grant asylum, "the Immigration Judge relied in part on the May 26, 1995, INS Asylum Gender Guidelines."[41] The judge granted asylum because she reasoned that R.A.'s persecution had occurred on account of both her political opinion and her membership in a particular social group, each of which are grounds for asylum according to the law. In terms of political opinion, the judge argued that R.A. was opposed to male domination and was subjected to domestic violence including rape, in retaliation. In making that argument, the judge seemingly relied on earlier case law through which battered women have been granted asylum. As Audrey Macklin explains, "a divergence appears to be emerging with respect to the treatment of domestic violence [as a basis for asylum] in the United States, on one hand, and Australia and Canada on the other. The latter link domestic violence to membership in a particular social group, while in the United States, some decision makers use the ground of political opinion in addition to or instead of particular social group."[42] In other words, in the United States, asylum claims by battered women are often evaluated in terms of whether the woman resisted subordination that was imposed upon her, and if she was battered in retaliation. If she was, she is potentially eligible for asylum on the basis of persecution for her political opinion. However, Macklin points to the limits and dangers of such reasoning:

> It seems bizarre to characterize a man's reason for beating his spouse as *her* real or imputed political opinion about her role and status in society. Among other things, it begets potentially invidious and artificial distinctions regarding men's motivation for beating their intimate

partners. . . . [Such] analysis appears predicated on the idea that there are "political" reasons for beating wives, and there are "personal" reasons for beating wives.[43]

Indeed, "domestic violence is not about what a woman believes but about her gender [status]."[44] Consequently, in Macklin's view, domestic violence is more appropriately linked to a woman's membership in a particular, gender-based social group than to her political opinion.

Unfortumately for R.A., a majority of the BIA echoed Macklin's argument about the shortcomings of using "political opinion" as a ground for granting asylum to battered women. They reasoned that the violence and rapes R.A. endured were not in retaliation for any political opinions she held, but because her husband believed that he had the right to behave that way. As the BIA expressed it, his actions "[do] not reflect . . . that he had any understanding of the respondent's perspective or that he even cared what the respondent's perspective may have been."[45] Thus, his actions reflected his own views rather than a response to hers. Since asylum can be granted only when the applicant shows that *she* holds an opinion for which she was persecuted—not when the persecutor holds a discriminatory view—the BIA overturned R.A.'s initial grant of asylum on the basis of political opinion.

The immigration judge had also granted asylum to R.A. because of her membership in a particular, gender-based social group. But as Macklin points out, U.S. courts have been reluctant to accept that gender on its own constitutes a "particular social group." Thus, they require that gender be defined more narrowly by adding other qualifiers. In conformity with this requirement, the judge in R.A.'s case defined her as a member of a social group comprising "Guatemalan women who have been involved intimately with Guatemalan male companions, who believe that women are to live under male domination."[46] Yet the BIA argued that this was not a socially meaningful category, and even if it was, "the respondent has not established that her husband has targeted and harmed her because he perceived her to be a member of this particular social group."[47] In other words, R.A. could not prove that the harm she suffered was on account of her membership in that social group.[48]

Ultimately, although R.A. suffered rapes and physical violence that the BIA acknowledged reached the level of persecution, she was denied asylum. This was because she did not establish to the BIA's satisfaction that her experiences of persecution were on account of one of the five grounds enumerated in refugee law. Unlike the immigration judge who had originally decided R.A.'s case, the majority also felt that "the D.O.J. [Gender] Guidelines . . . provide no definitive answers for a case such as the one before us."[49] R.A. was given thirty days to voluntarily depart from the United States.

The denial of R.A.'s claim generated such a response that in December 2000 the INS issued draft regulations designed to make it easier for victims of domestic violence to receive asylum in the United States. In January 2001 the U.S. Attorney General vacated the BIA's ruling on R.A.'s case and remanded the case to the BIA to reconsider when the proposed rule changes had been finalized.[50] Clearly, refugee/asylum criteria and the question of how they should most appropriately be applied to women's situations including rapes remain sites of contestation and continual revision.

Judges and courts generally seem to have received the message that rape can constitute persecution, which is a positive development.[51] But the BIA's initial denial of R.A.'s application reveals that only certain instances of rape are deemed to merit asylum, even when the rape is persecutory. Asylum applicants must also establish their membership in at least one of the five categories enumerated in refugee/asylum law for gaining asylum and must prove a connection between their membership and the persecutory rape. As R.A.'s case makes clear, this is not easily done. When a woman cannot establish to the court's satisfaction that there is a connection between her experiences of rape and one of these five grounds, she will be denied asylum. Thus, only in certain instances does rape get treated as a valid basis for asylum. In this way, the asylum process inscribes politically troubling differentiations among experiences of rape.[52]

Furthermore, in order to establish the connections between persecutory rape and one of the five grounds for asylum, women must present testimony. Their testimonies are elicited through processes that are paradigmatic of the confessional structure described by Foucault in *The History of Sexuality* (Vol. 1).[53] As Foucault indicates, the confessional structure is a crucial mechanism for deploying sexuality within wider circuits of power. In the context of the refugee/asylum system, nationalist ideology is one of the circuits of power that becomes activated by women asylum seekers' confessions or testimonies about their experiences of rape. According to Sherene Razack, the legal procedures that are used to elicit such testimonies "construct asylum seekers from the Third World either as unworthy claimants or as supplicants begging to be saved from the tyranny of their own cultures, communities and men."[54] By both demanding and producing images of third-world women as especially victimized by their cultures and communities, the testimonial dimensions of the asylum process reinscribes notions of Western superiority, civilization, and decency.[55] At the same time, "the West's implication in the contemporary patterns of global economic exploitation and the political contexts that produce the world's refugees" remains masked.[56] The ways that U.S. women are also subject to exploitation and abuse become minimized as well.

Because asylum testimonies resonate with these nationalist and imperialist discursive structures, Razack suggests that women who are unable to paint themselves as "a Third World Supplicant or an Exotic Female Other" are likely to fail in their applications.[57] Echoing her claim, Saeed Rahman from Pakistan, who received asylum because of persecution for sexual orientation, relates:

> the asylum process requires the painting of one's country in extremely racialist and colonialist ways in order to show [eligibility for asylum]. This requirement can cause great tension for the asylee. . . . When lawyers use terms like intolerant, police brutality, Islamic fundamentalism, etc., images of the Third World, underdeveloped folks, backwardness, and fanaticism are evoked. These images are, of course, very useful for obtaining asylum. However, for some asylees, it can be a difficult discussion. Some of us, as people of color and immigrants in this country, do not buy completely into the U.S. discourse on freedom and rights. We are also aware of the ways in which our histories have been shaped by the United States. For instance, in my case, I grew up under a military dictatorship in Pakistan which was strongly supported and maintained by the United States.[58]

Rahman's remarks underscore how eliciting asylum seekers' testimonies about sexual or sexuality-based persecution serves functions beyond merely exploring the validity of their claims. Rather, the process provides an opportunity to (re)construct colonialist, nationalist contrasts between the United States and other countries—while disavowing the United States' central role in creating and sustaining oppression in other countries, and minimizing the forms of oppression that are experienced by people who live in the United States.[59]

Other Limits on Rape as a Basis for Asylum

Systemic constraints also ensure that only a fraction of potentially eligible asylum cases, including those that involve raped women, are ever brought forward. The constraints are part of what Judith Butler characterizes as "the politics of violence" that operates "through regulating what will and will not be able to appear as an effect of violence."[60] The constraints stem from the fact that the refugee/asylum system operates at the juncture of a profound contradiction. As Bhabha explains, the refugee/asylum system "crystallize(s) the conflict between two founding principles of modern society: the belief in universal human rights which inhere in all individuals by virtue of their common dignity, and the sovereignty of nation states," including the right of states to deny admission to anyone, including people who have been persecuted.[61] This conflict, and the United States' history of often prioritizing nation-state considerations over individual human rights, is evident in the glaring disparity between the treatment of Haitians and Cubans who have sought refuge since 1959. The United States has generally welcomed Cubans, presuming that because they are fleeing Castro and Communism, they are fleeing persecution. By contrast, Haitians fleeing violence, repression, and military coups have frequently been interdicted at sea and returned to their country without any hearings on their claims to asylum. The cases of Haitians who reached the United States were often conducted without a fair process and then denied.[62] Alex Stepick writes of the differential treatment accorded to Haitians and Cubans in 1980:

> the U.S. government's justification for the differential treatment hinged on the distinction between political refugees and economic migrants. The argument did not withstand even superficial scrutiny. . . . In fact, the difference between the [treatment of] Cubans and Haitians . . . had less to do with individual motivations than with the country they left behind (Communist versus right-wing), the community that received them (politically powerful Cubans versus politically invisible Haitians), and their color (predominantly White Cubans versus Black Haitians).[63]

Stepick succinctly captures how foreign and domestic policy considerations and race relations significantly determine which women are given an opportunity to apply for asylum and how their applications are read—even though asylum applications are supposedly decided on a case-by-case basis using a neutral standard.

The Illegal Immigration Reform and Immigrant Responsibility Act (IIRIRA) of 1996 introduced a series of additional constraints that made it much more difficult for everyone, including raped women, to apply for asylum. First, IIRIRA introduced "expedited removal," under which people who arrive in the United States without documents or with false documents are summarily "removed" without a hearing or review. Understandably, the United States does not want to encourage unauthorized entries. But people fleeing persecution often have no choice but to enter without papers or with false papers. Thus, expedited removal means that people who are genuinely fleeing serious persecution may not have their cases heard.

The regulations do provide that if the entering foreigner indicates an intention to apply for asylum, or expresses fear of persecution, she or he will be referred to an official. The official will make a quick determination as to whether the person has a credible fear of persecution. If the decision is negative, the person will be "removed" from the United States unless she or he requests a review of the decision by an immigration judge.[64] Immigration judges' reviews are supposed to occur within twenty-four hours. The review "will be limited to determination of credible fear and may be conducted by telephone or video. If the immigration judge's review finds the alien not to have a credible fear, the rule states that the alien will be promptly removed."[65] Yet many arriving people do not know that they should mention their asylum claims when threatened with expedited removal, nor are they aware that they can ask for the initial asylum officer's decision to be reviewed by a judge.[66] Furthermore, as Helton and Nicoll note, "given that many gender-related [and sexuality-related] claims raise new, unusual and complex issues, an accelerated and abbreviated screening process does not inspire confidence that these claims will be given adequate consideration."[67] Certainly, women who have endured rape may find it impossible to convey their experiences through such an accelerated process.

Even those who are found to have a credible fear of persecution are often detained. Wendy Young explains:

> Despite [the government's] stated commitment to the protection of women fleeing gender-based persecution and other forms of violence, each year the U.S. government detains thousands of asylum seekers, including hundreds of women, pending the outcome of their immigration proceedings. Scattered throughout the country in detention centers and prisons, these women are often locked up for months and even years, cut off from their families, friends, and attorneys, while they await the outcome of a legal process they do not understand. Unlike the criminal inmates with whom they are frequently comingled, these women have committed no offense. Their only "crime" has been to seek refuge in a country that has long held itself out as a haven for the oppressed.[68]

While detained, asylum seekers remain vulnerable to rape and other abuses by guards and the criminals with whom they are sometimes commingled.[69] Thus, they risk a repetition of the violence that drove them to seek asylum in the first place.

For those who enter the United States legally (and without being detained), IIRIRA mandates that they must make an application for asylum within one year of entry or forfeit the possibility. This one-year rule has had a chilling effect on applications. For one thing, many people do not know about the rule and miss the deadline. Logistical difficulties, such as lack of pro bono or affordable legal representation, also prevent people from filing claims within one year. Many people who have been persecuted, including rape victims, suffer from post-traumatic stress disorder (PTSD) as a result of their experiences. PTSD, which is a normal response to abnormal experiences, makes it difficult for people to remember some or all the details of their experiences, especially within a one-year time frame. Yet such details are vital in order to build a convincing case.[70] With the one-year deadline, attorneys find themselves expected to force their clients to remember traumatic details when they are neither ready nor able, or risk losing the case.[71]

A final constraint on women's ability to apply for asylum, even after they have been raped on account of one of the five grounds enumerated in refugee/asylum law, is that they experience great difficulty leaving their countries. As Noemi Masliah explains,

> women generally travel much less and therefore have less opportunity to get where they can apply for asylum. Their ability to migrate is often affected by (1) cultural factors—women cannot travel alone; (2) economic factors—it is expensive to travel and women often have restricted access to money; (3) having fewer educational opportunities which would take them abroad to study; (4) having limited career opportunities which would require international travel, and (5) having childcare responsibilities at home.[72]

To sum up, rapes in contexts that provide opportunities for reiteration of nationalist and colonialist contrasts between the United States' supposed enlightenment and sending countries' supposed backwardness, that can be clearly linked to the five grounds for asylum as these are currently interpreted, and that are deemed unlikely to generate a substantial number of applicants are most likely to be acknowledged as a basis for asylum. Certainly, there are exceptions to these standards, but generally they establish the limits of rape as a basis for claiming asylum.[73]

Furthermore, interlocking constraints prevent many women from ever having an opportunity to present their experiences and claims for asylum. Here, then, we see that many potential claims are foreclosed from ever being brought, and among claims that are brought, larger discursive structures often ensure that women's testimonies of rape get read in ways that resonate with nationalist structures and projects.

Rape and the Border Patrol

Like the refugee/asylum system, the Border Patrol relies on constructions about female sexuality in order to perform its job and, in the process, to reproduce dominant forms of U.S. nationalism and imperialism. Yet the Border Patrol constructs sexuality differently than the refugee/asylum system does. A key difference is that Border Patrol agents have been implicated in incidents of rape and sexual abuse of undocumented women. Given that Border Patrol agents represent the U.S. government, their actions, and the government's response to them, provide crucial insight into the connections between rape and the maintenance of national borders. A recent court case brought by Blanca Bernal against the INS after she was raped by Border Patrol agent Larry Selders enables an analysis of these connections.

To fully understand Bernal's case, we need to situate it in relation to the history of U.S.-Mexico border, which was a creation of the U.S.-Mexico war, the Treaty of Guadalupe-Hidalgo (1848) that forced Mexico to cede nearly half of its territory to the United States, and the Gadsden Purchase (1853). Despite the fact that U.S. borders have continually changed and that the U.S.-Mexico border specifically was derived from war and conquest, people tend to view the border as natural, inevitable, and an area to be protected from incursion at all costs. As Néstor Rodríguez expresses it, "the state boundary between the United States and Mexico appears today as an immutable fact,"[74] constructed as such by processes including the activities of the Border Patrol. Rodríguez explains, "undoubtedly, the perceived absolute character of the border is related to the absolute power that maintains it. At U.S. border sites, this power is manifested through the presence and activities of the Border Patrol, Customs, and other federal agencies. . . . the 'necessary' character of the border is also produced by other processes of social construction,"[75] which include discourses of national security,[76] representations of the border as "out of control," and images of the border as the site through which Latino "aliens" (who are supposedly completely "Other" to "Americans") enter and threaten the United States.[77] Calls to reinforce the border have also become common responses to deindustrialization and a shrinking social safety net, and, since September 11, to fears of terrorism and the changing global order. In short, the U.S.-Mexico border is a material site produced through histories of war, conquest, and purchase, around which various discourses powerfully coalesce. In turn, these discourses legitimate the activities of the Border Patrol, which supposedly secures the border from incursion.[78]

The Border Patrol was created in 1924 to control the entry of people along U.S. land borders. Historically, a majority of its personnel and resources have always been located at the U.S.-Mexico border rather than the U.S.-Canadian border.[79] The Border Patrol has undergone enormous transformations since the late 1970s, including increased militarization and substantial growth in personnel. In terms of militarization, the expansion of the "war on drugs" in the 1980s generated cooperation between the Drug Enforcement Administration, the FBI, the Coast Guard, and the Border Patrol in carrying out border monitoring, thus ending the historical separation of police and military authority at the border.[80] Technology used to monitor the border was increasingly militarized and included "data links, computer systems, seismic, magnetic and infrared sensors, low-light television systems, airplanes, and helicopters."[81] By 1989 the Border Patrol had "issued M-16 automatic rifles, created counterinsurgency units and trained its agents in riot control."[82] "Experimental technologies previously off limits" began to be tested; these included "an electric current that stops a fleeing car, a camera that can see into vehicles for hidden passengers, and a computer that checks commuters by voiceprint."[83]

The INS budget ballooned in the 1990s, from $1.5 billion in 1994 to $3.9 billion in 1999.[84] Substantial amounts of the budget were spent on expanded technology for use at the border and increased detention facilities. For instance, at the San Diego/Tijuana border area, a triple fence was installed in an effort to prevent migrants from entering.[85] Checkpoints within the United States also multiplied. Roberto Martinez writes that "in San Diego, we are boxed in. We have checkpoints all around. You can't leave San Diego county without going through a checkpoint. Highway 94, I-8, I-15, I-5 [have checkpoints]. . . . They might as well move the whole border up to L.A."[86]

The number of Border Patrol agents also grew substantially. The Immigration Control and Reform Act (1986) provided funds to increase the number of Border Patrol agents from 2,500 to about 4,800.[87] The Illegal Immigration Reform and Immigrant Responsibility Act (1996) authorized the hiring of 1,000 additional Border Patrol agents per year during the period 1997–2001, more than doubling the number of agents. Legislation passed after September 11, 2001, authorized further hires.[88] According to the Justice Department, "the INS is now the largest Federal law enforcement agency [in the country]. . . . The immigration service has more than 15,000 officers authorized to carry weapons and make arrests, more than the Federal Bureau of Investigation, the Bureau of Prisons, the Customs' Service or the Drug Enforcement Administration."[89]

The massive buildup of technology and personnel and the integration of the Border Patrol with various military and police units transformed the border into a "low intensity conflict" war zone.[90] The impact of these changes has been deeply felt by legal U.S. residents and citizens of the border area, especially Latinos, who are constantly stopped, questioned, and often abused by Border Patrol agents based on their appearance, names, accent, and/or where they live.[91]

Migrants, both documented and undocumented, have also experienced the impact of the militarization of the border and expansion of Border Patrol personnel. According to a report issued by Amnesty International in 1998, migrants' human rights are often violated at this militarized border:

> The allegations of ill-treatment that Amnesty International collected include people struck with batons, fists, and feet, often as punishment for attempting to run away from Border Patrol agents; denial of food, water, and blankets for many hours while detained at Border Patrol stations and Ports of Entry for INS processing; sexual abuse of men and women; denial of medical attention; and abusive, racially derogatory and unprofessional conduct towards the public sometimes resulting in wrongful deportation of U.S. citizens to Mexico.[92]

Amnesty International also noted that some juveniles caught by the Border Patrol have been "beaten, punched, kicked and verbally insulted," as well as denied access to legal representation and detained under conditions that do not meet international standards.[93] Human Rights Watch documented the use of excessive force against migrants, including unjustified shootings that result in death.[94] These claims were corroborated by the American Friends Service Committee (AFSC), who observed in a 1998 report that Border Patrol agents "exhibit a penchant for cruelty and violence towards those they have been commissioned to hunt down and apprehend. The forms of conduct range from Border Patrol agents' labeling of undocumented immigrants they apprehend as 'tonks,' in reference to the sound a flashlight makes striking a human's skull, to unwarranted discharging of firearms."[95] The result of the use of firearms is death in far too many instances. For example, a joint Border Patrol–San Diego police taskforce formed the Border Crime Prevention Unit, and "from 1984 to 1989, members of the taskforce were involved in 26 shooting incidents in which 19 people were killed and 24 were wounded."[96]

Significantly, the rape and sexual abuse of immigrants—usually women but sometimes men—is consistently reported by all the groups who have examined human rights abuses at the border.[97] For example, Amnesty International reported that some women who had been detained by the INS underwent degrading vaginal searches performed by male officers and experienced sexual abuse and assault. Amnesty also noted that pressures were brought to bear upon the women to prevent them from filing complaints, and two women who did complain were accused of lying and threatened with prosecution.[98] Human Rights Watch stated in its first of five reports about the U.S.-Mexico border, which were issued between 1992 and 1997, that "human rights groups monitoring the border unhesitatingly state that sexual abuse is rampant. In a handful of cases, INS agents have been prosecuted for the rape of undocumented women, but more frequently it has not been reported."[99] Subsequent reports also contain accounts of undocumented women who were raped and sexually abused. The American Friends Service Committee reports on human and civil rights violations at the border also include such accounts.

Although rape and sexual abuse occurs, the system to hold Border Patrol agents accountable for such acts is weak at best. To some extent, this is because many abuses "occur in the field, along the border, in no man's land, where agents' suspicions are unlikely to be challenged, and where witnesses to their actions are likely to be scarce."[100] Human Rights Watch/Americas also noted that human rights violations continue because

> abusive Border Patrol agents are not held accountable. Agents who violate agency policies and the law avoid the consequences of their actions because INS procedures for receipt and review of complaints alleging violations are wholly inadequate. As a result, even if a victim or witness is resolute and able to overcome the many barriers to filing and pursuing a complaint, the structural flaws in the investigatory and disciplinary process virtually guarantee that even the most brutal agents will remain on the force.[101]

Amnesty International's 1998 report further explains,

> the complaint system, though better publicized than before, contin-
> ued to lack public confidence. Its procedures are complex, multi-
> jurisdictional and have failed to remedy injustices in the past. There is
> a perception that INS officers act with impunity. Complaint forms in
> Spanish or English were not readily available to those who might need
> them in the Border Patrol holding areas visited by Amnesty Inter-
> national, despite INS assurances since 1994 that this concern had been
> remedied.[102]

Julie Light also describes how the "code of silence among law enforcement officials is virtually unbreakable" and ensures that agents will not
testify against one another even when they have witnessed violence,
abuse, or human rights violations.[103] Further compounding the problem
is that "many of the officers charged with investigating such allegations
were once themselves field agents" who are reluctant to aggressively challenge the code of silence.[104]

The experiences of Blanca Bernal, an undocumented Mexican woman
who was detained by Border Patrol Agent Larry Selders in 1993, transported to a remote area, and raped, further illustrate how difficult it is to
secure accountability from the Border Patrol on matters of rape. According to the judgment issued by Frank R. Zapata, the district court judge
who ruled on Bernal's civil suit, the basic facts of Bernal's experience
were these:

> On September 3, 1993, Blanca Bernal and her friend Ana Gomez, both
> Mexican citizens, illegally entered the United States through a hole in
> the border fence, which separates Nogales, Sonora, from Nogales,
> Arizona. Ms. Bernal was 21 years old. After meeting some friends and
> visiting two restaurants, an on-duty male law enforcement officer ap-
> proached and detained the two women. The officer was wearing a
> green uniform and badge, which identified him as a U.S. Border Patrol
> Agent. The Agent also carried a pistol holstered at his waist and wore a
> name tag on his shirt, which identified him as Larry Selders. Agent
> Selders asked for their "papers," and when they could not produce any,
> he grabbed them both and pushed them into the back of a green and
> white Ford Bronco, a U.S. Border Patrol vehicle.
>
> As Agent Selders drove Ms. Gomez and Ms. Bernal out of town,
> he asked them, "Do you want to go to the office or to Mexico?" Both
> women responded, "To Mexico." Agent Selders then offered to return

and release the two women into Mexico instead of bringing them to the immigration office, where they would be locked up, "in exchange for one of us giving him sex." Both women responded to Agent Selders' proposition for sex by saying "No!" Agent Selders repeated the question and they repeated their answers. Agent Selders then stopped the truck and angrily told Ms. Gomez to get out. She left through the tailgate window, which Agent Selders had lowered by pressing a button. Ms. Bernal also tried to exit, but Agent Selders quickly raised the window before she could get out.

Agent Selders then told Ms. Bernal to crouch down, drove her to an isolated area some 20 to 30 minutes out of town, and stopped the vehicle. There he removed Ms. Bernal from the truck and jerked her around. He told her that he liked her a lot and that he was going to have sex with her. For several minutes the two tussled as Agent Selders attempted to undress Ms. Bernal. She implored him to leave her alone, but he would not. She scratched at Agent Selders and tried to push him away. However, he forcibly removed her clothing, grabbed her hair and left wrist, placed her on the tailgate of his vehicle and raped her.

After he finished, Ms. Bernal was crying hysterically. She found a napkin and tried to clean herself off. Both she and Agent Selders got dressed and he ordered her back into the vehicle. Ms. Bernal felt dirty and powerless. She got back into the vehicle through the rear door and Agent Selders drove her back into Nogales, Arizona, and dropped her off near the old courthouse. Agent Selders threatened Ms. Bernal not to say anything to anyone about what he had done.[105]

Bernal immediately reported her rape to the Nogales, Arizona, police and the Mexican consulate and sought medical treatment from a doctor who confirmed that she showed physical signs of forcible rape. By reporting her rape to the police and seeking a medical exam, Bernal followed the steps necessary to legally establish that a rape had occurred. Many women cannot or do not follow these steps, due to barriers such as legal status, cost, and shame. Their chances of obtaining accountability diminish accordingly. Yet even though Bernal followed all the procedures, accountability remained elusive. In a controversial plea bargain, Selders negotiated the initial charges of rape and kidnapping down to the much lesser charge of attempting to transport a woman for immoral purposes.[106] He was sentenced to one year in prison but served just six months. The federal government then charged him with violating Bernal's civil rights and with two counts of bribery for demanding sexual favors. On the basis of these charges, he was eventually sentenced to one year's imprisonment, but the sentence was amended to "time served," with the result that he served no additional time.[107] Bernal persisted by filing a civil suit against Selders and the INS, charging them with negligence that resulted in her being raped.

Bernal's suit revealed difficulties, beyond those described by Amnesty International and America's Watch, in getting the INS to respond to charges of rape by one of its agents. For one thing, the judge found the INS complicit, at the level of institutional practice, with allowing these rapes to be perpetrated. As Judge Zapata noted, Selders's position provided him with a uniform, gun, and badge, and the power of a law enforcement officer. As a law enforcement officer, he had the power to apprehend, detain, question, and transport individuals like Bernal and her friend. When he used these powers, they were not free to refuse or leave. His position also gave him the power to incarcerate or release them, which he used to try to obtain sex from them. When they refused to provide sex in exchange for release, he raped Bernal anyway.[108] His acts were committed while he was on duty, at locations within his patrolling area. In the judge's opinion, "Agent Selders' wrongful acts were performed within the scope of his employment. . . . Although the ultimate act of raping Ms. Bernal was done to satisfy Selders' personal desires, the conduct leading up to, in connection with, and following the rape, were done in the service of the Border Patrol. . . . Agent Selders was serving the Border Patrol while serving his own personal desires."[109]

Not only did Selders appropriate the powers of his position as a means for committing rape; according to the judge, his coworkers and supervisors had reason to anticipate that he was likely to do so. In 1989 he had sexually assaulted a Caucasian U.S. citizen, Ms. D. H. The assault was known in Selders's workplace because he was subsequently released from jail into his supervisor's custody. H.'s husband also called Selders's workplace to complain. H. eventually decided not to pursue charges against Selders, due to the expense of travel and lodging (her usual residence was Louisiana and the assault took place in Arizona).[110] Nonetheless, Bernal's attorney charged that the INS should have investigated, verified, or followed up on Selders's arrest and reported it to the Office of Professional Responsibility (OPR), the agency charged with investigating allegations of Border Patrol misconduct.[111] If that had been done, he claimed, Selders would likely have been removed from his duties and Bernal would not have been raped.

Instead, the patrol agent in charge of the Nogales station where

Selders worked reported Selders's arrest to the Tucson headquarters but did nothing to alter his duties or supervision or otherwise prevent him from continuing to behave as a sexual predator. The Tucson staff person who was responsible for reviewing the allegations of Agent Selders's sexual misconduct and making disciplinary recommendations to the chief patrol agent "failed to review the allegations of Selders' misconduct."[112] He "did not even read the Santa Cruz County Sheriff's Department Offense Report . . . until he began to formulate his opinion for this [Selders'] trial."[113] In violation of mandatory procedures, he also did not report Selders's arrest to the OPR.

The judge who heard Bernal's case concurred that if there had been an investigation, verification, or follow-up to Selders's arrest, "there was sufficient evidence to substantiate Ms. H.'s allegations of sexual assault against Agent Selders."[114] This would most likely have caused Selders to be permanently removed from his duties, with the result that he would not have been in a position to rape Bernal. Consequently, in the judge's opinion, the Border Patrol staff's failure to investigate, verify, or follow up on the arrest of Selders for the 1989 assault on H., and the failure to report his arrest to OPR for investigation, constituted forms of negligence that contributed to Bernal's rape.

Similar negligence occurred in another rape incident involving Selders. In this case, the victim was Ms. A. D., a Mexican national, who, with five others, illegally entered the United States in December 1988, through a hole in the fence.

> Ms. D. was the last one through the hole in the fence. An American man dressed in a Customs uniform picked her up. He was driving a white pick-up truck. . . . He asked for her papers. The man then drove her to Patagonia Lake and said, "Mine or into the water." He then sexually assaulted Ms. D. for approximately two and a half hours. Ms. D. returned to her home and told her sister what had occurred, exposing her breasts, which were bruised and purple. Ms. D. did not report the incident to the authorities then, because she was afraid she would lose her job and because she did not have a passport.[115]

In 1993 the incident came to the attention of the Office of the Inspector General (OIG), which had assumed OPR's duties of investigating allegations of Border Patrol misconduct, and OIG began an investigation.[116] D. provided a description of her assailant to the OIG, who contracted Border Patrol headquarters in Tucson. But the Tucson staff person with whom the OIG spoke did not mention Selders's prior arrest for sexual assault, or that Selders fit the description of D.'s assailant, even though he was aware of both facts. He later testified that he failed to provide this information because he "just didn't make the connection."[117] As a result, the OIG closed the investigation of D.'s case. However, if the OIG had known about Selders's prior arrest, and that he fit the description of D.'s assailant, they would not have closed the case. Instead, they would have recontacted her and given her a photo lineup that included Selders's picture. The judge expressed confidence that D. would have identified Selders from the lineup, since she had no difficulty identifying him in connection with Bernal's case. In the judge's opinion, her identification, combined with Selders's prior assault on H., would have resulted in Selders's permanent removal from the Border Patrol. But because the Tucson staff person failed to provide pertinent information to the OIG, none of these steps occurred. In the judge's opinion, the Tucson staff person's failure to provide pertinent information to the OIG also constituted negligence that directly contributed to Bernal's being raped.

Yet another incident in which Selders sexually assaulted a woman was also brought to light by Bernal's suit. This case involved Ms. L. B., a Mexican woman with legal temporary residence in the United States. On 2 August 1988 she traveled from Tucson to Nogales with her two young sons to visit relatives. At a hotel a man approached her and asked for their papers. B. gave him her "INS card," which he put in his shirt pocket. When she asked for it back, he refused and ordered her to follow him in her car. He drove to an isolated area and "ordered Ms. B. into his car, where he proceeded to assault her within viewing distance of her two small children, who were crying hysterically."[118] The man then told B. to be quiet about the assault or he would kill her. Returning her INS card, he threatened, "You will always be mine," since he had access to an INS computer and could find her any time. Shortly after the assault, he harassed B. by telephoning her at her home in Tucson.[119] Fearing for her life, B. moved.

B. told a private attorney about the incident. The attorney contacted the OPR and a Border Patrol agent, told them that a woman had been assaulted by someone whom she believed worked for the Border Patrol, and provided a description. The OPR responded that the victim had to come to their office to file a complaint, but B. did not do so. Although Bernal's attorney charged that the INS response to this case was also negligent, the court did not agree. Significantly, however, the court did not dispute that the assault happened, or that Selders was the perpetrator.

Bernal's case provided a rare, public look at INS procedures for responding to rapes perpetrated by its agents. In addition to the inadequacies that human rights groups have described, Bernal's case resulted in a finding that the INS was institutionally complicit in making rape possible and negligent in its response to incidents of rape and sexual assault that involved one of its agents.

Rapes That Remain Unrepresentable as Crimes

Although the INS has been criticized repeatedly for its inadequate procedures for receiving and addressing complaints about Border Patrol agents like Selders who engage in rape, sexual assault, and sexual abuse, it has failed to institute significant changes. This failure indicates a fundamental problem, which is that the rapes of undocumented women remain largely unrepresentable as crimes or even problems to address from the government's point of view. To understand why this is so, it is helpful to turn briefly to the history of another group of women—African Americans.

Historically, rape has been a central dimension of African American women's experiences in the United States but was also largely unrepresentable and inconceivable as a crime until relatively recently. Darlene Clark Hine suggests that "the true dimension and nature of this exploitation remains shrouded in denial, metaphor, ignorance and silence."[120] For women who endured rape and sexual exploitation, silence partly served as a survival strategy and mode of resistance.[121] But silence also stemmed from "the politics of denial" practiced by other, more privileged groups in the United States and from systemic institutionalized practices of denial.[122]

For example, according to Saidiya Hartman's analysis of the case of Celia, a slave woman hanged for murdering her master who repeatedly raped her, the law blamed slave women for their own victimization by constructing them as simultaneously submissive and seductive. In this way, the law masked the violence of the white patriarchal state that both produced and systematically dehumanized the racialized and gendered body of the African American slave woman. As Hartman explains, the law "provided a way of masking the antagonistic fissures of the society by ascribing to the object of property an ensnaring and criminal agency that acted to dissimulate the barbarous forms of white enjoyment permitted within the law."[123]

Equally, undocumented women tend to get blamed for their own victimization when they are raped. To understand why undocumented victims get blamed, we must grasp how immigration in general—and undocumented immigration in particular—is popularly conceptualized.

As Saskia Sassen explains, both popular understanding and U.S. immigration policy "place exclusive responsibility for the immigration process on the individual and hence make the individual the site for the exercise of the state's authority."[124] This individualizing approach ignores the fact that larger structures, including globalization processes and neocolonial relations, clearly also condition immigration. When immigration is treated strictly as an individual matter, without regard to these larger structures, undocumented immigrant women become constructed as the ones who originally broke the law and, therefore, as people who live outside the law. Leo Chavez summarizes: "as *illegal aliens* they are not legitimate members of the community. The 'illegal' component of this term underscores that they exist outside the legal system that governs society. *Alien* is synonymous with *outsider, foreigner,* and *stranger.* . . . the undocumented immigrant's image consists of a conglomeration of negative values and missing qualities. (Even the term *undocumented* stresses the *lack* of documentation.)"[125] Constructed as inherently criminal, imbued with negative qualities, and positioned outside the conventional boundaries of society, undocumented women cannot easily (if at all) call on the law or other social systems for protection from rape and sexual abuse.[126] When they suffer rape, it is seen as their own fault.[127] By blaming undocumented immigrants for their own victimization, while ignoring the larger structures that condition immigration, the violence of the government that is visible at the border and that produces categories of people as "illegal," rapable, and otherwise exploitable becomes disavowed. As David Lloyd explains: "the state requires a substrate which is counter to its laws and civility and which it represents as outrageous and violent, in order that the history of domination and criminalization appear as a legitimate process of civilization."[128]

Under these conditions, the rapes of undocumented women at the U.S.-Mexico border remain largely unrepresentable as crimes from the point of view of the U.S. government. At the same time, rape and sexual abuse continue. The question to ask, then, is what is rape's function? More specifically, in an era of increased globalization, what role does rape play in reconstructing national borders?

Initially in my research I assumed that rape functioned as a form of crude, violent, border defense strategy. Like barbed wire and canine units, it kept women out. But Bernal's case showed that keeping women out was not the result. After Selders raped her, he didn't deport her. He released her in downtown Nogales, Arizona, to continue on her way. In other cases about which I found information, rape often functioned similarly. For example, on 15 December 1995, Border Patrol Agent Charles Vinson sexually assaulted an undocumented Salvadoran woman near the Tijuana River, then let her continue into the United States.[129] In January 1996 "a San Diego immigration inspector [Frederick Toothman] pleaded guilty to bribery and civil rights charges for allegedly soliciting sex from seven women in exchange for resolving their immigration problems."[130] Resolving their immigration problems presumably entailed promising to make it possible for them to enter and remain in the United States—if they provided sex. Yet another case involved two Guatemalan women who eventually sued two Border Patrol agents for rape and sexual battery while in custody. "One agent released [them] into the United States after the attacks and gave them each $1."[131] In each of these instances immigration officials demanded (or took) sex from undocumented women and then released the women into the United States rather than deported them.[132]

If not to keep them out, then what ends does the rape of undocumented women serve, from the government's point of view? Feminist scholarship in general makes clear that rape is a technology for the violent (re)production of gender and sexuality hierarchies, norms, and identities. As Sharon Marcus explains, gender and sexuality are never essential, pre-given identities but rather identities constructed and inscribed on bodies through mechanisms that include rape or the threat of rape.[133] Rape is also a technology for (re)producing racial and ethnic differences, as we know from the genocidal rapes that occurred in Bosnia and Rwanda in the 1990s, and, closer to home, from the histories of white males' rapes of African and African American women. In such situations rape reconstructs racial, ethnic, and class divisions among men who struggle to assert mastery over one another by raping women, or by protecting "their" women from rape. In the process, access to women's bodies and sexualities becomes constructed as a matter for males, rather than females, to determine.[134] Therefore, rape also reiterates patriarchy and heterosexuality as compulsory norms. It equally reconstructs racial and class divisions among women. For example, the vulnerability of African American slave woman to rape helped to construct and sustain images of white middle-class womanhood as "pure" and valorized.[135]

Since rape is a technology for (re)producing hierarchical social relationships, it reconstructs borders. These borders are not reducible to the nation's territorial borders, however. Instead, they involve social, economic, political, psychological, and symbolic borders within the United

States that connect to sexuality, gender, race, and class inequalities. Yet at the same time, the reproduction of these internal borders articulates with practices for controlling the territorial border.[136] As Robert Chang writes, "the geopolitical border is supplemented by internal policing mechanisms" that mutually construct one another.[137] The interaction between the reproduction of the territorial and internal borders is evident at two levels, in instances of rapes of undocumented women. First, as technology for reproducing social borders, rape inscribes undocumented women within U.S.-based hierarchies of gender, sexuality, race, and class. But second, as we have seen, undocumented women have almost no mechanisms available to protest or contest these inscriptions, especially when rape is perpetrated by Border Patrol agents. The fact that raped undocumented women have virtually no mechanisms for protest means that rape is also a site for the inscription of documented versus undocumented status as salient. Therefore, rape at the border by the Border Patrol is a site for reinscription by the state of the social body as stratified by gender, sexuality, race, class, and legal status.

These violent inscriptions are repeated on the bodies of undocumented women living within the borders of the United States. For example, undocumented women comprise an important labor pool in areas such as domestic work, garment work, piecework at home, live-in elder or child care, factory operation, restaurant work, agriculture, and other jobs at the lower end of the service sector.[138] In these jobs, undocumented women work long hours for low (or no) wages, in circumstances where health, safety, and labor laws are consistently violated. Rape and sexual abuse are also persistent conditions of labor for many undocumented women in these jobs.[139]

The prevalence of sexual abuse in low-end service sector jobs where undocumented women tend to be concentrated is suggested by a recent suit brought by the Equal Employment Opportunity Commission (EEOC) against the United States' number-one lettuce grower, Tanimura and Antle.[140] The EEOC negotiated a $1,855,000 settlement in 1999 with Tanimura and Antle in order to terminate a sexual harassment suit. According to the EEOC,

> a Tanimura and Antle production manager subjected a female employee, Blanca Alfaro, to quid pro quo sexual harassment, i.e. required sexual favors as a condition for employment and the receipt of job benefits. . . . Alfaro was subsequently subjected to a hostile work environment, which included constant unwelcome sexual advances by

that production manager and another management employee. . . .
Alfaro was discharged in retaliation shortly after complaining about
the unwelcome advances.[141]

A male worker who tried to defend Alfaro was also dismissed.

The EEOC suit against Tanimura and Antle is important on several
counts. Alfaro worked in a sector that employs undocumented immigrant women workers.[142] The EEOC pursued her case precisely because
they recognized that immigrant women workers, both documented and
undocumented, are subjected to forms of harassment, including sexual,
that need to be addressed.[143] EEOC's William Tamayo explained: "agri-
business is California's largest industry and employs a million workers
each year. Farmworker women have raised civil rights issues to the EEOC,
and consequently, the Commission has made sexual harassment in the
agricultural industry a priority for civil rights enforcement."[144] Ida
Castro, the chairwoman of EEOC, further clarified that "protection from
sexual harassment for Latina farm laborers, the most vulnerable of workers" was one of the EEOC's current priorities.[145] The *San Francisco
Chronicle* also noted that "farmworker advocates have long complained
about sexual exploitation of women workers by foremen, who have
broad power to hire and fire individual laborers each season. 'To get a
job, it's not uncommon to hear stories of women having to put out,' said
Marc Grossman, a spokesman for the United Farm Workers."[146] Maria
Dominguez confirmed that "in 1988, about 59% of [farmworker] women
considered sexual harassment a problem in the fields. However, in 1993
approximately 90% of the [farmworker women] reported that this is a
major problem confronting women farm workers in the workplace."[147]
Dominguez also enumerated reasons why women may be reluctant to report harassment. These included language gaps, cultural difference, limited literacy that makes filing a complaint difficult, fear of economic retaliation, and, significantly, immigration status. Women who were in the
country without authorization "fear deportation if they bring a claim."[148]

That the EEOC settled the suit against Tanimura and Antle for a sum
that was the largest for such a case in the nation's history suggests that
they were able to effectively marshal evidence of systemic, institutionalized practices of sexual abuse.[149] The settlement covers workers who were
employed between September 1994 and February 1999, suggesting that
the problem had been ongoing.

The extent of the problem of sexual abuse and sexual harassment in
other service-sector industries that employ immigrant women, including

the undocumented, is continually suggested by research literature, though rarely centrally pursued.[150] As Julienne Malveaux notes,

> the earliest recorded cases of sexual harassment in American work-places were from the bottom of the occupational hierarchy, not the top. Private household workers, clerical workers, hospital service workers, and restaurant staff all earn pay at the bottom of the occupational scale. They are as likely, if not more so, to be sexually harassed as their professional sisters. And they are more likely to be women of color. They don't make good copy, they are not necessarily articulate, and one can't build a movement or "effect" around them.[151]

When women are undocumented as well, it is very difficult to get the problem recognized, much less changed. Thus, the EEOC's effort was extremely important. But the problem of sexual abuse and harassment in other industries that employ undocumented women is surely still significant and needs to be addressed.[152]

Drawing on Lisa Lowe's work, we could suggest that labor exploitation in which rape and sexual abuse are central dimensions of experience involves the construction and use of undocumented women's bodies as sites where sexual, gender, racial, proletarianization, and immigration processes all converge. These different dimensions of violent inscription into U.S. society cannot be analyzed in isolation from one another, and they also cannot be reduced to a strictly economic analysis, as scholarship about the undocumented is prone to do.[153]

Undocumented status renders women vulnerable to sexual abuse not just in the workplace but also in their homes and personal relationships. Indeed, their vulnerability challenges the public-private dichotomy and makes clear how immigration law mediates even so-called private or personal domains.[154] Abusive partners or husbands routinely threaten to call the INS if undocumented women resist their abuse. Even women who legally migrate to the United States as spouses are vulnerable to such abuse, because they are dependent on their husbands for legal status. Under the terms of the Immigration Marriage Fraud Amendments (IMFA) of 1986, a husband must file papers for his wife to receive conditional residency, and after two years he must file again, this time for her permanent residency.[155] When a husband does not file, the woman lapses into undocumented status. Advocates have shown that some husbands "have used their control over this [legalization] process as a means of further abusing their partners."[156] For example, Maria from the Dominican Republic was dependent for legal status on a U.S. citizen husband who abused her sexually and otherwise:

> Afraid of risking deportation, Maria endured her husband's treatment for months. After she finally fled, her spouse demanded that she return to his apartment for her immigration papers. At first she told him, "No, you're going to hit me." But then she realized that she had to go because she needed the papers. She described the consequences: "He beat me on the head. He sat on my stomach. He put a knife to my throat and raped me. Then he threw me naked on the street."[157]

In sum, undocumented women crossing the U.S. border risk being raped by a range of assailants, including U.S. Border Patrol agents. Blanca Bernal's case makes painfully clear the difficulties of mobilizing the discourses of crime or civil rights to challenge the Border Patrol's rapes of undocumented women. Yet her case also reveals other possible avenues for contestation. Most importantly, she won her civil suit and was awarded $753,000 in damages. According to her attorney, the award marks the first time that the rape of an undocumented Latina has been treated with the same seriousness as the rape of a Caucasian citizen woman. Her case also encouraged other women who had been assaulted by Selders to come forward to demand justice. But despite Bernal's victory, rapes at the border remain horrifyingly easy to perpetrate and largely unrepresentable as crimes or even problems for the government to address. These rapes serve as technologies that violently reinscribe social hierarchies of sexuality, gender, race, class, and legal status—not only at the border but also in workplaces and homes within the United States territory. The government's investment in these technologies is suggested by the amount of money that they spent defending itself in Bernal's case and the fact that it has appealed the judge's award to her.[158]

The Border Patrol, like the refugee/asylum system, utilizes constructions about female sexuality in order to fulfill its duties. Each system's utilization does not merely replicate but also reconstructs and recirculates particular sexual regimes. Focusing on how both systems respond to women's experiences of rape has enabled me to highlight some of the differences, but also points of convergence, in their constructions of female sexuality.

Certainly, there are marked differences between the systems' regimes for conceptualizing and responding (or not) to rape. Drawing on international human rights agreements and standards and responding to lobbying by feminist, human rights, and immigrant advocates, the refugee/

asylum system has recognized that rape is neither private nor inconsequential but rather a violent crime of political and social significance. As a result, some women who have endured rape have been granted asylum, which entitles them to remain legally in the United States, secure a range of protections, and access social support programs. The fact that some women can obtain asylum on this basis represents a notable shift in how rape is conceptualized within refugee/asylum policy. Nonetheless, many instances of rape are not considered to provide a legitimate basis for asylum. Therefore, women's experiences of rape become differentiated, in a manner that is politically troubling and likely to remain challenged by a wide spectrum of groups, including those seeking to either broaden or further restrict admission. Furthermore, multiple systemic constraints prevent many women from ever applying for asylum, even when they have valid claims.

Although the refugee/asylum system officially recognizes the political significance of rape, the same cannot be said for the Border Patrol. Human rights reports, personal testimonies, and criminal prosecutions make clear that women are often sexually abused and sometimes raped by Border Patrol agents. But rather than treating rapes by their agents as violent crimes, the Border Patrol has largely failed to institute a working system through which such crimes can even be reported. The Border Patrol's indifference is reinforced by multiple structures that silence, deny, or minimize the reality and significance of rape when undocumented women are concerned.[159] Although some individuals and organizations have drawn public attention to the rape of undocumented women and struggled for change, such rapes remain frighteningly easy to perpetrate with few consequences for the perpetrator.

Clearly, there are disjunctures within the state apparatus for managing immigration, as reflected by these divergent responses to rape. Yet there is also a point of convergence, which is that these responses variously contribute to the reproduction of exclusionary nationalism.[160] In regard to refugee/asylee women, their admission on the basis of rape narratives provides a means to reconstruct an imperialist image of the United States as enlightened and progressive, in supposed contrast to the "backward" countries and cultures from which the women have fled. The United States' role in the global conditions that have produced these women as refugees in the first place, and the monotonous realities of racism, (hetero)sexism, and class exploitation in the United States, are conveniently erased by the process. In terms of undocumented women, their experiences of rape and sexual abuse both stem from and enable the reiteration of sovereign territorial borders. Their experiences are also driven by, and further fuel, sexual, gender, racial, and class borders within the U.S. national territory. The fact that these rapes remain largely unrepresentable as a serious issue that the government should address suggests that exclusionary discursive systems play a crucial role in enabling exclusionary nationalism.

Although the increasingly global circulation of capital, goods, technologies, information, and services has seemed to threaten traditional notions of territorially distinct nations and national sovereignty, the government's strategies for managing immigration, including those for responding to immigrant women who have been raped, provide opportunities for reconstructing the salience of borders, both territorial and internal.[161]

Conclusion

Sexuality, Immigration, and Resistance

A search for scholarship that theorized the connections between lesbian/gay and immigration issues initially drove *Entry Denied*. But as I began researching the histories of lesbian and gay immigrants, the Proposition 187 campaign swept California like a sandstorm. Designed to deny basic services to undocumented immigrants, the campaign provided an occasion to refashion racial, gender, sexual, class, and nationality hierarchies of every kind. Proposition 187 supporters continually circulated exaggerated representations of uncontrolled childbearing by undocumented Latinas that was supposedly destroying the state. This image, and the devastating legislation that resulted, made clear that public anxieties about sexuality and immigration were easily harnessed together for repressive ends. Yet Proposition 187's imagery strikingly relied on the demonization of racialized female heterosexuality, rather than lesbian and gay sexuality, to wreak its damage. Both the imagery and legislation suggested that there were crucial overlaps between the struggles of immigrant lesbians and gays and undocumented heterosexual Latinas, working and often raising children in the United States. To further examine these intersections, my research was transformed into an exploration of the connections between government efforts to regulate women's sexuality, broadly conceived, and immigration. A crucial overlap between these regulatory efforts was evident in immigration laws and practices that controlled women's immigration possibilities on the basis of sexuality. Though these laws and practices produced groups of both preferred and excludable women immigrants, my research, reflecting the public tenor of the 1990s, focused primarily on excludable women.

Examining how immigration-control practices produce women who are excludable on the grounds of sexuality required me to simultaneously engage and challenge both immigration and sexuality scholarship. For example, my research was greatly enabled by the rich existing scholarship about racial, ethnic, and class immigration exclusion in the United States. Nonetheless, I had to work against tendencies in that scholarship that treat distinctions of sexuality, gender, race, class, nationality, and legal status as if they refer to empirical, preexisting identities that immigrants already have. Instead, my research suggested that the actual operation of immigration control not only depends on these categories but also greatly contributes to their manufacture.[1] Furthermore, this process of manufacture is part of the mechanics through which "modern" states consolidate themselves and then extend their reach by inserting newcomers into the disciplinary networks of carceral society.[2] Such an analysis in no way excuses the injustices experienced by newcomers. But it positions newcomers within changing and contested social relations, rather than treating them as the bearers of ahistorical sexual, gender, racial, class, or national characteristics.

My analysis of the interface between immigration control and identity categories was most thoroughly developed in relation to women's sexuality, though I also indicated its application to racial, ethnic, class, and nationality categories. *Entry Denied* suggests that although women's sexuality has been a central concern of federal immigration control since the late nineteenth century, immigration officials never simply "uncovered" sexual identities or proclivities that already preexisted within immigrant women. Rather, multiple practices and discourses that varied by time, location, and the individuals involved were brought to bear upon immigrant women, in ways that contributed to producing the sexual identities, acts, and norms around which immigration monitoring was organized and regularly redefined.

My focus on sexuality directly challenged the tendency in immigration scholarship to ignore sexuality altogether or else subsume it into accounts of gender. Indeed, gender immigration scholarship has not substantially explored sexuality either. This may be understandable because, as Eve Sedgwick suggests, "the question of gender and the question of sexuality, inextricable from one another though they are . . . are . . . not the same question."[3] Sedgwick's point, that sexuality requires analysis on its own terms, needs to be acknowledged and addressed within immigration scholarship. In taking up Sedgwick's call, immigration scholars will have to guard against the presumption of normative heterosexuality. As

Michael Warner explains, "het culture thinks of itself as the elemental form of human association, as the very model of intergender relations, as the invisible basis of all community, and as the means of reproduction without which society wouldn't exist."[4] *Entry Denied* challenges both the erasure of sexuality and the presumption of normative heterosexuality in immigration scholarship, by centering sexuality while also making clear that not everyone is heterosexual. Further, it argues that far from being "natural," hegemonic heterosexuality is anxiously manufactured and oppressively enforced by state institutions that include the immigration apparatus. Since hegemonic heterosexuality is produced through racial, ethnic, gender, and class exclusions, only certain immigrants' heterosexuality becomes acceptable, while others are slated for exclusion—along with the rest of the "peripheral" sexual groups. These arguments make clear that sexual concerns crucially structure immigration-control processes and, as a result, cannot be simply tacked on to existing research. Rather, the theoretical frameworks and methodologies of immigration scholarship must be substantially revised to take sexuality in *all its forms* into critical account. Until these changes happen, immigration scholarship will not only continue to mirror but also further reinforce hegemonic power relations, while at the same time overlooking crucial aspects of how immigration processes operate.

Entry Denied engages in dialogue not just with immigration but also with sexuality scholarship. Here my concern is the fact that sexuality scholarship rarely addresses immigration, despite compelling reasons to do so. For instance, immigration has profoundly transformed sexual politics, communities, and cultural production in the last quarter century, in ways that demand attention. Furthermore, both immigration and sexuality have been at the forefront of public debate and legislative intervention in that same time period. Consequently, examination of the ways that xenophobia and normative heterosexuality articulate one another is critical. Equally necessary are analyses of the ways that anxieties about immigration strengthen the ability of state apparatuses to allocate rights and opportunities in a manner that reinforces hierarchies that are gendered, racialized, and classed.[5]

Several shifts within sexuality scholarship promise to facilitate analyses about the interface between sexuality and immigration. For one, some scholars have initiated a rigorous interrogation of the categories, terminologies, and epistemologies through which much sexuality scholarship has been organized. These bear the traces of their emergence and circulation within specific locations, time periods, and relations of power that need to be problematized. For this reason, in chapter 4, I resisted applying the category "lesbian" to Quiroz, even for the purpose of creating an immigrant counterdiscourse on sexuality. My resistance owes to the fact that the category's genealogy and normative associations do not adequately acknowledge the histories of colonization, racialization, and gender and class subordination that shape immigrant women's lives and sexualities.[6] The very language of sexuality—the histories it bears, and the histories it erases—needs to be radically reworked for research on immigration and sexuality to flourish.

Such reworking, which includes finding ways to theorize sexuality in relation to other social axes, is underway in "queers of color" scholarship, among other locations. Reflecting this imperative, Eng and Hom write that "to endorse the centralization of sex and sexuality in lesbian/gay studies without serious consideration of how other axes of difference form, inform, and deform the queer subject . . . would be to cast the white, European, middle-class gay man as the unacknowledged universal subject of lesbian/gay and queer studies."[7] Other changes, including the growth of sexuality scholarship engaged in critical conversation with postcolonial, feminist, critical race, and globalization theories, also promise to facilitate the emergence of a rich scholarship about the interface between immigration and sexuality, to which *Entry Denied* contributes.

Besides engaging immigration and sexuality scholarship, *Entry Denied* also challenges troubling tendencies that span a range of scholarship. For example, evolutionary narratives persistently frame immigrant women's lives and sexualities within models of movement from "tradition to modernity" and "repression to liberation."[8] Scholars including Chandra Talpade Mohanty, Mirjana Morokvasic, and Martin F. Manalansan argue that these models recirculate ahistorical images of immigrant women as backward, passive, and dependent victims of third-world patriarchy.[9] They also inscribe a developmental narrative of sexuality that mirrors the developmental narrative through which emigrants' countries become represented as "backward" and underdeveloped. As Mirjana Morokvasic explains:

> Social reality is reconstructed on the basis of the common-sense stereotype which situates migrant women at one end of the tradition-modernity dichotomy. . . . [According to the stereotype], the two fundamental criteria of access to modernity are employment and contraception . . . contraception (birth control is in this type of literature reduced to contraceptives only) becomes a pedagogical tool which stimulates progress in other domains.[10]

In these narratives, immigrant women's sexuality becomes reduced to a simple question of procreation. The ways that immigrant women's procreation is often targeted for control by the governments of "sending" and "receiving" countries, the barriers that restrict their access to comprehensive reproductive health care, and the fact that many immigrant women utilize forms of birth control generally remain overlooked.[11] Unequal relations within the global economy, and questions about how these inequalities help to generate and sustain the sexual regimes that are criticized as "backward," are also obfuscated.[12] My analysis of the regulation of sexuality at the border refuses these developmental models and instead indicates the irreducibly socially and politically constructed nature of immigrant women's varied sexualities. Furthermore, I indicate the central role of the U.S. immigration-control apparatus in producing particular women's sexualities as signs of backwardness or danger to the U.S. nation.

Besides challenging evolutionary models of immigrant women's sexuality, I also refuse the standard evolutionary narrative that immigration exclusions (including those based on sexuality) have "ended" because the public has matured in tolerance and understanding. Such a narrative constructs exclusion primarily as a matter of incomplete knowledge or stereotypical thinking, to be corrected through appropriate pedagogical interventions. While I do not want to minimize the role of incomplete knowledge and stereotypes in enabling exclusions, *Entry Denied* argues that other factors also crucially sustain exclusion. In particular, I stress the role of "common-sense" forms of knowledge, administrative routines, and examination procedures in creating and maintaining exclusion. These factors make clear that supposedly neutral forms of rationality and bureaucracy continue to generate racializing, heteropatriarchal, and imperialist epistemologies and relations of power that demand to be interrogated and transformed. In making these arguments, my analysis goes against the grain of much immigration scholarship, both liberal and conservative, but new analytic approaches are crucial if we are to seriously address how sexual, gender, racial, class, and national-origin exclusions are being reinscribed through current immigration-control strategies.

Repeating against the Grain

To develop these arguments without overgeneralizing the significance of different immigrant women's experiences—while nonetheless indicating that there are important connections among various immigrant groups' histories—each chapter of *Entry Denied* is built around specific case files, which are then situated in relation to larger histories. I relied on previously published or publicly available case files and official documents, rather than ethnographic data, as a means to read the immigration-control apparatus against itself and, at the same time, to shield from view immigrant women whose lives are deeply affected by the practices that I describe but who cannot afford to come to the attention of the government. Consequently, I do not theorize immigrant women's agency, except to the extent that it is visibly inscribed in official documents—which in some cases, it is.[13]

Immigrant women's agency in regard to the immigration-control practices, discourses, and knowledge regimes that *Entry Denied* describes can be conceptualized through Judith Butler's analysis of repetition. Butler suggests that social construction "is neither a single act nor a causal process initiated by a subject and resulting in a fixed set of effects"[14] but rather operates through compelled repetition of norms. The compulsory nature of repetition means that one is not free to refuse, yet there is always the possibility of repeating in ways that challenge the dominant order.[15] Thus, Butler envisions "repetition of hegemonic forms of power which fail to repeat loyally, and, in that failure, open possibilities for resignifying the terms of violation against their violating aims."[16]

Immigrant women's (and men's) agency is certainly exercised through the possibilities presented by repeating against the grain of official immigration-service requirements. Immigrants often produce documents, answers, information, and forms of appearance that only *seem* to conform to INS requirements. Yet immigration officials have always been aware of this behavior and attempted to guard against it. Consequently, there is a long history of struggle between immigrants who present themselves as legitimate applicants for admission and officials' efforts to determine whether the applicant truly matches immigration-service criteria for admission. For example, early Chinese immigrants were frequently accused of perpetrating fraud when they presented themselves as eligible for admission on the basis of kinship ties to Chinese people who were already living in the United States. Salyer, who evaluated the evidence for this claim, acknowledges that there were indeed quite a number of instances of fraud, but she also notes that popular perceptions of the Chinese as inherently deceitful resulted in exaggeration of the extent of fraud. She also argues that Chinese exclusion laws were so harshly implemented that they actually fueled fraud, because fraud was often the only way for even legitimate kin to gain entry. Substantiating Salyer's analysis is an account in *Island* of how genuine kin were sometimes denied entry to the United States, whereas fraudulent kin were admitted because they knew how to convince officials of their right to enter. An immigration inspector related:

> What happened was that in many cases where they were not real [but fictive kin], they were so well-coached that their testimonies jibed. Whereas in legitimate cases, they hadn't gone to the trouble of making up coaching books and preparing for it. They were the ones that got the wrong answers, because they thought it was going to be cut and dry.[17]

Similarly, congressional hearings in the 1980s about immigration marriage fraud underlined the difficulty of differentiating between "fraudulent" and "genuine" marriages. At the hearings, Commissioner of Immigration Alan Nelson described how immigrants mobilized the play of appearances to secure admission:

> The arrangers will carefully coach the participants on how to evade detection and pass any Service scrutiny. Detailed crib sheets may be provided which outline the questions commonly asked at INS interviews, or the spouses may be subjected to a "dry run" interview by an attorney to assure that they can answer any questions posed without faltering. Apartment keys are exchanged, and sometimes a joint bank account is opened to give the appearance of legitimacy. Identification may be changed to reflect the female's new married name. The spouse may be deliberately introduced to the landlord, building superintendent or neighbors so that he or she is known in the building should INS agents make inquiries.[18]

These concerns resulted in the passage of more stringent immigration laws and stricter practices of inspection.

Immigrant subversion also operates around the creation and use of forged documents and performances that are staged between documents, immigrants, and individuals like INS agents, the police, or employers.[19] Performances sometimes help forged documents to seem real or employers who hire undocumented workers to seem innocent.[20] The continuous play between "seeming" and "being" real, whether in terms of kinship claims, documents presented, or otherwise, has generated immigration histories that are difficult to recover using conventional historical methods.[21] Though these histories are often quickly dismissed as instances of lawless fraud, "fraud" itself can be usefully read as a competing system of knowledge that is brought against the state. Thus, fraud is another form of repeating differently—though the form is, of necessity, officially excoriated.[22] Such histories make clear that the immigration system has never been able to fully arrogate control of the meanings of the categories through which the border gets policed. Yet although histories of immigrant challenges using the political process, courts, and ethnic lobbies have been written, this level of subversion remains largely unrecorded. *Entry Denied* suggests the necessity and value of further exploring such forms of subversion and linking them to shifts in regimes for surveillance, normalization, and discipline based on sexuality, race, gender, and economics. The limits of such subversion must also be theorized; as Judith Butler cautions, we should "question whether parodying the dominant norms is enough to displace them; indeed, whether [such performances] cannot be the very vehicle for the reconstruction of hegemonic norms."[23]

In addition to further exploring histories of immigrants' resistance to and subversion of exclusion, other scholarship is necessary if we are to thoroughly rethink immigration histories in light of sexual regulation. For example, we need more studies that analyze how sexuality is negotiated within immigrant communities that are dealing with displacement and discrimination. According to Oliva Espín, communities often focus on preserving cultural tradition through controlling the gender and sexual behavior of women. At the same time, outsiders judge immigrants through stereotypes about the sexuality of the community's women. Thus, immigrant women find themselves caught "between the racism of the dominant society and the sexist expectations of [their] own community" as they attempt to negotiate competing sexual norms, identities, and expectations.[24] These processes, which situate sexuality at the heart of conflicts associated with immigration, demand further research and theorization.

We also need to examine how public discourses on sexuality legitimate the exclusion, condemnation, or acceptance of particular migrants, and how these discourses become appropriated, transformed, and redeployed. We need to inquire how U.S. constructions of citizenship reproduce sexual norms that affect migrants, and reciprocally, how discourses about dangerous migrant sexualities legitimize the subordination of minoritized U.S. communities. We need to understand how migrants create new modes of sexual identification, subjectivity, consumption, and coalition, which draw from and transform racial, ethnic, sexual, and cultural communities. Moreover, we need to theorize how these new modes of identification and subjectivity problematize dominant U.S. sexuality categories, epistemologies, and related practices. We need to analyze how migrant and citizen sexual practices and ideologies transform one another through unevenly structured exchanges.

These questions must be addressed in terms of female, male, and transgender sexualities, in light of the dynamics and contradictions of imperial histories, contemporary globalization, and mass migration. *Entry Denied* has sought to initiate critical inquiry into these issues. How readers take up the questions will significantly affect future scholarship and also contribute to reshaping the state's regulation of sexuality and immigration.

Appendix

Sexuality Considerations in the Refugee/Asylum System

In 1980 Congress passed the Refugee Act. The Act recognized the "permanence of refugee exoduses" and attempted to develop systemic rather than ad hoc processes for the admission and resettlement of refugees in the United States.[1] The Act also incorporated the 1951 UN definition of a refugee as one who experienced or had a well-founded fear of persecution on account of race, religion, nationality, membership in a particular social group, or political opinion, thus bringing the United States into line with international standards. However, to gain admission as a refugee, individuals not only have to conform to the international definition but also to fall within the United States' "special humanitarian concern" priorities for particular regions. The United States currently has five categories of special humanitarian concern, but all five do not apply to every region.[2] Refugee status, which must be obtained before one arrives in the United States, entitles the individual to a range of public benefits that are intended to facilitate resettlement, as well as the possibility of legal permanent residence.

The Refugee Act also included provisions that allowed the Attorney General to grant asylum to individuals living within the United States who seemed to have a valid claim, based on the refugee criteria. Under the law, as many as 5,000 asylees were eligible to become legal permanent residents each year. The provisions seemed generous, but their inadequacy was revealed within weeks of the signing of the Act. Zucker and Zucker explain that "Castro opened the port of Mariel and a flood of would-be Cuban refugees, to be joined by a smaller stream of Haitian refugees, began to wash up on our shores. It was immediately clear that the Refugee

Act, significant as it was, has dealt too perfunctorily with asylum."[3] By 1995 nearly half a million individuals in the United States were waiting for their asylum claim to be decided.[4] Although asylum cases are technically decided on the same basis as refugee ones, asylum applicants generally face a much higher burden of proof than refugees and are often presumed to be simply "economic migrants" rather then genuine refugees.[5] As with refugees, foreign and domestic policy considerations also significantly shape the outcome of asylum cases, even when individuals provide strong evidence of persecution.

In the mid-1980s concern emerged about how gender and sexuality were being addressed in refugee and asylum policies. The modal refugee was presumed to be "someone heroically trying to assert his (typically male) individuality against an oppressive state."[6] Consequently, women experienced difficulties having their cases presented and adjudicated appropriately. The difficulties arose because there was no explicit recognition of the gendered forms of persecution that women often experience, and it was unclear how refugee and asylum case law applied in many of their cases. Importantly, gendered persecution often involved either sexual violence or violence that used women's sexuality against them. For example, Nancy Kelly lists the following instances of gender-specific persecution: "systemic individual or mass rape, forced pregnancy, abortion, prostitution, genital surgery, beating while pregnant, or dowry burning."[7] Kelly's example suggests that although gender and sexuality cannot be conflated, they are nonetheless often closely linked in the persecution of women. Through attention to gender persecution, sexuality issues gained attention in the refugee/asylum system.

During the 1990s questions of sexuality attained increasing prominence in refugee and asylum cases. Below is a listing of the major aspects of sexuality that have been addressed to date. Sexuality remains a continually changing, highly contested area of refugee and asylum law.

Gender Persecution

Jacqueline Bhabha succinctly captures the problematic that gender persecution cases entail: "can a woman successfully claim asylum when her society of origin denies her (and women in general) freedoms considered fundamental according to international human rights norms? Conversely, can an insistence that she conform to norms prevailing in her country of origin amount to persecution?"[8] These questions have been conflictingly addressed in asylum cases. Several prominent U.S. cases involved Muslim women who objected to mandatory dress codes such as veiling but faced persecution if they failed to conform. Other cases involved women who dissented from gender norms in the realm of sexuality (described below). Thus, gender persecution cases often involved, but also extended beyond, issues of sexuality.[9]

Female Genital Mutilation

In March 1994, in *Oluloro*,[10] an immigration judge in Portland, Oregon, suspended the deportation of a Nigerian woman on the grounds that the likely imposition of female genital mutilation (FGM) on her U.S. citizen children, if they moved to Nigeria, constituted extreme hardship.[11] This was not an asylum case per se, but it brought the issue of FGM to public and judicial attention.[12]

Subsequently, there were several instances in which immigration judges granted asylum to women on the basis of their fear of facing FGM, but these decisions were not published since the cases did not go as far as the Board of Immigration Appeals (BIA). The fact that FGM was not automatically a basis for gaining asylum was painfully illustrated by a 1995 case involving a woman from Sierra Leone. The woman was politically opposed to FGM. She feared that if she returned to Sierra Leone, FGM would be imposed on her three daughters and she would be persecuted because she had publicly criticized her own mutilation. The judge denied her application for asylum, ruling "respondent cannot change the fact that she is female but she can change her mind with regards to her position towards the FGM practices."[13]

The most significant U.S. asylum case involving FGM was that of Fauziya Kasinga, a young woman from the Tchamba-Kunsuntu tribe in Togo, which required young women to undergo FGM at the age of fifteen.[14] Initially, Kasinga was not subjected to FGM because of the protection of her powerful father, but after he died, her aunt and her husband-to-be decided that she should undergo the procedure. At seventeen she fled Togo, traveled through Ghana and Germany, and eventually reached the United States, where she had relatives. Caught by the INS, she was detained in poor conditions for more than a year and was refused when she applied for asylum.[15] But a public outcry forced a reconsideration. In reconsidering Kasinga's case, the BIA had to decide several issues: "whether FGM, as practiced in Togo, constitutes persecution; whether the applicant, a young woman of the Tchamba-Kunsuntu Tribe who had not experienced FGM, is a member of a particular social group; and whether she has a well-founded fear of persecution on account of her membership in this group."[16] The BIA eventually awarded asylum to

Kasinga. However, their written decision held that asylum should be granted to those fleeing FGM only when "the practice, visited upon a resistant recipient, is so extreme as to shock the conscience of the society from which asylum is sought" and where it was inflicted "in a manner condemned by civilized governments."[17] This phrasing perpetuated racist and colonialist imagery and suggested that only limited instances of FGM should be regarded as a basis for asylum. Furthermore, the BIA narrowly defined the social group to which Kasinga belonged as comprising "young women of the Tchamba-Kunsuntu Tribe who have not had FGM as practiced by that tribe, and who oppose the practice." Thus, women facing FGM who did not belong to Kasinga's tribe would struggle to have their cases considered. Overall, the BIA's decision in Kasinga's case ensured that significant numbers of women who faced FGM were unlikely to apply for or be granted asylum in the United States.[18]

The Illegal Immigration Reform and Immigrant Responsibility Act of 1996, which was signed into law on 30 September 1996, made it a crime to practice FGM on minors.

FGM remains a contentious issue, especially because it is so easily used to stereotype African and Middle Eastern women and countries, thus breathing life into colonialist stereotypes and relationships.[19] At the same time, women seeking asylum because of FGM do not necessarily receive it, and connections are rarely made between FGM and "such American practices as domestic violence, sterilization and contraceptive abuse, unnecessary cosmetic surgeries, and the genital 'mutilation' that is routinely performed on intersexed or hermaphrodite children . . . [all of which are forms] of patriarchal violence intended to enforce strict gender lines and behavior."[20]

Forced Sterilization and Abortion

The Illegal Immigration Reform and Immigrant Responsibility Act of 1996 (IIRIRA) states that "a person who has been forced to abort a pregnancy or undergo involuntary sterilization, or who has been persecuted for failure to undergo such procedure or for other resistance to a coercive family population control program shall be deemed to have been persecuted on account of political opinion."[21] Furthermore, a person with a well-founded fear that he or she will be forced to undergo such a procedure, or will be subject to persecution for the failure of or resistance to such a procedure, is also considered to have a well-founded fear of persecution on account of political opinion.

Primarily addressed to asylum applicants from China, IIRIRA resolved a long series of conflicting interpretations about whether China's one-child population policy should be considered a legitimate ground for claiming asylum. Charles E. Schulman notes that in a 1994 case involving this question, the judge cited "*nine* inconsistent [U.S. policy] declarations concerning the validity of Chinese asylum claims based on opposition to coercive population control policies."[22] These inconsistencies were tied to shifts in foreign and economic relations between China and the United States.

Audrey Macklin observes that although IIRIRA legislates that those resisting China's one-child policy shall be deemed to have been persecuted on account of political opinion, "curiously, the legislation did not actually articulate what the opinion consisted of."[23] She notes that women should, in theory, be the primary beneficiaries of the legislation, because women are usually the ones who suffer most forced sterilizations and all forced abortions. But "ironically, the leading cases from the highest courts of Canada, the United States, and Australia all involve male claimants allegedly fleeing forcible sterilization, perhaps because men are more likely than women to have the resources to flee. One cannot but remark how sex inequality in the 'private sphere' informs not only who is more likely to undergo coercive violation of reproductive capacities, but also who has the opportunity to claim refugee protection on that account."[24] The Center for Reproductive Law and Policy also points out that "Congress's decision to single out forced abortion and sterilization, while giving no special consideration to refugees fleeing other coercive reproduction policies such as forced pregnancies and forced childbirth, offers a far from thorough protection of refugees' reproductive rights."[25]

Rape

Increasingly, refugee and asylum cases have recognized rape as a form of persecution. The INS's Gender Guidelines, issued in 1995, acknowledge that rape "may serve as evidence of past persecution on account of one or more of the five grounds."[26] The Guidelines also caution asylum officers that "the appearance of sexual violence in a claim should not lead adjudicators to conclude automatically that the claim is an instance of purely personal harm."[27]

However, it is important to understand that rape per se is not necessarily considered persecutory or a ground for asylum. Rather, rape as a means to persecute someone because of race, religion, nationality, membership in a social group (which has to be defined more narrowly than the category "women"), or political opinion is what courts generally acknowledge and address. This approach to analyzing rape was underscored when the BIA elevated as precedent a decision in which they awarded asylum to a Haitian woman who had been gang-raped and beaten in retaliation for her political activities.[28]

An issue that remains contested is how to appropriately frame and analyze the rapes of men and transgender people under existing refugee and asylum law.[29]

See chapter 5 for further discussion.

Gays and Lesbians

Until 1990 lesbians and gay men were barred by law from immigrating to the United States. Consequently, even when they faced forms of persecution such as rape, electroshock therapy, forced incarceration, beatings, hard labor, state-sanctioned execution, and forced marriages because of their sexual orientation, they were unable to apply for asylum on the grounds of persecution.

After 1990 those seeking asylum still faced great difficulty in persuading judges that they were persecuted on account of their membership in a social group. As an immigration spokesperson bluntly expressed it, "Can someone who has an inclination to do something that a majority does not think is right be defined as part of a social group? I think that would be debatable."[30] As a result, most lesbian and gay claims for asylum were rejected. One important exception was the case of Cuban-born Fidel Armando Toboso-Alfonso, who argued for withholding of deportation on the grounds that he would be persecuted for homosexuality if he were forcibly returned to Cuba. His claim succeeded in part because of the United States' historic animosity toward Cuba. Granting asylum to Cubans—even gay ones—seemed to validate claims about the evils of Communism under Castro.

In 1994 Attorney General Janet Reno announced that lesbians and gay men *should* be considered to comprise a social group for purposes of applying for asylum and elevated the Toboso case as a precedent.[31] This decision finally opened the door to lesbians and gay men who were facing persecution to apply for asylum.

Even though the door has opened, the process remains difficult. Noemi Masliah explains that it "imposes an obligation on the applicant not only to come out to a feared bureaucratic agent, but to prove the truth of his or her sexual orientation. Also, the applicant has to establish that he or she identifies with the social group called homosexuals. The applicant has to present . . . this very private aspect of his or her life by way of testimony, personal affidavit, and affidavits of others. This in most cases is psychologically, culturally, and emotionally invasive and difficult—even traumatic—and probably alone works to deter many lesbians and gay men from even thinking of applying."[32]

There remains a significant disparity between the number of cases filed by gay men versus lesbians, which shows the existence of ongoing gender barriers (described in chapter 5) in asylum access.[33]

Transgender Status

In the 1990s the asylum system also addressed claims by a small number of transgender individuals seeking protection from persecution. Fatima Mohyuddin offers the following general definition of who may be considered transgender: "transgender is an umbrella term that encompasses male and female cross dressers, transvestites, pre-operative and post-operative transsexuals, transsexuals who choose not to have genital reconstruction and intersexuals."[34] Transgender claims for protection have often failed in the U.S. court system, in part because they challenge dominant norms that presume binary gender and a neat equivalence between biological gender, gender identity, and sexual orientation. While case law that protects on the basis of biological sex or sexuality should theoretically provide a framework within which to protect transgender people from persecution, in practice this has often not happened. This is because gender protection laws are often implicitly based on notions of immutable, binary gender categories. Since transgender people do not fit within these gender models, courts sometimes decide that gender protection laws are inapplicable to them.[35] Nondiscrimination laws addressing sexual orientation often do not adequately protect transgender people either.

These difficulties were illustrated by the experiences of Mexican-born Geovanni Hernandez-Montiel, who initially applied for asylum in the United States in 1995. From a young age, Hernandez-Montiel, who was born as a biological male, felt that s/he was gay and displayed a "feminine" manner of dress and self-presentation. As a result, s/he was expelled from the Mexican school system, forcibly institutionalized by family, raped twice by the Mexican police when s/he was fourteen, and knifed by a group of young men. In 1993, at the age of fifteen, s/he fled to the United States but was arrested and forced to return to Mexico. S/he fled again in 1994 and filed an application for asylum and withholding of deportation in 1995. An immigration judge accepted Hernandez-Montiel's testimony as "credible," "sincere," and "forthright."[36] Nonetheless, the immigration judge, and later the Board of Immigration Appeals, denied asylum to Hernandez-Montiel. As Taylor Flynn summarizes, both found Hernandez-Montiel's testimony credible; both were undoubtedly aware that sexual orientation persecution provides a legitimate ground for granting asylum; but both reasoned that although Hernandez-Montiel was persecuted, it was not on account of sexual orientation but rather because of her/his manner of dress—which, in their opinion, s/he could change.[37] The Ninth Circuit Court reversed these decisions, however. The reversal occurred in part because the court's analysis established the interconnections between sexual orientation and gender identity, as reflected by Hernandez-Montiel's manner of dress. Thus they found that Hernandez-Montiel's manner of dress was not merely an issue of "fashion" about which s/he should make a different decision but rather an expression of gender identity that was fundamental to Hernandez-Montiel's personhood. This analysis allowed Hernandez-Montiel to finally obtain the protection that s/he needed. While the difficulties s/he experienced reveal the barriers facing asylum applicants whose claims cannot be accommodated under binary, stable notions of either gender or sexuality, the case also established an important precedent for other transgender asylum claims. A number of other transgender asylum cases have also been granted.[38]

HIV

The Immigration Act of 1891 excluded any immigrant who was "suffering from a loathsome or contagious disease," and medical exclusions have continued in various forms to the present. In June 1987 the Public Health Service (PHS) added AIDS infection to the list of dangerous contagious diseases. Senator Jesse Helms proposed that HIV be substituted for AIDS on the list, and when his proposal became law the government began to require that all applicants for legal permanent residence undergo an HIV test.

In 1991 the Secretary of Health and Human Services suggested that HIV should be removed from the list of medical exclusions, on the grounds that it was not contagious but instead transmitted through specific behaviors. However, political and public pressures prevented the change.

In November of that year, after a military coup deposed democratically elected President Aristide, thousands of Haitians fled their country. Many were intercepted at sea by the U.S. Coast Guard, who conducted onboard interviews to determine which persons, in their view, had a credible fear of persecution. Michael Ratner suggests that "hasty, onboard interviews of terrified and exhausted survivors pulled from the sea were likely to result in unreliable judgments about who could be safely repatriated."[39] Consequently, advocates went to court to enjoin the Coast Guard from forcibly repatriating any Haitians. During the ensuing legal battle, Haitians picked up by the Coast Guard were held at the United States Naval Station at Guantanamo Bay, Cuba. When advocates lost their legal challenge, the government began forcibly repatriating the Haitians whom they deemed to lack a credible fear of persecution. Those who were deemed to have a credible fear, however, were tested for HIV. Refugees who tested HIV-negative were brought to the United States to apply for asylum. Those who tested HIV-positive were required to undergo a second, more strict screening about whether their fear of persecution was well founded. A double standard for refugee protection was clearly in place, and it hinged on HIV status.

Those who tested HIV-positive and had a well-founded fear of persecution remained incarcerated in Guantanamo Bay in what Ratner characterizes as "the world's first HIV detention camp."[40] Judge Johnson, who eventually ruled that the refugees should be brought to the United States, described the conditions in which they had lived for more than a year: "they live in camps surrounded by razor barbed wire. They tie plastic garbage bags to the sides of the building to keep the rain out. They sleep on cots and hang sheets to create some semblance of privacy. They are guarded by the military and are not permitted to leave the camp except under military escort. The Haitian detainees have been subjected to predawn military sweeps as they sleep by as many as 400 soldiers dressed in full riot gear. They are confined like prisoners and are subject to detention in the brig without a hearing for camp rule infractions."[41] The judge further noted that "the detained Haitians are neither criminals nor national security risks. Some are pregnant mothers and others are children. Simply put, they are merely unfortunate victims of a fatal disease.... The Haitians' plight is a tragedy of immense proportion and their continued detainment is totally unacceptable to this court."[42] The judge ordered that they should be brought to the United States for emergency medical treatment and further processing, and that the failure to do so was an impermissible abuse of the Attorney General's discretion.

When Bill Clinton became president, he pledged to end HIV immigration exclusion. By February 1993 the PHS had completed a draft of regulations that would have removed HIV from the list of excludable contagious diseases. But to preempt such a change, legislation was introduced in Congress that "mandate[d] the exclusion of HIV-positive aliens applying for immigrant visas, refugee visas, and adjustment to permanent resident status."[43] The legislation held that as a matter of law—regardless of any medical opinion to the contrary—HIV infection constituted "a communicable disease of public health significance." As a result, the Immigration and Nationality Act was amended to exclude all HIV-positive noncitizens from the United States.[44]

Consequently, HIV-positive immigrants cannot, except in rare instances, become legal permanent residents (much less citizens). Waivers are available under certain limited circumstances.[45] Refugees or asylum applicants who test positive for HIV are also denied the right to remain in the United States unless they can meet the stringent waiver requirements. As Margaret Somerville and Sarah Wilson underscore, "it is sobering to think that this could mean that the political need to be seen to act against HIV infection and AIDS may be given priority over the protection of persecuted people."[46]

Contradictorily, since 1994 a very small number of applications for asylum have been granted to people who have been persecuted for having HIV or AIDS.

Trafficking and Violence

There has been some consideration of how immigration and refugee law could be used to protect women who are trafficked to the United States for sex work. Historically, immigration laws render such women superexploitable and unable to access even basic rights, because they enter improperly or without inspection, and their occupations render them excludable and deportable. In seeming acknowledgment of these difficulties, President Clinton signed the Trafficking Victims Protection Act (TVPA) on 28 October 2000. While the Act does not clearly define trafficking, it makes available up to 5,000 newly created T visas per year for people who can show that (1) they are victims of "severe trafficking"; (2) they are in the United States on account of such trafficking; (3) they have assisted in the investigation and prosecution of traffickers or are less than fifteen years old; and (4) they would suffer "extreme hardship involving unusual and severe harm" if removed from the United States.[47]

Although the TVPA offers some hope for trafficked women, an article in *The Hindu* sounds a note of caution. It observes that although the Act claims that some 50,000 women a year are trafficked to the United States, only 5,000 at most are eligible for T visas, and only after they "establish [their] victim credentials." Women who consent to some degree to come to the United States for sex work but then unexpectedly find themselves in situations where their human rights are severely violated remain unable to avail of T visas. Thus, the Act provides assistance to women based on their "chastity, purity, and innocence" rather than on the extent to which their human rights have been violated.

According to *The Hindu*, another problematic aspect of the Act is that "little distinction is drawn between migration and trafficking." Thus, antitrafficking efforts become "a guise for not only keeping people out, but also casting suspicion on those who go to the U.S. to work as nannies, domestic labour, dancers, factory workers or restaurant workers. All these groups of workers are placed in a suspect category and subject to scrutiny at borders." Finally, the Act focuses on countries of origin, which, as the article aptly notes, "are invariably regarded as 'foreign'" and allows the United States to establish standards through which these countries must prove they have taken steps to combat trafficking or face loss of non-humanitarian economic support. "There is an assumption that traffickers exist out there, in the rest of the world, and the U.S. will cleanse the rest of the world through punitive economic responses." This moralistic and jingoistic attitude is problematic, but even more troubling is the fact that such "economic punishments have been proven to harm more people than they help and do almost nothing to curtail the practice, but push it further underground, and invariably, render the subject of trafficking even more vulnerable and dependent on non-state agents."[48]

In addition to the TVPA, Congress also passed the Violence Against Women Act (VAWA) of 2000. This created a new U visa, available to "immigrants who are either victims of, or possess information concerning, a wide range of criminal activities including: rape; torture; trafficking; incest; domestic violence; sexual assault; abusive sexual contact; prostitution; sexual exploitation; female genital mutilation; hostage holding; peonage; involuntary servitude; slave trade; kidnapping; abduction; unlawful criminal restraint; false imprisonment; blackmail; extortion; manslaughter; murder; felonious assault; witness tampering; obstruction of justice; perjury; or attempt, conspiracy, or solicitation to commit one of these offenses."[49] Furthermore, "a federal, state or local official must certify that an investigation or prosecution would be harmed without the assistance of the immigrant or, in the case of a child, the immigrant's parent. No more than 10,000 U visas may be issued each year."[50] The effects of this law also remain to be seen.

In December 2000 the INS issued draft regulations that were designed to make it easier for victims of domestic violence to apply for asylum, by essentially recognizing them as members of a distinct social group. As chapter 5 demonstrated, domestic violence cases often include elements of sexual abuse, violence, or torture.[51]

In the 1990s the refugee/asylum system became a major site for the production of discourses about, and mechanisms for monitoring and adjudicating, sexuality. The results have been contradictory. On one hand, instances of serious persecution and abuse that are either based on sexuality or use sexuality as their instrument have become acknowledged and sometimes addressed. On the other hand, the adjudication of sexuality frequently replicates racist, colonialist, sexist, and classist relationships and imagery. Thus, sexuality continues to provide "an especially dense transfer point for relations of power" in the refugee/asylum system, which necessitate critical scrutiny and strategic intervention.[52]

Notes

Introduction

1. Within that majoritarian framework, my narration of the history of lesbian and gay exclusion was just one more instance of how minorities insist on relating grievances that have nothing to do with "ordinary" Americans and everything to do with the excesses of the minorities themselves.

2. I am using the terms "minor" and "minoritized" in ways that reference a larger but related debate about what is a "minority" literature or discourse. The term "minority" refers not to an essential or pre-given status but instead to a specific position that is produced within a matrix of domination and oppression. According to JanMohamed and Lloyd, the domination/oppression relationship produces cultural minority groups through "damage [that is] more or less systematically inflicted. . . . The destruction involved is manifold, bearing down on variant modes of social formation, dismantling previously functional economic systems, and deracinating whole populations at best or decimating them at worst. In time, with this material destruction, the cultural formations, languages, and diverse modes of identity of the 'minoritized people' are irreversibly affected, if not eradicated, by the effects of their material deracination from the historically developed social and economic structures in terms of which alone they 'made sense'" (4). In turn, this generates forms of cultural-, identity-, and political-production that respond to and implicitly critique the dominant, as well as generating articulations "of alternative practices and values that are embedded in the often-damaged, -fragmentary, -hampered, or -occluded works of minorities" (8). These minority productions, in turn, are frequently reappropriated in commercialized form by the dominant group. See "Towards

a Theory of Minority Discourse: What Is To Be Done?" by Abdul R. JanMahomed and David Lloyd in JanMohamed and Lloyd, eds., *The Nature and Context of Minority Discourse* (New York: Oxford University Press, 1990). Though the situation of lesbians and gay men is not equivalent to the cultural minorities that Jan-Mohamed and Lloyd describe, the notion that minority status is produced through specific social relations and histories of domination/oppression can be usefully retained and applied.

3. Richard Green, "'Give Me Your Tired, Your Poor, Your Huddled Masses' (of Heterosexuals): An Analysis of American and Canadian Immigration Law Policy," *Anglo American Law Review* 16 (1987), 142.

4. Ellen Ross and Rayna Rapp, "Sex and Society: A Research Note From Social History and Anthropology," in Carole S. Vance, ed., *Pleasure and Danger* (Boston: Routledge and Kegan Paul, 1983), 153.

5. Thus, I focus the federal government's management of immigration control, which began in the late nineteenth century.

6. See Nira Yuval Davis and Floya Anthias, eds., *Woman, Nation, State* (New York: St. Martin's Press, 1989), and Tamar Mayer, ed., *Gender Ironies of Nationalism: Sexing the Nation* (New York: Routledge, 2000).

7. A book that valuably examines the intersection of sexual, gender, race, and class exclusions in immigration law is Jacqueline Bhabha and Sue Shutter, *Women's Movement: Women Under Immigration, Refugee, and Nationality Law* (Stoke-on-Trent: Trentham Books Limited, 1994). The authors' focus is on the United Kingdom, though.

8. An example of the changing social construction of Chinese identity is that in 1854 the California Supreme Court classified the Chinese as Indians. See Michael Omi and Howard Winant, *Racial Formation in the United States* (New York: Routledge, 1986), 75. On Chinese exclusion, see Sucheng Chan, *Entry Denied* (Philadelphia: Temple University Press, 1991); Charles McClain, *In Search of Equality: the Chinese Struggle Against Discrimination in Nineteenth-Century America* (Berkeley: University of California Press, 1994); Lucy Salyer, *Laws Harsh as Tigers* (Chapel Hill: University of North Carolina Press, 1995); and Alexander Saxton, *The Indispensable Enemy: Labor and the Anti-Chinese Movement* (Berkeley: University of California Press, 1971), among others.

9. As Neil Gotanda notes, the Magnuson Act of 1943, which supposedly repealed Chinese exclusion, constructed Chineseness as a matter of ancestry rather than country of birth. By contrast, "white" Europeans' identities were defined by country of birth. Thus, the Magnuson Act constructed Chinese identity in a racializing and Orientalizing fashion. See Neil Gotanda, "Exclusion and Inclusion. Immigration and American Orientalism," in Evelyn Hu-DeHart, ed.,

Across the Pacific: Asian Americans and Globalization (Philadelphia: Temple University Press, 1999), 129–51.

10. Quoted in Salyer, *Laws Harsh as Tigers*, 56–57.

11. Writing on the ways that the white racial category has been constructed by law in naturalization cases, Ian Haney Lopez makes a similar point. He notes, "the individuals who petitioned for naturalization forced the courts into a case-by-case struggle to define who was a "white person" [since naturalization was restricted to free white people, later extended in 1870 to include people of African ancestry]. More importantly, courts were required in these prerequisite cases to articulate rationales for the divisions they were creating. . . . the courts . . . had to explain the bases on which they drew the boundaries of Whiteness. The courts had to establish by law whether, for example, a petitioner's race was to be measured by skin color, facial features, national origin, language, culture, ancestry, the speculation of scientists, popular opinion, or some combination of these factors. Moreover, the courts had to decide which of these or other factors would govern where the various indices of race contradicted one another. In short, the courts were responsible for deciding not only who was White, but why someone was White" (2–3). Immigration officials had to make similar decisions about people they processed. See Ian Haney Lopez, *White By Law: The Legal Construction of Race* (New York: New York University Press, 1996).

12. See for example Gina Buijs, ed., *Migrant Women: Crossing Boundaries and Changing Identities* (Oxford: Berg, 1993); Sucheng Chan, "The Exclusion of Chinese Women," in Chan, ed., *Entry Denied*; Donna Gabaccia, *From the Other Side: Women, Gender, and Immigrant Life in the US, 1820–1990* (Bloomington: Indiana University Press, 1994); Evelyn Nakano Glenn, *Issei, Nisei, Warbride: Three Generations of Japanese American Women in Domestic Service* (Philadelphia: Temple University Press, 1986); Delores Mortimer and Roy S. Bryce-Laporte, eds., *Female Immigrants to the United States: Caribbean, Latin American, and African Experiences* (Washington, D.C.: Smithsonian Institution, RIIES Occasional Papers No.2, 1981); Rita J. Simon and Caroline Brettell, *International Migration: The Female Experience* (Totowa, N.J.: Rowman and Allanheld, 1986). For an overview of trends in feminist immigration scholarship, see Silvia Pedraza Bailey, "Women and Migration," *Annual Review of Sociology* 17 (1991), 303–25.

13. It treats sexuality not as a pre-given identity that merely awaited "discovery" by diligent officials, but rather as changingly constructed through monitoring procedures, and as a site for social conflict and challenges.

14. There is a single reference to migration in *The History of Sexuality* (Vol. 1), where Foucault claims that newly emerging institutions and branches of power became harnessed to the project of calculating and managing life.

According to Foucault, the study of migration was one such emerging area of knowledge. See Foucault, *The History of Sexuality* (Vol.1) (New York: Vintage Edition, 1990), 140.

15. Ann Laura Stoler, *Race and the Education of Desire: Foucault's* History of Sexuality *and the Colonial Order of Things* (Durham: Duke University Press, 1995).

16. For critical assessments other than Stoler's of Foucault's approach to matters of race, see Bob Carter, "Rejecting Truthful Identities: Foucault, 'Race,' and Politics," in Moya Lloyd and Andrew Thacker, eds., *The Impact of Michel Foucault on the Social Sciences and Humanities* (New York: St. Martin's Press, 1997), 128–46; Abdul JanMohamed, "Sexuality On/Of the Racial Border: Foucault, Wright, and the Articulation of 'Racialized Sexuality,'" in Domna Stanton, ed., *Discourses of Sexuality* (Ann Arbor: University of Michigan Press, 1992); and Robert C. J. Young, "Foucault on Race and Colonialism," *New Formations* 25 (summer 1995), 57–65. On Foucault's treatment of gender, see Irene Diamond and Lee Quinby, eds., *Feminism and Foucault: Reflections on Resistance* (Boston: Northeastern University Press, 1988); Susan J. Hekman, ed., *Feminist Interpretations of Michel Foucault* (University Park: Pennsylvania State University Press, 1996); Jana Sawicki, *Disciplining Foucault: Feminism, Power, and the Body* (New York: Routledge, 1991). Foucault's framework presents other difficulties for this project, too—for instance, when he dismisses law as primarily a repressive mechanism, whereas immigration law is clearly not just repressive but also profoundly generative of disciplined bodies and identities. See Alan Hunt and Gary Wickham, *Foucault and the Law: Towards a Sociology of Law as Governance* (London: Pluto Press, 1994). Foucault's work also presents difficulties for conceptualizing resistance. On this point, see Stuart Hall, "Who Needs Identity?" in Stuart Hall and Paul Du Gay, eds., *Questions of Cultural Identity* (London: Sage, 1996).

17. Foucault, *The History of Sexuality* (Vol. 1), 140.

18. See Michel Foucault, "On Governmentality," in Graham Burchell, Colin Gordon, and Peter Miller, eds., *The Foucault Effect: Studies in Governmentality* (Chicago: University of Chicago Press, 1991), for discussion of changing rationalities of state. See also the concluding section of Foucault's *The History of Sexuality* (Vol. 1).

19. Foucault, *The History of Sexuality* (Vol. 1), 145.

20. Thus, immigration control was also integrally tied to the economy. The literature on the connections between immigration control and the economy is enormous.

21. Quoted in Siobhan Somerville, *Queering The Color Line* (Durham: Duke University Press, 2000), 15. Some years later, W.E.B. Du Bois famously observed,

in a different but directly related formulation, that "the problem of the twentieth century is the problem of the color line."

22. This is one of several points explored by Judith Butler in "Sexual Inver-
sions," in John Caputo and Mark Yount, eds., *Foucault and the Critique of Institutions* (University Park: The Pennsylvania State University Press, 1993).

23. Sandra Lee Bartky, "Foucault, Femininity, and the Modernization of Patriarchal Power," in Irene Diamond and Lee Quinby, eds., *Feminism and Foucault,* 61.

24. Foucault, *The History of Sexuality* (Vol. 1), 24.

25. Ibid., 47.

26. Ibid., 43.

27. Foucault's first reference to peripheral sexualities occurs in the section
of *The History of Sexuality* (Vol. 1) called "The Perverse Implantation." There he
claims that the discursive explosion around sexuality in the eighteenth and nineteenth centuries was accompanied by two modifications. One was "a centrifugal
movement with respect to heterosexual monogamy . . . the legitimate couple
with its regular sexuality had a right to more discretion. It tended to function as
a norm, one that was stricter, perhaps, but quieter" (38). In tandem with this
change, the sexuality of "children, mad men and women, and criminals; the sen-
suality of those who did not like the opposite sex" (38) came under scrutiny. He
refers to these as "peripheral sexualities" (39).

28. Thanks are due to Jasbir K. Puar for helpful comments on this point.

29. Michel Foucault, *Discipline and Punish: The Birth of the Prison* (New
York: Pantheon, 1977), 184.

30. Foucault, *The History of Sexuality* (Vol. 1), 105.

31. Foucault, *Discipline and Punish,* 297. Thus, contrary to the assumption
that individuation entailed progressive liberation from old-world traditions and
inherited social identities, Foucault argued that individuation provided the very
means to weave immigrants into webs of surveillance and control.

32. Herbert Dreyfus and Paul Rabinow, *Michel Foucault: Beyond Structural-
ism and Hermeneutics,* 2d ed. (Chicago: University of Chicago Press, 1983), 153.

33. Colin Gordon writes: "The same style of analysis, [Foucault] argued, that
had been used to study techniques and practices addressed to individual human
subjects within particular local institutions could also be addressed to techniques and practices for governing populations of subjects at the level of a political sovereignty over an entire society. . . . At the same time, moving from the
former to the latter meant something different from returning to a theory of the
state in the form demanded and practiced by Foucault's Marxist critics. Foucault
acknowledged the continuing truth of the reproach that he refrained from a

theory of the state, 'in the sense that one abstains from an indigestible meal.' . . .
Foucault holds . . . that the state has no essence. The nature of the institution of
the state is, Foucault thinks, a function of changes in practices of government,
rather than the converse." See Colin Gordon, "Introduction," in Burchell, Gordon,
and Miller, eds. *The Foucault Effect: Studies in Governmentality,* 4.

34. Symbolizing their liminal status are immigrants' green cards, which
identify them as legal residents. The latest version of these cards contains a
micro-dot with portraits of the heads of all the presidents of the United States.
The symbolic implications of having to carry these portraits are stunning, hint-
ing as they do at the existence of profound processes of surveillance and peda-
gogy that are intended to form aliens into citizen-subjects. See Michael D. Towle,
"High Tech Green Card Called a Way to Curb Fraud," the *Contra Costa Times,*
22 April 1998, D.1. The micro-dots are intended to differentiate "genuine" green
cards from "fakes."

35. See Linda Bosniak, "Membership, Equality, and the Difference that Alien-
age Makes," *New York University Law Review* 69 (December 1994), 1047–149.
These restrictions have varied over time. Furthermore, they intersect with racial, gender, and class restrictions that allocate rights and entitlements in a
stratified manner to those living within the United States. But the core point is
incontrovertible—legal immigrants do not have exactly the same rights as citizens. Those who are living in the United States without legal residency face even
more restrictions.

36. A President's Crime Commission survey discovered that "91 percent of
all Americans have violated laws that could have subjected them to a term of
imprisonment at one time in their lives." If we take this finding as a general standard, then potentially 91 percent of all immigrants may be deportable. Of course,
we also know that who actually becomes labeled and treated as a criminal is a
political matter, with the poor and people of color being overwhelmingly likely
to become labeled and treated in that way. Therefore, the provisions of immigration law could increase disparities among immigrants on the basis of wealth
and racial status. See Jeffrey Reiman, "The Rich Get Richer and the Poor Get
Prison," in Karen E. Rosenblum and Toni-Michelle C. Travis, eds., *The Meaning
of Difference* (New York: McGraw Hill, 1996), 295.

37. Margaret H. Taylor and T. Alexander Aleinikoff, "Deportation of Criminal Aliens: A Geopolitical Perspective," at http://www.iadialog.org/taylor.html.

38. Mirta Ojito, "Change in Laws Sets Off Big Wave of Deportations," *New
York Times,* 15 December 1998, A1.

39. See Anthony Lewis, "Abroad at Home: The Mills of Cruelty," *New York
Times,* 14 December 1999, A27.

40. *Refugee Reports* June–July 2001, vol. 22, no. 6, p. 6. The cases that generat-

ed this ruling were *Immigration and Naturalization Service v. St. Cyr* (00-787) and *Calcano-Martinez v. Immigration and Naturalization Service* (00-1011).

41. This ruling was generated by the cases of *Reno et al v. Ma* (00-38) and *Zadvydas v. Underdown and Immigration and Naturalization Service* (99-7791). However, the Supreme Court decisions "did not deal with the many others who did not plead guilty but were [nonetheless] convicted of crimes and still face automatic deportation even when the offenses were minor or committed decades earlier" (Susan Sachs, "Cracking the Door for Immigrants," *New York Times* Sunday, 1 July 2001).

42. See especially sections 411 and 412 of the Act.

43. Thus, "in Mississippi, a 20-year-old student from Pakistan said he was stripped and beaten in his cell by inmates who were angry about the attacks, while guards failed to intervene or give him proper medical case." Other similar cases have been reported. See Richard Serrano, "U.S. Strikes Back; Many Held in Terror Probe Report Rights Being Abused," *Los Angeles Times,* 15 October 2001, p. A1. See also related stories by Serrano, "U.S. Strikes Back; The Investigation; Ashcroft Denies Wide Detainee Abuse," *Los Angeles Times,* 17 October 2001, p. A4; "Response to Terror," *Los Angeles Times,* 25 October 2001, p. A3. Other stories include Judy Peres, "Concerns Rise of Civil Rights Being Ignored," *Chicago Tribune,* 16 October 2001; Seth Stern, "Lawyers Potential Abuse of Visa Laws to Hold Suspected Terrorists," *Christian Scientist Monitor,* 18 October 2001; "Detainees Held in Secrecy Without Access to Attorneys or Civil Liberties," *Washington Post,* 15 October 2001. An Amnesty International Report found that detainees were often held without access to their families or attorneys and in many cases had not been told why they were being held. See http://www.amnesty.org.

44. Foucault's image of an archipelago also serves as an apt reminder that immigration processing in the late nineteenth and early twentieth centuries was most often conducted on islands: Ellis Island on the East Coast and Angel Island on the West Coast. The use of islands for processing immigrants entailed strategic calculations about how best to use geography to ensure control of particular populations. As upcoming chapters show, geographic calculations remain central to the organization of immigration today, albeit in changed form.

45. In 1998 the INS doubled its detention capacities. It has also subcontracted with public jails and private correctional companies to hold people who entered without authorization, as part of the growth of what Angela Davis calls "the prison industrial complex." In states like California a pilot program is in place to cross-check prison inmates' residency status and to ensure the deportation of noncitizens once their time is served.

46. See Robert S. Chang, "A Meditation on Borders," in Juan Perea, ed., *Immigrants Out!* (New York: New York University Press, 1997), 249. See also

Chang's book *Disoriented: Asian Americans, Law, and the Nation State* (New York: New York University Press, 1999).

47. Immigration control, then, is always "inseparable from internal policing mechanisms, formal and informal." (Chang, *Disoriented*, 39.) Extending Lisa Lowe's analysis in *Immigrant Acts* (Durham: Duke University Press, 1996), Chang also traces how the history of the exclusion of Asians, and of their incorporation as subordinated minorities, constructs Asians as perpetual foreigners in the dominant imaginary, no matter how many generations they have lived here. As Chang writes, "it is in part through the figure of Asian immigrants and their descendents as perpetual internal foreigners that the national community has been able to identify itself. Without Asian Americans, they (the 'real' Americans) would not know who they were" (*Disoriented*, 38). Lisa Lowe elaborates, "in the last century and a half, the American *citizen* has been defined over and against the Asian *immigrant*, legally, economically, and culturally" (*Immigrant Acts*, 4). Lowe further analyzes how such a style of imagining legitimated the incorporation of Asians as subordinated minorities who could be exploited, while at the same time attempting to resolve the contradictions between capitalist exploitation and claims of representative democracy. Orientalism has also sanctioned imperialist economic relations and war in Asian countries. For a rich discussion of the connections between immigration control and the subordination of Mexican-origin people in the United States, see David Gutierrez, *Walls and Mirrors* (Berkeley: University of California Press, 1995).

48. Benedict Anderson, *Imagined Communities* (London: Verso, 1991), revised edition, 4.

49. Roxanne Lynn Doty, "The Double Writing of Statecraft: Exploring State Responses To Illegal Immigration," *Alternatives* 21 (1996), 180. Through immigration control, the seeming naturalness and timelessness of the nation, territory, and citizenry is continually (re)constructed.

50. Doty, "The Double Writing of Statecraft," 180.

51. Chang, "A Meditation on Borders," 246. According to John Torpey, immigration control is also one of the key mechanisms through which the state has constituted itself *as* a state: "I argue that, in the course of the past few centuries, states have successfully usurped from rival claimants such as churches and private enterprises, the 'monopoly of the legitimate means of movement'—that is, their development as states has depended on effectively distinguishing between citizens/subjects and possible interlopers, and regulating the movements of each." See John Torpey, *The Invention of the Passport: Surveillance, Citizenship, and the State* (Cambridge: Cambridge University Press, 2000), 1–2. Torpey also valuably criticizes the tendency in much immigration scholarship to take the ex-

istence of states for granted, thus "fail[ing] to see the ways in which regulation of movement contributes to constituting the very 'state-ness' of states" (6).

52. Thus, in 1983, the Fifth Circuit Court ruled that "Congress has unbounded power to exclude aliens. Congress can exclude aliens from entering the United States for discriminatory and arbitrary reasons, even those which might be condemned as a denial of equal protection if used for purposes other than immigration." See *Matter of Longstaff*, 716 F. 2d 1439 (5th Cir. 1983).

53. Among many others, Bill Ong Hing clearly addresses this point, as suggested by his book's title: *Making and Remaking Asian America through Immigration Policy, 1850–1990* (Stanford: Stanford University Press, 1993). The title of Loius DiSipio's and Rudolfo O. de la Garza's book, *Making Americans, Remaking America* (Boulder: Westview Press, 1998), also alludes to the fact that immigration "makes" Americans within particular boundaries.

54. Thus, women become "the material or the ground" for patriarchal nation-building projects that are "neither about nor for women." See Hyunah Yang, "Re-Membering the Korean Military Comfort Women: Nationalism, Sexuality, and Silencing," in Elaine H. Kim and Chungmoo Choi, eds., *Dangerous Women: Gender and Korean Nationalism* (New York: Routledge, 1998), 130. Alan Finlayson succinctly summarizes the problem this way: "men can never 'be' the nation— they can only 'have' it—while women can never 'have' the nation because they 'are' it." See Alan Finlayson, "Sexuality and Nationality: Gendered Discourses of Ireland," in Terry Carver and Véronique Mottier, eds., *Politics of Sexuality: Identity, Gender, Citizenship* (New York: Routledge, 1998), 98.

55. Floya Anthias and Nira Yuval-Davis, "Introduction," in Yuval-Davis and Anthias, eds., *Woman, Nation, State*, 10. Echoing these authors, Tamara Mayer writes: "'Purity,' 'modesty' and 'chastity' are common themes . . . when a nation is constituted in opposition to the Other there emerges a profound distinction not only between us and them, but more pointedly, between our women and theirs." See Tamar Mayer, "Introduction," in Mayer, ed., *Gender Ironies of Nationalism*, 10.

56. Yang, "Re-Membering The Korean Military Comfort Women," 130.

57. M. Jacqui Alexander, "Erotic Autonomy as a Politics of Decolonization," in Chandra Talpade Mohanty and M. Jacqui Alexander, eds., *Feminist Genealogies, Colonial Legacies, Democratic Futures* (New York: Routledge, 1997), 65.

58. Alexander, "Erotic Autonomy," 64–65.

59. Pete Wilson, "An Open Letter to the President of the United States on Behalf of the People of California," *New York Times*, 10 August 1993, A11. Emphasis in the original.

60. Catherine P. Kingfisher, "Rhetoric of (Female) Savagery: Welfare Reform

in the United States and Aotearoa/New Zealand," *NWSA Journal* 11, no. 1, (spring 1999), 12.

61. Gwendolyn Mink, "Feminists, Welfare Reform, and Welfare Justice," *Sojourner* 24, no. 2 (October 1998), 26. Mink further explains, "the issue is not whether government should assist mothers in collecting payments from fathers. Of course it should. Neither is the issue whether child support enforcement provisions in welfare policy help mothers who have or desire child support awards. Of course they do. Nor is the issue whether it is a good thing for children to have active fathers—of course it can be. The issue is coercion, coercion directed toward mothers who have eschewed patriarchal conventions—whether by choice or from necessity." See Mink, "Feminist Themes in the Personal Responsibility Act," *Sojourner* 24, no. 2 (October 1998).

62. Mink, "Feminist Themes."

63. When the PRA came up for renewal in 2002, President Bush's proposals included allocating $300 million to promote heterosexual marriage by women on welfare.

64. The ways that immigration and welfare reform laws operate in tandem to control poor and minority women's heterosexualities and childbearing is suggested by the fact that 1996 welfare reform penalized not just poor and minority U.S. women but also made legal immigrants, with few exceptions, ineligible for most public forms of assistance. The Illegal Immigration Reform and Immigrant Responsibility Act, passed the same year, increased income requirements for anyone sponsoring a family member for immigration to the United States, with the result that poorer immigrants in the United States are unable to bring their families over. For a trenchant critique of the connections between welfare, immigration control, and structural adjustment programs imposed on debtor nations, see Grace Chang, *Disposable Domestics* (Boston: South End Press, 2000).

65. Kimberlé Crenshaw et al., "Introduction," in Crenshaw et al., eds., *Critical Race Theory: The Key Writings That Formed the Movement* (New York: The New Press, 1995), xvi.

66. Ibid., xv.

67. Ibid.

68. David Reimers, *Still the Golden Door: The Third World Comes to America* (New York: Columbia University Press, 1985), 72–73.

69. Naomi Zack, *Thinking about Race* (Belmont, Calif.: Wadsworth, 1998), 44.

70. Salyer succinctly captures this point, writing "legislation alone did not secure restrictionists' objectives, however. The way that laws were interpreted and enforced proved equally important." See Salyer, *Laws Harsh as Tigers,* xiv.

71. Foucault, *Discipline and Punish,* 191.

72. Ibid., 189.

73. Ibid., 190.

74. Jacqueline Maria Hagan, *Deciding To Be Legal: A Maya Community in Houston* (Philadelphia: Temple University Press, 1994), 101.

75. Nina Glick Schiller, Linda Basch, and Cristina Szanton Blanc, "Towards A Definition of Transationalism: Introductory Remarks and Research Questions," in *Towards a Transnational Perspective on Migration: Race, Class, Ethnicity, and Migration Reconsidered* (New York: New York Academy of Sciences, 1992), 1–2.

76. Patricia Pessar, ed., "Introduction," in *Caribbean Circuits: New Directions in the Study of Caribbean Migration* (New York: Center For Migration Studies, 1997), 4.

77. Ibid.

78. Ibid., 4–5.

79. Roger Rouse, "Making Sense of Settlement," in *Towards a Transnational Perspective on Migration,* 45.

80. Nina Glick Schiller, Linda Basch, and Cristina Szanton Blanc, "Towards a Definition of Transnationalism," 12.

81. Donald M. Nonini and Aihwa Ong, "Introduction: Chinese Transnationalism as an Alternative Modernity," in Ong and Nonini, eds., *Ungrounded Empires: The Cultural Politics of Modern Chinese Transnationalism* (New York: Routledge, 1997), 26.

82. Of course, as Pessar cautions, "having concluded that the bimodal, settler-sojourner model fails to capture the transnational dynamics of Caribbean [and other] migration, we should avoid falling into the opposite trap. Clearly, not all migrants enjoy equal access to the statuses and resources needed to participate in a full range of transnational social, economic, and political projects. . . . It is still the case that some immigrants will come to settle permanently in the home or host country and gradually diminish ties with other locales, while others will steadfastly refuse to choose, constructing lives in and between both societies." See Pessar, "Introduction," 9–10.

83. Another task for future research is the analysis of how aspects of immigration processing have inflected the consciousness and sparked the resistance of various U.S. racial and ethnic communities and of various governments that have been concerned (or not) about the treatment of "their" nationals.

1. Entry Denied

1. Philip Brian Harper, Anne McClintock, José Esteban Muñoz, and Trish Rosen, "Introduction," "Queer Transexions of Race, Nation, and Gender" a special issue of *Social Text* nos. 52–53 (fall 1997), 1.

2. William S. Bernard, "A History of U.S. Immigration Policy," in Richard Easterlin, David Ward, William S. Bernard, and Reed Ueda, *Immigration* (Cambridge: The Belknap Press of Harvard University, 1982), 84.

3. Lucy Salyer, *Laws Harsh as Tigers,* 1.

4. Salyer, *Laws Harsh as Tigers,* 5; Congressional Research Service, *History of the Immigration and Naturalization Service* (Washington, D.C.: U.S. Government Printing Office, 1980), 7.

5. Congressional Research Service, *History of the Immigration and Naturalization Service,* 7.

6. Salyer, *Laws Harsh as Tigers,* 6.

7. E. P. Hutchinson, *A Legislative History of American Immigration Policy 1798–1965* (Philadelphia: University of Pennsylvania Press, 1981), 506.

8. The words "any relative or personal friend" were deleted by the Act of 1891. The word "family" was retained.

9. Hutchinson, *A Legislative History,* 505.

10. David M. Schneider, *American Kinship: A Cultural Account,* 2d ed. (Chicago: University of Chicago Press, 1980), 33.

11. Kath Weston, *Families We Choose* (New York: Columbia University Press, 1997), xiii.

12. M. Jacqui Alexander, "Erotic Autonomy as a Politics of Decolonization," in M. Jacqui Alexander and Chandra Talpade Mohanty, eds., *Feminist Genealogies,* 65.

13. Within this regime, as Yang succinctly summarizes, "nation is equated with the male subject position, and women's sexuality is reified as the property of the masculine nation." Hyunah Yang, "Re-Membering the Korean Military Comfort Women: Nationalism, Sexuality, and Silencing," in Elaine H. Kim and Chungmoo Choi, eds., *Dangerous Women,* 130.

14. *Immigration Investigation,* 51st Congress, 2d Sess., House of Representatives, Report no. 472, Select Committee on Immigration and Naturalization, hearing held 12 March 1890, published 14 January 1891, 114.

15. *Immigration Investigation,* 495. A witness heartily agreed with the adoption of this policy because "it is astonishing how many of these cases come over here, women sent over pregnant just to get rid of them" (*Immigration Investigation,* 600). Though the witness may well have exaggerated, his comment points to the larger history whereby women have attempted to deal with problem pregnancies through immigration. Full exploration of this issue has not been undertaken to date but would be very valuable.

16. Except in the unlikely event that his act resulted in criminal charges being filed and these charges somehow came to the attention of the immigration service.

17. George Peffer, *If They Don't Bring Their Women Here* (Urbana: University of Illinois Press, 1999), 26–27.

18. After 1924 all Chinese (and Asian) spouses became ineligible to enter the United States. In 1925 the Supreme Court extended entry rights to Chinese wives of Chinese merchants who were living in the United States, but denied that same right to Chinese wives of Chinese American citizens. An amendment in 1930 allowed Chinese wives of Chinese Americans to enter the United States, but only if marriage had taken place before the Act of 1924 was approved. Not until 1943, when the Chinese Exclusion Act was repealed and Chinese people became eligible to naturalize, were general spousal reunification benefits extended to Chinese immigrants. See Sucheng Chan, "The Exclusion of Chinese Women, 1870–1943," in Sucheng Chan, ed., *Entry Denied*, 94–146.

19. Michael Omi and Howard Winant, *Racial Formation in the United States,* 64–65.

20. Lisa Lowe, *Immigrant Acts,* 177–78, n.6.

21. Perhaps not coincidentally, this was the same year that the Page Law passed.

22. Quoted in Frederick Grittner, *White Slavery: Myth, Ideology, and American Law* (New York: Garland, 1990), 45.

23. Arlene R. Keizer, "A 'Cage of Obscene Birds': Slavery and the Deployment of Sexuality," paper presented at the American Studies Association National Conference, Detroit, 15 October 2000.

24. For more on antipolygamy, see Joan Smith Iverson, "A Debate on the American Home: The Anti-Polygamy Controversy, 1880–1890," in John C. Fout and Maura Shaw Tantillo, eds., *American Sexual Politics* (Chicago: University of Chicago Press, 1993), 123–40. For discussion of why polygamy is deemed a challenge to the national order, see Shane Phelan, "Structures of Strangeness: Citizenship and Kinship," in her *Sexual Strangers: Gays, Lesbians, and the Dilemmas of Citizenship* (Philadelphia: Temple University Press, 2001), 63–81. See also Peggy Pascoe, *Relations of Rescue* (Oxford: Oxford University Press, 1990).

25. Quoted in Mark Haller, *Eugenics: Hereditarian Attitudes in American Thought* (New Brunswick: Rutgers University Press, 1963), 79.

26. Haller, *Eugenics,* 54. See also Linda Gordon, *Woman's Body, Woman's Right: A Social History of Birth Control in America* (New York: Grossman, 1976), 116–58; and Angela Y. Davis, *Women, Race, and Class* (New York: Vintage, 1983), 202–21.

27. Omi and Winant, *Racial Formation in the United States,* 173, n.11.

28. Congressional Research Service, *History of the Immigration and Naturalization Service,* 9. There was also a massive expansion of the civil service between 1865 and 1891, as the number of federal jobs tripled. The rise of the

federally controlled immigration system was part of that expansion. See Mary Beth Norton et al., *A People and a Nation. A History of the United States,* brief ed., 4th ed. (Boston: Houghton Mifflin, 1996), 387.

29. Congressional Research Service, *History of the Immigration and Naturalization Service,* 9.

30. According to Hutchinson, the United States wanted to exclude criminal immigrants—except those who had been charged with clearly politically motivated crimes. The provisions regarding moral turpitude represented an effort to differentiate between these two sorts of crimes and to exclude anyone except those convicted of political offenses.

31. Jonathan Katz, in *Gay American History: Lesbians and Gay Men in the USA* (New York: Avon, 1976), shows that African Americans and immigrants were disproportionately jailed for "crimes against nature," including sodomy. The 1880 census listed sixty-three people who were incarcerated on that basis. "Nineteen of these are 'Native white' and male; one is female. Eleven of these are listed as 'Foreign born white' males. Thirty-two of these are 'colored' males. The relative number of white and 'colored' prisoners . . . is, of course, extremely disproportionate to the racial character of the general population" (57). The number of foreign-born men imprisoned is also disproportionate. Of the 11 foreign born, they are specified as: 2 from Germany, 2 from England, 3 from Ireland, 1 from Italy, 2 from Mexico, and 1 from Russia. The 1890 census included an enumeration of those jailed for offenses "against public morals," including crimes against nature. A total of 224 people were listed, including 45 foreign-born "whites." Of the 78 "Colored" U.S.-born people convicted, 76 were listed as "Negro" and 2 as Chinese (61). Of the 101 U.S.-born whites who committed these crimes, 7 had one foreign-born parent and 32 had two foreign-born parents.

32. *Grounds for Exclusion of Aliens Under the Immigration and Nationality Act. Historical Background and Analysis,* Committee of the Judiciary, U.S. House of Representatives, 100th Congress, 2d Sess., September 1988 (Washington, D.C.: U.S. Government Printing Office, 1988), 13.

33. Under the law, anyone who imported (or tried to import) a woman for prostitution or who held (or tried to hold) a woman for prostitution could be charged with a felony and jailed (Jane Perry Clark, *The Deportation of Aliens from the United States to Europe* [New York: Columbia University Press, 1931], 232).

34. Alan Kraut, *Silent Travelers: Genes, Germs, and the 'Immigrant Menace'* (New York: Basic Books, 1994), 272–73.

35. Quoted in Kraut, *Silent Travelers,* 63.

36. David M. Brownstone, Irene M. Franck, and Douglass L. Brownstone, *Island of Hope, Island of Tears* (New York: Rawson and Wade Publishers, 1979), 226.

37. File 54513/6, National Archives, Washington, D.C. (Accession # 60A600).

38. Hutchinson, *Legislative History*, 422.

39. Ibid., 420, my emphasis.

40. Clark, *The Deportation of Aliens*, 232. In 1909 the Supreme Court struck down the provisions against harboring women for purposes of prostitution, in *Keller v. United States*.

41. The subject files of the immigration service are listed on microfiche T458 at the National Archives in Washington, D.C. Under the subject heading "immoral aliens" is the following entry, showing debate about whether men could also be found immoral: "#54,645-181, Secty State fwds ltr frm UCS Bluefields, Nicaragua req infm if that part of I/Laws excld frm entry to U.S. persons of immrl character applies to men as well as women, 2-12-1919." I requested a copy of this information from the National Archives, but staff were unable to locate it.

42. Immigration laws presumed that the spouse coming to the United States was a woman following a pioneering husband.

43. Donna Gabaccia, *From The Other Side*, 27–41; Doris Weatherford, *Foreign and Female* (New York: Shocken Books, 1984); Feri Felix Weiss, *The Sieve or Revelations of the Man Mill, Being the Truth about American Immigration* (Boston: The Page Company, 1921); Brownstone, Franck, and Brownstone, *Island of Hope*.

44. Weatherford, *Foreign and Female*, 176.

45. Edward Corsi, *In the Shadow of Liberty* (New York: Arno Press, 1969), 81.

46. Lillian Faderman, *Odd Girls and Twilight Lovers* (New York: Penguin, 1991), 41–45.

47. Katz, *Gay American History*, 380.

48. Ibid. Katz also mentions other passing immigrant women, including Murray Hall, a Scottish woman who became a Tammany Hall politician, "played poker at the clubs with city and state officials," smoke and drank with male cronies, and married twice (354).

49. See Grittner, *White Slavery*, 39, 50, 62.

50. Ibid., 64.

51. Ibid.

52. George Kibbe Turner, "Daughters of the Poor," *McClure's Magazine* (November 1909), 45–61.

53. *Grounds for The Exclusion of Aliens*, 15.

54. Grittner, *White Slavery*, 94.

55. Grittner, *White Slavery*, 102.

56. Lynching allegedly occurred in response to African American men "sexually threatening" white women. In fact, such incidents were rare, and lynching more generally functioned as a tool to terrorize black communities and individual blacks who challenged racism. Some blacks were lynched for being successful

shopkeepers and businessmen. "In other cases, a dispute over wages or some other kind of assertive behavior might provoke a group of whites to target a black for murder. Often, it was not the rape of a white woman but the sexual assault of a black woman [by a white man] that set a lynching in motion." John D'Emilio and Estelle B. Freedman, *Intimate Matters: A History of Sexuality in America*, 2d ed. (Chicago: University of Chicago Press, 1997), 217.

57. Ibid., 221.

58. Ann Lucas, "The Dis-ease of Being a Woman: Rethinking Prostitution and Subordination," Ph.D. diss., Jurisprudence and Social Policy Program, University of California, Berkeley, 1997, 64.

59. Katz, *Gay American History,* 80.

60. Kitty Calavita, *Inside The State: The Bracero Program, Immigration, and the I.N.S.* (New York: Routledge, 1992), 7.

61. Salyer, *Laws Harsh as Tigers,* 133.

62. The impact of eugenics on immigration monitoring was beyond question; eugenics "experts" had been invited to assist in the inspection of immigrants at Ellis Island after the press claimed that regular inspections were permitting too many undesirables to enter. See Kraut, *Silent Travelers,* 73–75.

63. Hutchinson, *Legislative History,* 422. The idea that polygamy was un-Western (and unwhite) was reiterated by observers such as immigration inspector Feri Felix Weiss, who characterized the circumstances of European women who were coming to the United States through sponsorship by the Mormon Church as akin to being placed in a harem. Weiss related, "Many letters of despair were received from time to time from girls in Utah and Idaho, describing their helpless condition as the fifth or sixth wife of some old and cruel Mormon" (Weiss, *The Sieve,* 179).

64. Kraut, *Silent Travelers,* 276.

65. Quoted in Richard Green, "'Give Me Your Tired,'" 140.

66. Ibid., 141. According to Haller, the term "constitutional psychopathic inferior" emerged through eugenics. Eugenicists began administering Binet intelligence tests to various populations, including those labeled as delinquents. Their results suggested that "feeble-mindedness" was a primary cause of all sorts of delinquency, including, but not restricted to, sexual forms. "From the testing of delinquents came the discovery and labeling of a new type of social menace, variously called the moral imbecile, psychopath, constitutional inferior, or (most commonly) defective delinquent. The defective delinquent was a feebleminded person—usually a moron since lower varieties of the feebleminded lacked the necessary intelligence—who had antisocial and criminalistic tendencies. The 'typical' defective delinquent acted without forethought, without remorse, driven by passions he was unable to control or understand. Such persons

were the perpetrators of brutal murders and sex assaults and were incorrigible in their criminalistic tendencies" (Haller, *Eugenics*, 104).

67. Robert Podnanski, "The Propriety of Denying Entry to Homosexual Aliens: Examining the Public Health Service's Authority over Medical Exclusions," *University of Michigan Journal of Law Reform* 17 (1983–84), 333–34.

68. Clark, *The Deportation of Aliens*, 236.

69. Ibid.

70. Ibid., 235.

71. Hutchinson, *Legislative History*, 421.

72. Clark, *The Deportation of Aliens*, 235. This severe response to immigrant prostitution was mirrored by domestic policies. In response to the war, "pressure was placed on cities near military bases to close their red light districts and the army established 5-mile 'pure zones' to keep prostitutes away from the camps." Women suspected of prostitution near military bases were summarily dealt with: "the military suspended writs of habeas corpus, arrested women en masse, and forcibly held more than fifteen thousand in detention centers for periods averaging ten weeks. No men were arrested for patronizing prostitutes." These measures were intended to ensure troops' readiness for combat. See D'Emilio and Freedman, *Intimate Matters*, 212.

73. In regard to prostitution, D'Emilio and Freedman relate that by 1920, "the red light district had passed into history; the system of commercialized prostitution that had reigned in American cities for almost half a century had been destroyed. . . . [But although red light districts closed], prostitution did not end. Instead, it changed its form and locale, with streetwalkers and call girls becoming more typical. The new structure made the working class prostitutes more vulnerable to police harassment, and shifted control of her day-to-day life from the madame who ran the brothel to the male pimp who controlled her street activities with the threat, sometimes fulfilled, of violence. Ideals of male continence won little acceptance." D'Emilio and Freedman, *Intimate Matters*, 213.

74. "Immigration and Naturalization Legislation," Appendix 1 of the *Statistical Yearbook of the Immigration and Naturalization Service* (Washington, D.C.: U.S. Government Printing Office, 1991), A.I-5.

75. According to Bill Ong Hing, "the Western Hemisphere included Canada, Mexico, Central America, South America, and the 'adjacent islands' of Saint Pierre, Miquelon, Cuba, the Dominican Republic, Haiti, Bermuda, the Bahamas, Barbados, Jamaica, the Windward and Leeward Islands, Trinidad, Martinique, and other British, French, and Netherlands territory or possessions in or bordering on the Caribbean Sea." See Bill Ong Hing, *Making and Remaking Asian America through Immigration Policy, 1850–1990*, 249, n.203.

76. Hutchinson, *Legislative History*, 511.

77. John Higham, *Strangers in the Land: Patterns of American Nativism, 1865–1925* 2d ed. (New Brunswick: Rutgers University Press, 1988), 324.

78. Ibid.

79. In 1922–23 the Supreme Court ruled that Asian Indians and Japanese immigrants were "aliens ineligible to become citizens." The Act of 1924 excluded all "aliens ineligible for citizenship," without explicitly naming Asians.

80. Calavita, *Inside the State,* 7.

81. Hutchinson, *Legislative History,* 511.

82. The system avoided problems that were arising because of the numerical ceilings imposed on immigration since 1921. Because of numerical ceilings, ships waited until the stroke of midnight on the days when new quotas became available, then raced into the harbors to try to ensure that *their* passengers were processed before all the quota was used up. Jane Perry Clark describes what happened to one passenger who was presented for processing after the quotas were filled: "An Armenian reaching the United States in 1923 and finding the immigration quota in which he belonged filled and himself excluded, provided a modern version of the flying Dutchman. By American regulations under the Quota Act of 1921 he could not enter the United States, and by Turkish regulation he could not re-enter Turkey once he left, so like the Dutchman he seemed condemned to wander the seven seas." See Clark, *The Deportation of Aliens,* 23.

83. John Torpey, *The Invention of the Passport,* 120.

84. Ibid.

85. Congressional Research Service, *History of the Immigration and Naturalization Service,* 2.

86. Norton et al., *A People and a Nation,* 532.

87. Norman L. Zucker and Naomi Flint Zucker, *The Guarded Gate: The Reality of American Refugee Policy* (San Diego: Harcourt Brace Jovanovich, 1987), 23–24. The failure to aid Jews through the immigration system is perhaps best exemplified by the story of the *St. Louis,* a ship that left Germany in 1939, carrying 930 Jewish refugees. "Denied entry to Havana, the *St. Louis* headed for Miami, where coast guard cutters prevented it from docking. The ship was forced to return to Europe. Some of these refugees took shelter in countries that were later overrun by Hitler's legions" and perished. See Norton et al., *A People and a Nation,* 532.

88. Norton et al., *A People and a Nation,* 532.

89. Ibid., 534.

90. Congressional Research Service, *History of the Immigration and Naturalization Service,* 53.

91. Norton et al., *A People and a Nation,* 543.

92. Paul Spickard, *Mixed Blood* (Madison: University of Wisconsin Press, 1989), 135.

93. Zucker and Zucker, *The Guarded Gate*, 31.

94. Ibid., 32.

95. Calavita, *Inside the State*, 21.

96. Ibid., 50.

97. See Elaine Tyler May, *Homeward Bound* (New York: Basic Books, 1988).

98. D'Emilio and Freedman, *Intimate Matters*, 286.

99. John D'Emilio, "The Homosexual Menace: The Politics of Sexuality in Cold War America," in D'Emilio, *Making Trouble* (New York: Routledge, 1992), 64.

100. Quoted in Green, "Give Me Your Tired," 141.

101. Other provisions of the Act of 1952 reiterated what were, by then, standard exclusions based on sexuality. For instance, immigrants coming to the United States to engage in "immoral" sexual acts remained excluded. The Act also excluded prostitutes, procurers, and those receiving the proceeds of prostitution.

102. Hutchinson, *Legislative History*, 332.

103. According to Nelia Sancho, the Japanese army forced "an estimated 200,000 Chinese, Korean, Filipino, Malaysian, Indonesian, and Dutch women and girls" into sexual slavery in countries that they occupied during World War II (145). Jewish women were also forced into sexual slavery by the Nazis. See Nelia Sancho, "The Comfort Woman System during World War II: Asian Women as Targets of Mass Rape and Sexual Slavery," in Ronit Lentin, ed., *Gender and Catastrophe* (London: Zed Books, 1997), 144–54.

104. See U.S. Senate, *Report of the Proceedings, Hearings Held Before the Subcommittee on Immigration and Naturalization of the Committee of the Judiciary, on S.1006, S.2369, to Amend the Immigration and Nationality Act*, 30 July 1957, 17, 19. Of the eighty randomly selected private bills for relief from the 84th Congress that I reviewed, ten involved women who were barred due to prostitution. Most were European, though several were Mexican or Canadian. None were Asian. The men were all U.S. citizens, and their race and ethnicity were not specified. The experience of war, and the fact that U.S. servicemen were filing on the women's behalf, trying to bring them to the United States as wives or fiancées, significantly defined the information that was contained in these ten bills and the way the requests were viewed. All but one of the men had met these women while serving in the U.S. armed forces abroad. Several had cohabited and borne children together, and most eventually married. The bills highlighted the fact that the women had been connected to prostitution, but gave no indication that the men had patronized prostitutes, although no doubt some of them had. Indeed, it is likely that some of these men met their wives or fiancées precisely

through patronizing prostitutes. For instance, the bill filed for a thirty-four-year-old Mexican woman, who reportedly turned to prostitution to support herself and her son in Tijuana, states that she met her husband "when he was brought to her room by another Mexican woman."

105. The family ties that provided a basis for immigration preference were these: being the unmarried son or daughter of a U.S. citizen; being the spouse or unmarried son or daughter of a U.S. resident; being the married son or daughter of a U.S. citizen; or being the brother or sister aged at least twenty-one of a U.S. citizen. Citizens' spouses were nonquota immigrants who remained able to enter outside of quota limits or preferences.

106. David Reimers, *Still the Golden Door: The Third World Comes to America*, 73.

107. Ibid.

108. In hindsight, it is clear that congressional calculations were inaccurate. Asians and Latin Americans became the major groups to immigrate to the United States by the 1970s (see Reimers for discussion of why that happened). But this does not invalidate the fact that the 1965 revision were intended to preserve European dominance in immigration.

109. The use of the heterosexual family as an instrument of racial purpose, evident in the 1965 INA, also cropped up in Daniel Patrick Moynihan's *The Negro Family: The Case For National Action* (popularly known as the Moynihan Report), released in the same year. Moynihan was the Assistant Secretary of Labor and the Director of the Office of Policy Planning and Research. In the report, "Moynihan described Black culture as a 'tangle of pathology' that is 'capable of perpetuating itself without assistance from the white world.' The chief culprit, Moynihan asserted, was Blacks' matriarchal family structure. . . . Moynihan thus endowed poor Black women—the most subordinated members of society—with the power of a matriarch" (Dorothy Roberts, *Killing The Black Body* [New York: Pantheon Books, 1997], 16). Many interpreted the report as grounds for shifting the blame for black poverty onto black women's sexual and gender behaviors, which were characterized in ways that extended long-standing stereotypes, while minimizing the fact that systemic inequalities in housing, education, employment, and other arenas were powerfully at the root of black poverty. At the same time, the 1965 INA's promotion of the heterosexual immigrant family was intended to serve not just racial and gender but also economic purposes. Lawmakers calculated that immigrant heterosexual families would boost consumer spending without constituting a significant source of labor competition (because they presumed that wives and children would not be in the workforce). See Reimers, *Still the Golden Door*, 71; United States, Congress. House. 88th Congress, 2d Session. *Hearings on H.R. 7700 and 55, Identical Bills*

to Amend the Immigration and Nationality Act, and for Other Purposes (Washington, D.C.: U.S. Government Printing Office, 1964).

110. Saskia Sassen, "Why Migration?" *Report on the Americas* 26, no. 1 (July 1992), 14–19.

111. At the end of the 1970s "the latest in a long line of purity movements took shape" (D'Emilio and Freedman, *Intimate Matters*, 345). The movement burst onto the national scene through the 1980 presidential election and shaped immigration and domestic policies in important ways over the next two decades.

112. Grace Chang, *Disposable Domestics*, 55–92.

113. Several mothers responded by bringing a class action suit against the INS in 1988, charging that the INS violated IRCA through their method of implementation, and that INS regulations discriminated on the basis of sex. The suit was dismissed in 1998, due to provisions of 1996 immigration law that limited the courts' ability to review legalization issues *(Zambrano v. INS)*.

114. Once again, "immoral immigrants" who failed to value American institutions—rather than the effects of globalization, downsizing, government cutbacks, growing numbers of women in the labor force, home-grown racism and sexism and their effects—were seen as the cause for changing marriage patterns.

115. *Immigration Marriage Fraud, Hearing Before the Subcommittee on Immigration and Refugee Policy of the Committee of the Judiciary,* U.S. Senate, 99th Congress, 1st Sess., 26 July 1985 (Washington, D.C.: U.S. Government Printing Office, 1986), 29. For further discussion of dominant cultural anxieties about the impact of immigrant marriage patterns on American institutions and values, see Bonnie Honig, *Democracy and the Foreigner* (Princeton: Princeton University Press, 2001), 86–92.

116. *Immigration Marriage Fraud*, 50.

117. See Michelle J. Anderson, "A License to Abuse: The Impact of Conditional Status on Female Immigrants," *Yale Law Journal* 102 (1993), 1401–30. Also, Leti Volpp, *Working with Battered Immigrant Women* (San Francisco: Family Violence Prevention Fund, 1995).

118. Salyer, *Laws Harsh as Tigers*, 247. Salyer writes, "Even the in-depth questioning developed to detect fraud in Chinese cases has survived in a different context, and is now used to test the validity of marriages between aliens and American citizens."

119. Personal conversation, Joane Nagel, Detroit, Mich., 14 October 2000.

120. Sandra Eschenbrenner, "Immigration—Aliens—The Invalidation of a Homosexual Marriage for Immigration Purposes," *Suffolk Transnational Law Journal* 7 (1) (1983), 267–68, 273. The case is *Adams v. Howerton*, 673 F. 2d 1036 (9th Cir. 1982).

121. A. Lynn Bolles, "Goin' Abroad: Working-Class Jamaican Women and Migration," 75–76, in Dolores M. Mortimer and Roy S. Bryce-Laporte, eds., *Female Immigrants to the United States: Caribbean, Latin American, and African Experiences* (Washington, D.C.: Research Institute on Immigration and Ethnic Studies, 1981), 56–84.

122. Grace Poore, "Three Movements in A-Minor," *Trikone Magazine* (1997), 11. Poore also lists the strategies that she developed for safely participating in queer communities, despite her immigrant status: "if I couldn't sign petitions, I distributed them; if I couldn't attend meetings, I organized them; if I couldn't do civil disobedience, I wrote." But within a queer politics that stresses visibility and outness, without recognizing the dangers that outness presents to immigrants, people like Poore are often seen as traitors, rather than as effective strategists who have devised ways to participate in communities despite the constraints imposed by their immigrant status. At the same time, queers in immigrant communities remain vulnerable to accusations that they are harming the community or have been "corrupted" by U.S. cultural influences. These charges, although homophobic (though not necessarily "more" homophobic than the mainstream), also reflect a response to the racism, colonialism, and class exploitation under which many immigrant communities labor. As a result, lesbian and gay immigrants are placed in complex, contradictory positions and tend to be excluded from most support structures. Mark Chiang valuably suggests that the narrative of homosexuality as an effect of "Western" corruption "has less to do with the homophobia or traditionalism of ethnic communities than with discourses of nationalism and their particular mechanisms for defining and enforcing normative definitions of community and identity. . . . Although homosexuality in [dominant] American culture is primarily perceived as a form of deviance from prescribed *gender* identities—connoting a threat that arises from within national borders—Wat and Shah suggest that for Asian communities in both Asia and the United States, the phantasmic danger that homosexuality poses to national/ ethnic identity may supersede other axes of alterity. The figure of the homosexual becomes a sign for the Western domination that enters from without and disrupts the communities' ability to reproduce the structures of social relations. The homophobia that lesbians and gays of color face in their ethnic communities finds its corollary in the racism that they confront in gay communities that are primarily white." See Mark Chiang, "Coming Out into The Global System," in David Eng and Alice Hom, eds., *Q&A: Queer in Asian America* (Philadelphia: Temple University Press, 1998), 378.

123. Michael Ratner, "How We Closed the Guantanamo HIV Camp: The Intersections of Politics and Litigation," *Harvard Human Rights Journal* 11 (spring 1998), 195.

124. Similar debacles were avoided through the cynical expedient of implementing a policy of forcibly repatriating all Haitians who were intercepted at sea, without trying to determine whether any had valid claims for asylum.

125. This argument conveniently overlooks how undocumented immigrants are often actively recruited by U.S. employers and ignores research that describes the economic and social contributions of the undocumented, such as that by Fix and Passel. See Michael Fix and Jeffrey Passel, *Immigration and Immigrants: Setting the Record Straight* (Washington, D.C.: Urban Institute, 1994).

126. Dorothy Roberts, "Who May Give Birth to Citizens? Reproduction, Eugenics, and Immigration," in Juan Perea, ed., *Immigrants Out!* (New York: New York University Press, 1997), 207.

127. Roberts, "Who May Give Birth," 210.

128. They resulted not only in changes to immigration law but also in the passage of official English legislation; repeal of affirmative action programs; efforts to end bilingual education; attacks on ethnic studies programs; and strategies to undermine unions.

129. D'Emilio and Freedman, *Intimate Matters,* 145. Murray, with Hernstein, publicized these concerns through publication of *The Bell Curve,* a supposedly scientific inquiry into alleged racial and economical differentials in IQ, which became a *New York Times* best-seller.

130. Roberts, "Who May Give Birth," 214.

131. In February 2001, Rep. Jerold Nadler (D-NY) introduced the Permanent Partner Immigration Act (HR 690), which would amend the Immigration and Nationality Act to include recognition of same-sex couples. It seems unlikely that the bill will make it out of committee hearings.

132. In the aftermath of September 11, 2001, most public and political expressions of grief strongly relied on images of heterosexual families (generally white, citizen, and not particularly poor) as the primary victims of the attacks and the instruments through which a response should be organized and legitimized. As David Eng writes, "the narrative of white heteronormativity leaves no public space, no public speech, for those liminal groups—lesbians and gays and undocumented migrant workers, for example—who perished in the tragedies, but whose degraded social status, hard to affirm in life, became impossible to acknowledge in death" (David Eng, "The Value of Silence," *CLAGS News* 11, no. 3 [fall 2001]: 9). Moreover, representations of the threat of terrorism assumed markedly sexualized forms. As Jasbir Puar describes, "posters that appeared in midtown Manhattan only days after the attack show a turbaned caricature of bin Laden being anally penetrated by the Empire State building. The legend beneath reads, 'The Empire Strikes Back,' or 'So you like skyscrapers, huh, bitch?' . . . American retaliation promises to turn bin Laden into a fag" (Jasbir

Puar, "Towelheads, Diapers, and Faggots: Reviving the Turban," in *CLAGS News* 11, no. 3: 6). Americans who wore turbans and/or were perceived as being of Arab descent became subjected to forms of violence, including murder, in which heteropatriarchy, racism, and imperialism were complexly imbricated. Moreover, Andrea Smith has observed, the discourses and institutionalization of a homeland security apparatus after September 11 presumed that danger is "out there" and safety is "at home"—obscuring the ways that sexualized, racialized, gendered, and economic forms of violence, in which the U.S. state is complicit, are lived in homes, workplaces, and public spaces in the United States and at the border (Andrea Smith, presentation at the conference "On the Line: Gender, Sexuality, and Human Rights in the Américas," at the University of California, Santa Cruz, 9 March 2002). Sylvanna Falcón observes that the events of September 11 have resulted in funding cuts to nonprofit organizations, including those critical of U.S. policies and practices regarding sexuality, race, gender, and economics (presentation at "On the Line: Gender, Sexuality and Human Rights in the Américas"). Finally, as many have noted, the bombing of Afghanistan was legitimated in part through claims that the United States was "liberating" Afghani women. While Taliban oppression seems indisputable, the United States' self-presentation as "liberator" cynically deploys heteronormative gender and sexual discourses and practices that disavow its own eminent investment in militarized, violent heteropatriarchy.

2. A Blueprint for Exclusion

1. U.S. Immigration and Naturalization Service, *Statistical Yearbook of the Immigration and Naturalization Service, 1991*, A1-2.

2. Three of the five provisions of the Page Law dealt with prostitution. E. P. Hutchinson summarizes, "The first section made it a duty of consular officials at any port from which subjects of China, Japan, or other Oriental nations were to depart for the United States to determine whether such travel was 'free and voluntary,' and to ascertain whether any such travelers were under contract or agreement to serve for 'lewd and immoral purposes' in the United States, and in the latter case, to refuse to grant the required permit for travel. The third section of the act forbade the importation of women for prostitution, outlawed all contracts and agreements for such importation, and made illegal importation a felony subject to imprisonment of up to five years and a fine of up to $5,000. The fifth section included 'women imported for the purposes of prostitution' as one of the excluded classes." See E. P. Hutchinson, *Legislative History*, 419–20. About the provisions for convicts and contract laborers, see Salyer, *Laws Harsh as Tigers*, 260 n. 76, and Peffer, *If They Don't Bring Their Women Here*, 8.

3. As chapter 1 shows, laws subsequently mandated the exclusion of prosti-

tutes of every nationality, "immoral" women, single women who "arrived in a state of pregnancy," lesbians and gay men, polygamists, and other people considered undesirable as immigrants on sexual grounds.

4. John D'Emilio and Estelle Freedman, *Intimate Matters,* xvii.

5. Judy Yung, *Unbound Feet: A Social History of Chinese Women in San Francisco* (Berkeley: University of California Press, 1995), 18.

6. Yung, *Unbound Feet,* 21–22. Sucheng Chan sums up the experiences of Chinese immigrants by saying that their lives were shaped by prejudice, economic discrimination, political disenfranchisement, immigration exclusion, physical violence, and social segregation. See Chan, *Asian Americans: An Interpretive History* (Boston: Twayne Publishers, 1991), 45.

7. Benson Tong, *Unsubmissive Women: Chinese Prostitutes in Nineteenth-Century San Francisco* (Norman: University of Oklahoma Press, 1994), 4–5. Similarly, Judy Yung writes: "The scarcity of women in the American West, the suspension of social and moral restraints, and the easy access to wealth during the early years of the gold rush attracted women from different parts of the world. The first prostitutes to arrive were women from Mexico, Peru, and Chile; these were followed by women from France and other European countries, as well as women from American cities such as New York and New Orleans" (*Unbound Feet,* 26).

8. Yung, *Unbound Feet,* 31. Sucheng Chan corroborates this analysis, writing that "during the gold rush and for several decades thereafter, prostitutes of many nationalities lived and worked in San Francisco. Municipal authorities tried sporadically to suppress prostitution and they singled out Chinese women for special attention from the beginning" ("The Exclusion of Chinese Women," 97). See also Tomás Almaguer, *Racial Fault Lines* (Berkeley: University of California Press, 1994), 177–78.

9. Benson Tong notes that the city of San Francisco passed another antiprostitution ordinance in 1869, this time directing that the doors of brothels should be kept shut (presumably so that passers-by could not see what was going on inside, and perhaps to also prevent women from advertising).

10. Jacqueline Barker Barnhardt, *The Fair but Frail: Prostitution in San Francisco 1849–1900* (Reno: University of Nevada Press, 1980), 49.

11. Quoted in Sucheng Chan, "Exclusion and Chinese Women," 103.

12. George Peffer, *If They Don't Bring Their Women Here,* 33.

13. *Chinese Immigration; Its Social, Moral and Political Effects,* Report to the California State Senate of its Special Committee on Chinese Immigration (Sacramento: State Printing Office, 1878), 272.

14. *Report of the Joint Special Commission to Investigate Chinese Immigration,* Rpt. 689, 44th Cong., 2d Sess., Senate (Washington, D.C.: USGPO, 1877), 19. (Hereafter *Report.*)

15. *Report*, 19.

16. *Report*, 1097.

17. *Report*, 14.

18. *Report*, 143.

19. *Report*, 143.

20. *Report*, 652.

21. Stuart Creighton Miller, *The Unwelcome Immigrant: The American Image of the Chinese* (Berkeley: University of California Press, 1966), 112.

22. Audrey Smedley, *Race in North America* (Boulder: Westview Press, 1993), 269.

23. Quoted in Miller, *The Unwelcome Immigrant*, 154.

24. De Gobineau was one of the preeminent scientific racists of the nineteenth century.

25. *The Moral and Intellectual Diversity of the Races*, from the French by Count A. De Gobineau, with an analytic introduction and copious historical notes by H. Hotz (Philadelphia: J.B. Lippincott and Co., 1865), 385, 386, 287. My emphasis.

26. Chandra Talpade Mohanty, "Under Western Eyes: Feminist Scholarship and Colonial Discourses" in Chandra Talpade Mohanty, Ann Russo, and Lourdes Torres, eds., *Third World Women and the Politics of Feminism* (Bloomington: Indiana University Press, 1991), 51–80.

27. Miller, *The Unwelcome Immigrant*, 166.

28. Ibid., 163.

29. Quoted in Siobhan Somerville, "Scientific Racism and the Emergence of the Homosexual Body," in *Journal of the History of Sexuality* 5, no. 2 (1994), 246.

30. Eleanor Miller, Kim Romenesko, and Lisa Wondolkowski, "The United States," in *Prostitution: An International Handbook of Trends, Problems, and Policies*, ed. Nanette J. Davis (Westport, Conn.: Greenwood Press, 1993), 309.

31. Judith Walkowitz, *Prostitution and Victorian Society: Women, Class, and the State* (Cambridge: Cambridge University Press, 1980).

32. Gayle S. Rubin, "Thinking Sex: Notes for a Radical Theory of the Politics of Sexuality," in *The Lesbian and Gay Studies Reader*, ed. Henry Abelove, Michele Aina Barale, and David M. Halperin (New York: Routledge, 1993), 17–18.

33. Deborah Rhode, *Justice and Gender: Sex Discrimination and the Law* (Cambridge: Harvard University Press, 1989), 261.

34. Gail Hershatter, *Dangerous Pleasures: Prostitution and Modernity in Twentieth-Century Shanghai* (Berkeley: University of California Press, 1997), 5. Kamala Kempadoo affirms that "we view prostitution not as an identity . . . but as an income-generating activity or form of labor for women and men. . . . Sex work . . . is not always a steady activity but may occur simultaneously with other

income-generating work such as domestic service, informal commercial trading, market vending, shoeshining, or office work. Sex work can also be quite short lived or part of an annual cycle of work." Kamala Kempadoo, "Introduction: Globalizing Sex Workers Rights," in Kempadoo and Jo Doezema, eds., *Global Sex Workers* (New York: Routledge, 1998), 3. On migrant sex workers, see the section "Migrations and Tourism" in *Global Sex Workers*. See also the section "Migration and Prostitution" in Gail Pheterson, ed., *A Vindication of the Rights of Whores* (Seattle: The Seal Press, 1989). See also Than Dam Troung, *Sex, Money, and Morality: The Political Economy of Prostitution and Tourism in South East Asia* (London: Zed Books, 1990).

35. According to Priscilla Alexander, tiers in the sex industry include street-walking, massage parlors, bar and café prostitution, brothels, and "call girl" or escort services. Priscilla Alexander, "Prostitution: A Difficult Issue For Feminists," in Frederique Delacoste and Priscilla Alexander, eds., *Sex Work: Writings By Women in the Sex Industry* (Pittsburgh, Pa.: Cleis Press, 1987), 189–90. These tiers may have been modified since Alexander described them, with new tiers emerging.

36. Hershatter, *Dangerous Pleasures*, 4.

37. Ruth Rosen, *The Lost Sisterhood: Prostitution in America, 1900–1918* (Baltimore: The Johns Hopkins University Press, 1982), xiii.

38. Alternatively, poor families might put their daughters up for adoption rather than sell them. Adoption took two forms: as a future daughter-in-law, which was considered a betrothal, or as a real daughter, in which case the girl became part of the family. See Sue Gronewold, *Beautiful Merchandise: Prostitution in China 1860–1936* (New York: Haworth Press, 1982), 39.

39. See Peffer, *If They Don't Bring Their Women Here*, 71.

40. For more information on the sex/gender system in nineteenth-century China, see Gronewold, *Beautiful Merchandise*; Kay Ann Johnson, *Women, the Family, and Peasant Revolution in China* (Chicago: University of Chicago Press, 1983); Olga Lang, *Chinese Family and Society* (New Haven: Yale University Press, 1946); Rubie S. Watson and Patricia Buckley Ebrey, eds., *Marriage and Inequality in Chinese Society* (Berkeley: University of California Press, 1991). On marriage resistance among women in Guangdong, which was the home of most early Chinese immigrants to California, see Janice Stockard, *Daughters of the Canton Delta* (Stanford: Stanford University Press, 1989). According to Gronewold (and contrary to dominant U.S. ideologies of the time), "the rite of marriage was almost universally regarded as a sad occasion" for Chinese women (p. 41).

41. Gail Hershatter puts the point more forcefully, arguing that both prostitution and marriage have to be situated on a shared continuum of claims to women's sexual services. See Gail Hershatter, "Prostitution and the Market in

Women in Early 20th Century Shanghai," in Watson and Ebrey, eds., *Marriage and Inequality in Chinese Society*, 258. Hershatter's essay examines "similarities between marriage and prostitution in Shanghai, as well as the movement of individuals from one to the other" (259).

42. Sanger characterizes the existence of these 71 as "an announcement so disgraceful to humanity that . . . it would scarcely be credited." He also offers an analysis of why, in his view, married women might work as prostitutes: "Sufficient [sic] has been proved to show that in many cases, prostitution among married women is the result of circumstances which must have exercised a very powerful influence over them. The refusal of a husband to support his wife, his desertion of her, or an act of adultry with another woman, are each occurrences which must operate injuriously upon the mind of any female, and, by the keen torture that such outrages inflict on the sensitiveness of her nature, must drive her into a course of dissipation. Many women thus circumstanced have actually confessed that they made the first false step while smarting from injuries inflicted by their natural protectors, with the idea of being revenged upon their brutal or faithless companions for their unkindness. Morality will argue, and very truly, that this is no excuse for crime; but much allowance must be made for the extreme nature of the provocation, and the fact that most of these women are uneducated, and have not sufficient mental or moral illumination to reason correctly upon the nature and consequences of their voluntary debauchery, or even to curb the violence of their passions." See William W. Sanger, *The History of Prostitution: Its Extent, Causes, and Effects Throughout the World* (New York: Eugenics Publishing Company Edition, 1937), 475–76.

43. Tong, *Unsubmissive Women*, 159.

44. Peggy Pascoe, *Relations of Rescue* (New York: Oxford University Press, 1990), 95.

45. Pascoe, *Relations of Rescue*, 96. Pascoe adds, "their employment as sexual 'slaves'—the fact that so troubled mission women—did not in itself lead them to request help; for the most part, they contacted missionaries only when they felt that their owners had treated them particularly badly."

46. Sucheng Chan, *This Bittersweet Soil: The Chinese in California Agriculture, 1860–1910* (Berkeley: University of California Press, 1986), 390. Chan also includes statistics on the small numbers of married Chinese women who worked as prostitutes, according to census data for the Sacramento Delta in 1880 and 1900. See 392–93.

47. Note that my argument about prostitutes as a category is similar to Foucault's about the emergence of the category "homosexual."

48. George Peffer, "Forbidden Families: Emigration Experiences of Chinese

Women under the Page Law, 1875–1882," *Journal of American Ethnic History* 6, no. 1 (fall 1986), 33.

49. Peffer, "Forbidden Families," 32. David Bailey, the American consul in Hong Kong between 1875 and 1877, asked these questions of women applicants who appeared at the consulate on the day that he got word of the Page Law's passage. Over time, he likely altered the questions somewhat, but this is one sample of what the questions covered.

50. Peffer, "Forbidden Families," 31–35; Tong, *Unsubmissive Women*, 34–77. According to Peffer, these procedures were developed by David Bailey. Peffer relates that Bailey's successor, Sheldon Loring, who served until 1879, was also reasonably diligent in following these procedures, as was his successor, John Mosby, until 1881. After 1881 Mosby decided that he would no longer examine Chinese women departing on non-U.S. vessels, even if they were bound for the United States, and in June 1882 he declared that he had abolished the entire procedure established by his predecessors. However, Mosby's abolition of procedure "occurred too near the implementation of the [1882 Chinese] Exclusion Act to exert an impact on Chinese female immigration" (54). See Peffer, *If They Don't Bring Their Women Here*, 43–56.

51. Testimony of Col. F. A. Bee, in U.S. District Court, Northern California District, *In The Matter of Wah Ah Chin and Others for Their Discharge on Writ of Habeas Corpus*, No. 2495, March 1882, 19.

52. According to the ship's captain, Colonel Bee also had duplicates of the women's paperwork and photographs in his possession when he boarded the ship, which had presumably been sent to him from Hong Kong.

53. Testimony of Col. F. A. Bee, *In The Matter of Wah Ah Chin and Others*, 19–20.

54. Ibid., 20.

55. Foucault, *Discipline and Punish*, 191.

56. Ibid., 172.

57. Tong suggests that most of the women "belonged to a different cultural and legal environment and had been brought up to believe that all 'foreign devils' were 'barbarians'—a belief reinforced by their agents during the voyage to America." This would have discouraged many of them from seeking assistance from U.S. officials. (*Unsubmissive Women*, 64.)

58. *Report*, 987.

59. Miller, *The Unwelcome Immigrant*, 14. Miller writes that "the allegedly universal dishonesty in China [was] mentioned by 37 [of 50] of the sample" of traders' accounts and echoed in books published by diplomats. See *The Unwelcome Immigrant*, 29–30.

60. Yung, *Unbound Feet*, 66.

61. In the years following the Page Law, control of space and detailed questioning were combined in acute forms to try to produce the "truth" of all Chinese immigrants' testimonies. For instance, "during his term as collector [of the port of San Francisco] between 1889 and 1893, Timothy Phelps devised a system of investigation which attempted to expose fraudulent testimony. The inspectors questioned the applicant and his [or her] witness separately and in great detail about their family and village in China. Inspectors would ask questions such as, How many steps were there out of the family's back door? How many houses were there in the village? Did the mother have bound feet? If discrepancies existed in the testimony, the inspectors assumed that the parties did not know each other and that the applicant's claim was false. Chinese immigrants dreaded the inspector's investigations. Over the years, the inspector's drilling became longer and more refined" (Salyer, *Laws Harsh as Tigers,* 59). These interrogations easily lasted weeks and even months, and while they were going on, immigrants were kept carefully separated from family and friends. They were detained either in the Pacific Mail steamship shed, or, after 1910, on Angel Island. In these locations, their movements were carefully circumscribed. For instance, exercise was barely permitted and sharply supervised so that immigrants could not talk to anyone else. Parcels and visitors were denied. Even food parcels were denied, because officials feared that information that coached immigrants in what to say to officials might be included in the food. Stories of ingenious Chinese methods for smuggling coaching information are legion; one story, related in an immigration report, sheds light on the reasons for the restrictions against outside food. According to the report, "the device adopted to deliver the coaching letter was this: the letter was written in small characters on a slip of tissue paper, which was rolled tightly and placed inside of a large peanut shell, the two halves of which were carefully glued together, and then placed in a bag and sent to the Chinaman." (See *Facts Concerning the Enforcement of Chinese Exclusion Laws,* House Document 847, U.S. House of Representatives, 59th Congress, 1st Sess., 25 May 1906 [Washington, D.C.: U.S. Government Printing Office], 10.) Contact with Chinese staff was also restricted to the greatest degree possible, for fear that staff had been paid to pass on coaching information. The authors of *Island* also relate that "a different interpreter was used for each session" of a case, to forestall collusion. See Him Mark Lai, Genny Lim, and Judy Yung, *Island: Poetry and History of Chinese Immigrants on Angel Island, 1910–1940* (San Francisco: HOCDOI, 1982), 22.

62. Under the Chinese Exclusion Act of 1882, this class bias would be extended to men.

63. Foucault explains, "it is not simply in terms of a continual extension that

we must speak of this discursive growth; it should be seen rather as a dispersion of centers from which discourses [on sexuality] emanated, a diversification of their forms, and the complex deployment of a network connecting them." See *The History of Sexuality* (Vol. 1), 34.

64. As John Torpey expressed it, the principle involved is that "the person's body is used *against* him or her." *The Invention of the Passport*, 17.

65. See *Report*, 392–93.

66. Testimony of Col. F. A. Bee, *In The Matter of Wah Ah Chin and Others*, 24.

67. Ibid. Bee further told the court that "I have never sent any males back. We have sent females" (24).

68. Torpey, *The Invention of the Passport*, 117–18.

69. On the use of Bertillionage in the United States, see Donald C. Dilworth, ed., *Identification Wanted: Development of the American Criminal Identification System, 1893–1943* (Gaithersburg, Md.: International Association of Chiefs of Police, 1977); Alan Sekula, "The Body and the Archive," in Richard Bolton, ed., *The Contest of Meaning: Critical Histories of Photography* (Cambridge: MIT Press, 1989), 343–89; Shawn Michelle Smith, *American Archives* (Princeton: Princeton University Press, 1999), 68–93. I have found little information about the use of Bertillionage as a technique for immigration control. The one reference I found concerned using Bertillionage to control Chinese immigrants' entry, specifically between 1903 and 1906. See *Facts Concerning the Enforcement of Chinese Exclusion Laws*, 31.

70. According to Paul Rabinow, "the first practical use of fingerprints took place in Bengal. As Major Ferris of the India Staff Corps put it, 'the uniformity in the colour of the hair, eyes, and complexion of the Indian races renders identification far from easy.' The proverbial 'prevalence of unveracity' of the Oriental races provided another motivation for these gentlemen to perfect a reliable identification system, one whose basis lay in a marker beyond or below the cunning will of the native or criminal." (See Paul Rabinow, "Galton's Regret," in Rabinow, *Essays on the Anthropology of Reason* [Princeton: Princeton University Press, 1996], 113.) Although fingerprints are a mark of the body that cannot be altered and result in precise identifications, Rabinow relates that Galton's regret was precisely that fingerprints could not reveal anything about the "race" or "inner character" of the person.

71. Daniel W. Sutherland, "The High-Tech ID Menace," *The American Spectator* 32, no. 2 (February 1999), 60. Teeth X rays have been recently used as a means to determine the age of people seeking asylum who claim to be minors but are suspected of lying. See Chris Hedges, "Crucial INS Gatekeeper: The Airport Dentist," *New York Times*, 22 July 2000, A1.

72. See Chris Hedges, "Crucial I.N.S. Gatekeeper: The Airport Dentist," *New York Times*, 22 July 2000, A1, A14.

73. Sekula, "The Body and the Archive," 348.

74. Chan, "The Exclusion of Chinese Women," 100, my emphasis.

75. Reports of the Immigration Commission, *Importation and Harboring of Women for Immoral Purposes* 61st Congress, 3d Sess., Senate Document 753 (Washington, D.C.: U.S. Government Printing Office, 1911), 71. My emphasis.

76. Robyn Wiegman refers to "the cultural training that quite literally teaches the eye not only how but what to see" (22), and she analyzes the role of visual regimes in "making race real" (21) in *American Anatomies: Theorizing Race and Gender* (Durham: Duke University Press, 1995). See especially "Economies of Visibility," 21–78.

77. Readers should keep in mind that beliefs that bodies can be divided unambiguously into male and female are culturally constructed, and, furthermore, there are differences between seeming to have a body that is culturally coded as male or female versus an individual's own bodily identifications.

78. Lucie Cheng Hirata, "Free, Indentured, Enslaved: Chinese Prostitutes in Nineteenth-Century America," in Lucie Cheng Hirata and Edna Bonacich, eds., *Labor Immigration under Capitalism: Asian Workers in the U.S. Before World War II* (Berkeley: University of California Press, 1984), 410.

79. Sander Gilman, *Difference and Pathology: Stereotypes of Sexuality, Race, and Madness* (Ithaca: Cornell University Press, 1985), 94.

80. Ibid., 95–96.

81. Gilman, *Difference and Pathology,* 98; Steven Jay Gould, *The Mismeasure of Man* (New York: Norton, 1981), 129.

82. According to Mark Haller, "The Massachusetts Commission for the Investigation of White Slave Traffic, in one of the most significant investigations of Vice, gave Binet tests to one hundred young prostitutes and two hundred experienced prostitutes. Not only did more than half test feebleminded, but the behavior of the prostitutes confirmed what the tests indicated: 'The general lack of moral insensibility, the boldness, egotism, and vanity, the love of notoriety, the lack of shame or remorse, the absence of even a pretense of affection for their own children or their parents, the desire for immediate pleasure without regard for consequences, the lack of forethought or anxiety about the future—all cardinal symptoms of feeblemindedness—were strikingly evident in every one of the 154 women.'" (See Mark H. Haller, *Eugenics: Hereditarian Attitudes in American Thought,* 103.) Eugenicists became directly involved in immigration administration. For instance, in 1912 Henry Goddard, a leading eugenicist, was invited to assist at Ellis Island in selecting immigrants who might be feeble-

minded or mentally deficient and should be denied entry. See Alan M. Kraut, *Silent Travelers*, 74.

83. Yung, *Unbound Feet*, 24.

84. Gail Hershatter, for instance, has documented that courtesans in Shanghai sometimes had bound feet. See *Dangerous Pleasures*, 84. See also Wang Ping, *Aching for Beauty: Footbinding in China* (Minneapolis: University of Minnesota Press, 2000).

85. Yung, *Unbound Feet*, 24.

86. See Fernando Henriques, *Prostitution and Society*, 3 vols. (London: McGibbon and Kee, 1962, 1963, 1968), for a history of how prostitutes have used (or been required by authorities to use) clothing and other visual signs as a means to differentiate themselves.

87. See Walkowitz, *Prostitution and Victorian Society*, 26. See also Christine Stansell, *City of Women: Sex and Class in New York, 1789–1860* (New York: Knopf, 1986), 187, where she writes, "fancy dress signified a rejection of proper feminine behaviors and duties. For [working class] girls who donned fine clothes, dress was en emblem of an estimable erotic maturity, a way to carry about the full identity of an adult, and a sign of admission into heterosexual courting."

88. *Report*, 1146.

89. For Foucault, the "individual" is not understood in a humanist sense, but as a position that is produced through subjectification that constitutes one as an individual in a specific way, and that links one into wider relations of power. See *Discipline and Punish*, 190.

90. This process was not implemented immediately after the Page Law but developed later in the nineteenth century.

91. Lai et al., *Island*, 110.

92. Salyer notes, "The longer the exclusion laws were in existence, the longer the 'paper trail' that was completed.... Eventually, administrators created a system for cross-referencing files making it possible to compare, for example, the testimony of a man, his brothers and sons to see if there were any material discrepancies to suggest fraudulent relationships. Ironically, the documents created by officials to curb the possibility of fraud became valuable commodities and, in some ways, expanded the opportunities for those who wished to enter the United States illegally. 'Paper' [i.e. fraud] sons and daughters entered successfully because the immigration authorities had in their files documents in which fathers had earlier attested to their children's birth in China. Illegal immigrants could purchase doctored birth certificates with their own photographs substituted [or, if there had not really been a birth at all, they purchased the slot of a child who had been fictitiously registered]." See Salyer, *Laws Harsh as Tigers*, 150.

The ironies were also noted by an inspector, who related, "What happened in many cases where they were not real sons but paper [i.e. fraud] sons, they were so well coached [i.e. taught how to respond to the inspector's questions] that their testimonies jibed. Whereas in legitimate cases, they hadn't gone to the trouble of making up coaching books and preparing for it. They were the ones who got the wrong answers because they thought it was going to be cut and dry." When genuine claimants offered "wrong" answers, they were not usually allowed to land. See Lai et al., *Island*, 114.

93. Foucault, *Discipline and Punish*, 190.

94. Ibid., 149.

95. Silvia Pedraza, "Origins and Destinies: Immigration, Race, and Ethnicity in American History," in Pedraza and Rubén G. Rumbaut, eds., *Origins and Destinies: Immigration, Race, and Ethnicity in America* (Belmont, Calif.: Wadsworth Publishing, 1996), 10.

96. The most massive governmental writing about immigrants is perhaps the forty-volume Dillingham Commission Report, produced in 1911.

97. Sekula, "The Body and the Archive," 348.

98. Sekula, "The Body and the Archive," 351. On nineteenth-century visual images of the Chinese in U.S. print media, see Phillip L. Choy, Lorraine Dong, and Marlon K. Hom, eds., *Coming Man: Nineteenth-Century American Perceptions of the Chinese* (Seattle: University of Washington Press, 1995).

99. Smith, *American Archives*, 7.

100. Ibid., 5.

101. Ibid., 7, 5.

102. Therefore Torpey rightly critiques immigration scholars who take state structures for granted rather than understanding how state control over movement has helped to constitute and maintain the state *as* a state in an ongoing way. See Torpey, *The Invention of the Passport*, 3, 6.

103. Ibid., 17.

104. Foucault, *Discipline and Punish*, 191.

105. Furthermore, immigration scholarship based on case files (and government documents in general) must also question the extent to which reliance on these documents generates narratives that exclude the perspectives of those who are rendered "unrepresentable" by and within the state. See my essay "The 1965 Immigration and Nationality Act: An 'End' to Exclusion?" in *positions: east asia cultures critique* 5, no. 2 (fall 1997), 501–22, for discussion of this point.

106. Today, women continue coming to the United States, under conditions ranging from consent to severe coercion, to engage in sex work. In seeming acknowledgment of the extreme difficulties that face victims of coercion, President Clinton signed the Trafficking Victims Protection Act (TVPA) on 28 October

2000. The Act does not clearly define trafficking but nonetheless, makes available up to 5,000 newly created T visas per year for people who can show that (1) they are victims of "severe trafficking"; (2) they are in the United States on account of such trafficking; (3) they have assisted in the investigation and prosecution of traffickers or are less than fifteen years old; and (4) they would suffer "extreme hardship involving unusual and severe harm" if removed from the United States (*Refugee Reports* 21, no. 10, October 2000, 4).

Additionally, the expanded Violence Against Women Act (VAWA) of 2000 created a new U visa, available to "immigrants who are either victims of, or possess information concerning, a wide range of criminal activities including: rape; torture; trafficking; incest; domestic violence; sexual assault; abusive sexual contact; prostitution; sexual exploitation; female genital mutilation; hostage holding; peonage; involuntary servitude; slave trade; kidnapping; abduction; unlawful criminal restraint; false imprisonment; blackmail; extortion; manslaughter; murder; felonious assault; witness tampering; obstruction of justice; perjury; or attempt, conspiracy, or solicitation to commit one of these offenses" (*Refugee Reports,* October 2000, 5). Furthermore, "a federal, state or local official must certify that an investigation or prosecution would be harmed without the assistance of the immigrant or, in the case of a child, the immigrant's parent. No more than 10,000 U visas may be issued each year" (4). See *Entry Denied*'s appendix for further discussion.

3. Birthing a Nation

1. Ichioka relates, "In Japan, marriage was never an individual matter, but always a family affair. Heads of household selected marriage partners of family members through intermediaries or go-betweens. An exchange of photographs sometimes occurred in the screening process, with family genealogy, wealth, education, and health figuring heavily in the selection criteria. . . . If families mutually consented, engagement and marriage ensued." See Yuji Ichioka, *The Issei* (New York: The Free Press, 1988), 164.

2. Ibid.

3. A majority of Japanese immigrants to the continental United States settled in California, which is why I focus on that area.

4. Gayle Rubin, "Thinking Sex: Notes for a Radical Theory of the Politics of Sexuality," in Abelove, Barale, and Halperin, eds., *The Lesbian and Gay Studies Reader,* 13.

5. Lauren Berlant has analyzed how "the generational form of the family has provided the model for the national future" (Berlant, *The Queen of America Goes to Washington City* [Durham: Duke University Press, 1997], 18). This model helps to explain, on one hand, the state's promotion of heteropatriarchal marriage,

and on the other, the state's fear of childbearing by racialized minorities and the poor, and its excoriation of sexualities that are deemed threatening to hetero-patriarchy. For further discussion, see Lee Edelman, "The Future Is Kid Stuff: Queer Theory, Disidentification, and the Death Drive," *Narrative* 6, no. 1 (January 1998): 18–30.

6. Ronald Takaki, *Strangers from a Different Shore,* (New York: Penguin, 1989), 48.

7. Ibid., 47–48.

8. See Sucheng Chan, *Asian Americans,* 9–11; Takaki, *Strangers from a Different Shore,* 42–53.

9. Evelyn Nakano Glenn, *Issei, Nisei, Warbride,* 30.

10. Yuji Ichioka, "Ameyuki-san: Japanese Prostitutes in Nineteenth-Century America," *Amerasia* 4, no. 1 (1977), 2.

11. Ichioka, "Ameyuki-San," 1; Elaine H. Kim, *With Silk Wings: Asian American Women at Work* (San Francisco: Asian Women United of California, 1983), 122.

12. Arnold Shankman has traced images of Japanese immigrants in the African American press from 1867 to 1933. His work makes it clear that exclusionist rhetoric was racially differentiated. African Americans, like their white counterparts, favored immigration restriction (because of economic competition); unlike whites, however, they were utterly opposed to restriction "that would prevent the black and yellow people from Asia and Africa from entering the country solely because their skins were not white" (451). And although 1905 signaled the start of an unrelenting anti-Japanese restrictionist campaign within the mainstream, Shankman records that "the negative image of Japan and her people that appeared in the black press abruptly changed in 1905, when Russia lost the Russo-Japanese War. No longer were the Japanese described as improvident, ignorant, careless, or superstitious; instead they were seen as courageous people. . . . Blacks, who had often heard about the alleged inferiority of the darker races, exulted in the Japanese victory" (440). See Arnold Shankman, "'Asiatic Ogre' or 'Desirable Citizen'? The Image of Japanese Americans in the Afro-American Press, 1867–1933," in *Nativism, Discrimination, and Images of Immigrants,* vol. 15 of the American Immigration and Ethnicity series, ed. George Pozzetta (New York: Garland Publishing, 1991), 437–58. Little research has been done about how exclusionist ideologies were differentiated by race, gender, class, or ethnicity; more information about this would be an extremely valuable corrective to the current tendency to explore exclusion primarily from the perspective of white males. On African American views of the Japanese generally, see Reginald Kearney, *African American Views of the Japanese: Solidarity or Sedition?* (Albany: State University of New York Press, 1998).

13. Roger Daniels, *The Politics of Prejudice: The Anti-Japanese Movement in California and the Struggle for Exclusion* (New York: Atheneum, 1972), 20–45.

14. Glenn writes, "Gulick's data show that 45,706 females were admitted to the continental United States between 1909 and 1924, of whom 33, 628 were listed as wives. . . . by 1920, there was one female for every two males." See *Issei, Nisei, Warbride*, 31. According to Takaki, 66,926 Japanese women entered Hawaii and the mainland combined between 1908 and 1924. See *Strangers from a Different Shore*, 47.

15. Dorinne Kondo, *Crafting Selves* (Chicago: University of Chicago Press, 1990), 268.

16. Sharon Sievers, *Flowers in Salt* (Stanford: Stanford University Press, 1983), 111.

17. As Kondo summarizes, "women, in fulfilling their appropriate gender roles, placed themselves in loyal service to the state." *Crafting Selves*, 267.

18. Kondo, *Crafting Selves*, 268–69. Also ironic was that the Code's norms of female domesticity and subordination drew from Western models, in an effort to show that Japan was equal to the West. The ways that the Code linked gender, family, and state control were also inspired by Western examples. See Sievers, *Flowers in Salt*, 105–07. Sievers also makes clear that "through the language of the decade seemed more traditional, often Confucian, the institutions that permitted increasing control over the population were borrowed from authoritarian models in the West." (88) Thus, Japanese state patriarchy did not involve "timeless tradition," but an active reworking by the state of gender norms, to some degree in light of Western standards and the demands of "modernization."

19. Kondo, *Crafting Selves*, 170.

20. Kyoko Yoshizumi, "Marriage and Family: Past and Present," in Kumiko Fujimura-Fanselow and Atsuko Kameda, eds., *Japanese Women: New Feminist Perspectives on the Past, Present, and Future* (New York: Feminist Press, 1995), 187. According to Yoshizumi, registration became universally required under the Meiji government for two reasons: to eliminate tax evasion and avoidance of military service (187). This process parallels the processes for registering and inscribing all individuals that was discussed in the previous chapter as integral to the development of the modern state apparatus.

21. See Doris Weatherford, *Foreign and Female*, 176–79; Donna Gabaccia, chapter 3, *From the Other Side*.

22. Her file is to be found in Box 953, the National Archives, San Bruno, California.

23. Case # 14517/25-6, Box 953, National Archives, San Bruno, California.

24. Iseno's ability to read and write was also consonant with the fact that

Japanese immigrants at that time tended to be better educated and arrive with more money than their European counterparts.

25. This designation reflects an earlier moment in the official U.S. articulation of racial categories than the contemporary form "Asian" and predates the 1922 Supreme Court decision that the Japanese were neither Caucasian nor African American and therefore were ineligible for naturalization.

26. Their letterhead includes, "Object: evangelization of the Japanese on the Pacific Coast."

27. Ichioka, *The Issei*, 165.

28. Holding the woman until her husband called for her was in line with mainstream constructions of domesticity and paralleled what happened to European wives. For information about the processing of European wives during this time period, see the chapter "Here Comes The Bride" in Feri Felix Weiss's *The Sieve*. Weiss, an immigrant himself, also served as an immigration inspector. The practice of hiring immigrants to be inspectors reflects a very interesting calculation and economy of power. See also David M. Brownstone, Irene M. Franck, Douglass M. Brownstone, *Island of Hope, Island of Tears*. For an account of the very contrasting treatment received by Chinese wives, see Him Mark Lai, Genny Lim, and Judy Yung, *Island*, as well as Sucheng Chan, "The Exclusion of Chinese Women, 1875–1943," and chapter 2 of this book.

29. Kazu Ito, *Issei: A History of Japanese Immigrants in North America* (Seattle: Executive Committee for the Publication of Issei, 1973), 201.

30. Wives were also "advised to walk alongside their husbands, not behind them, so as to avoid the negative stereotype of Japanese women being enslaved by Japanese men." Ichioka, *The Issei*, 185.

31. Glenn, *Issei, Nisei, Warbride*, 47.

32. Although immigrants may have recrafted gender and sexual norms to some degree, this is not intended to suggest that U.S. dominant cultural norms were anything but patriarchal too.

33. V. S. McClatchy, "Japanese Immigration and Colonization: Brief Prepared for Consideration by the State Department," 1921. Included in V. S. McClatchy, ed., *Four Anti-Japanese Pamphlets* (New York: Arno Press, 1978), 65.

34. McPhelan served as mayor of San Francisco and as a United States senator; his anti-Asian activities "dated back to the 1880s" (Daniels, *The Politics of Prejudice*, 81).

35. Daniels, *The Politics of Prejudice*, 95–99.

36. McClatchy, "Japanese Immigration and Colonization," 20.

37. Ibid., 30.

38. Ibid., 2. McClatchy also writes, "Japanese colonization has commenced

in states other than California, and is certain to develop in time, throughout the Union, the dangers already present in California, and in Hawaii" (23).

39. See Elaine H. Kim and Eui-Young Yu, *East to America* (New York: New Press, 1996), 366.

40. Benjamin B. Ringer, *"We The People" and Others* (New York: Tavistock Publications, 1983), 780.

41. Ibid., 779–81.

42. The idea of immigration as a means to effect a biological change, conceived in racial terms, is explained in Lothrop Stoddard's popular book, *The Rising Tide of Color against White World Supremacy* (New York: Charles Scribner's Sons, 1920). According to Stoddard, immigration transformed the United States into a white settler society. As a result, countries like the United States "have become part of the white race heritage, which should be defended to the last extremity. . . . They are the true bulwarks of the race, the patrimony of future generations who have a right to demand of us that they shall be born white in a white man's land" (226). Here again we see in operation the metaphor of the nation's continuity secured by, for, and through children. The relationship between childbearing and whiteness is also quite plain.

43. Foucault, "On Governmentality," in *The Foucault Effect: Studies in Governmentality,* ed. Graham Burchell, Colin Gordon, and Peter Miller, 100. *The History of Sexuality* (Vol. 1) further elaborates that "the old power of death that symbolized sovereign power was now carefully supplanted by the administration of bodies and the calculated management of life" (139–40).

44. Foucault, *The History of Sexuality* (Vol. 1), 105.

45. McClatchy, "Japanese Immigration and Colonization," 34.

46. Ibid., 47.

47. Ibid., 49.

48. Stoddard, *The Rising Tide of Color,* 261.

49. Ibid., 262.

50. Ibid., 263.

51. Ibid., 268.

52. "If races are to conserve their best qualities, they can receive into their mate selection circles only races closely related, by blood, to themselves."*American History in Terms of Human Migration,* Extracts from Hearings before the Committee on Immigration and Naturalization, House of Representatives, 70th Cong., 2d Sess., 7 March 1928 (Washington, D.C.: U.S. Government Printing Office, 1928), 7.

53. McClatchy, "Japanese Immigration and Colonization," 42.

54. Ibid., 43.

55. Stoddard, *The Rising Tide of Color*, 256.

56. Nazli Kibria, "Migration and Vietnamese American Women: Remaking Ethnicity," in Maxine Baca Zinn and Bonnie Thornton Dill, eds., *Women of Color in U.S. Society* (Philadelphia: Temple University Press, 1994), 248. Of course, complete assimilation is never possible for people who are marked as "racial minorities" in white America.

57. Therefore, as Kibria explains, "[mothers] have been seen in two capacities. On one hand, immigrant [mothers], viewed as staunch supporters of immigrant traditions, have been viewed as barriers to assimilation. Alternatively, they have been seen as important intermediaries or vehicles of integration into dominant society." Kibria, "Migration and Vietnamese American Women," 248.

58. For example, interventions into Mexican mothers' dietary practices were believed to be necessary because "the typical noon lunch of the Mexican child, thought to consist of 'a folded tortilla with no filling,' became the first step in a life of crime. With 'no milk or fruit to whet the appetite,' the child would become lazy and subsequently 'take food from the lunch boxes of more fortunate children' in order to appease his/her hunger. 'Thus,' reformers alleged, 'the initial step in a life of thieving is taken.'" See George Sanchez, "Go After the Women: Americanization and the Mexican Immigrant Woman, 1915–1929," in Ellen DuBois and Vicki L. Ruiz, eds., *Unequal Sisters* (Routledge, 1990), 257.

59. The cooking of cabbage soup was determined to be the root cause of the dampness of Polish homes and the peeling of wallpaper, which could be corrected through a program that "carr[ied] the English language and American ways of caring for babies, ventilating the house, preparing American vegetables, instead of the inevitable cabbage, right into the new homes." See John McClymer, "Gender and 'The American Way of Life': Women in the Americanization Movement," *Journal of American Ethnic History* 10, no. 3 (spring 1991), 12.

60. Glenn, *Issei, Nisei, Warbride*, 199.

61. At that time, Southern and Eastern Europeans were popularly considered "lesser" versions of the "white race," and Mexicans were similarly viewed. Japanese, however, were seen as belonging to an entirely separate "race."

62. McClatchy, "Japanese Immigration and Colonization," 74.

63. There is an enormous literature on how schools replicate social inequalities. See, for example, the work of Paolo Freire, John Ogbu, bell hooks, Michelle Fine, Henry Giroux, and Stanley Aranowitz, to name just a few.

64. See Ichioka, "Nisei Education and Dual Nationality," in *The Issei*, 196–210; see also Takaki, *Strangers from a Different Shore*, 212–29.

65. An analysis of Japanese exclusion that pays attention to the very different gender interests entailed in labor struggles is long overdue. Daniels's book only

hints at the extent to which white labor interests were also male interests. White women clearly played an important role in exclusion, but the specific nature of their participation, and their reasons for desiring Japanese exclusion, have yet to be systematically analyzed. At minimum, attention to the differential position of white men, white women, African American men, and African American women in the labor market would help to illuminate the intersection of racial *and* gender dynamics that fueled exclusionist labor agitation.

66. Of course, analysis of the ways that family labor reinforced gender and generational inequities is also necessary.

67. McClatchy, "Japanese Immigration and Colonization," 53. McClatchy's argument seems to suggest that the Japanese were better workers and therefore deserved economic advancement rather than exclusion. But Stoddard explained why this was not the correct conclusion to draw: "The argument runs that, since the Oriental laborer is able to underbid the white laborer, the Oriental laborer is the fittest and should therefore be allowed to supplant the white man in the interests of human progress. This is of course merely clever use of the well known fallacy which confuses the terms 'fittest' and 'best.' The idea that, because a certain human type fits in certain ways with a particular environment (often an unhealthy, manmade social environment), it should be allowed to drive out another type endowed with much richer potentialities for the highest forms of human evolution, is a sophistry as absurd as it is dangerous." Citing Professor E. A. Ross, he further explains: "It is a case of a man fitted to get the most out of good conditions refusing to yield them to a weaker man able to withstand bad conditions." See Stoddard, *The Rising Tide of Color,* 273, 274.

68. McClatchy, "Japanese Immigration and Colonization," 63.

69. McClatchy, "Japanese Immigration and Colonization," 4. Later in the pamphlet, he claims they control "one eighth of all the State's irrigated acreage" (55).

70. The bearing of children within legitimate marriage is integrally connected to the transmission of property and identity. In the United States, where interracial and same-gender marriage has been forbidden by law, marriage as a conduit for transmission of property and identity has shored up what Foucault refers to as "the homeostasis of the social body" in regard to racial, gender, class, and sexual boundaries (*The History of Sexuality,* Vol.1, 107). African Americans have often been particularly dispossessed by this weave between race, sex, marriage, and transmission of property and identity. (See Abdul JanMohamed, "Sexuality on/of the Racial Border: Foucault, Wright, and the Articulation of 'Racialized Sexuality,'" in Domna Stanton, ed., *Discourses of Sexuality,* 94–116. See also Patricia J. Williams, "On Being the Object of Property," in *Alchemy of Race and Rights* (Cambridge: Harvard University Press, 1991), and Roberts,

Killing the Black Body. But, ironically, children born to Japanese immigrant couples in a society intent on maintaining homeostasis actually provided a means to temporarily challenge racist efforts to dispossess the Japanese of property.

71. McClatchy, "Japanese Immigration and Colonization," 57.

72. Ibid., 42.

73. Ibid., 74. After 1916 the Japanese government did stop conferring automatic Japanese citizenship on children of Japanese couples born in the United States—partly to appease restrictionists who questioned the political loyalty of these children. Ichioka relates that "the Japanese Diet amended the Japanese Nationality Act in 1916. The first amendment allowed the parents or guardians of Nisei who were 14 years old or younger to renounce their youngsters' Japanese citizenship on their behalf; it also allowed those Nisei who were 15 or 16 years old to renounce it for themselves. Male Nisei who were 17 years old or more, however, were subject to a precondition. They could forswear their Japanese citizenship only if they had fulfilled their Japanese military duties." A 1924 amendment to the Japanese Nationality Act allowed retroactive renunciation of Japanese citizenship without preconditions; it also abolished automatic Japanese citizenship based on paternal descent. See Ichioka, *The Issei*, 204, 206.

74. "There are in the continental United States today not less than 35,000 American born Japanese (Gulick); and in Hawaii not less than 60,000 (See Joseph Timmons, Exhibit XV). Under the Expatriation law of Japan, every one of these children, on whom is freely conferred the privileges of American citizenship, could have made application, through parents or guardians, at any time before reaching seventeen years of age, for permission to expatriate. According to an official statement from the Japanese government (Exhibit XXIII), exactly 73 have so applied and the government had granted the request in 64 cases. . . . These figures show that less than one in a thousand of our citizens of Japanese parentage are in a position where they can exercise their American citizenship rights for the benefit of this government and not for the benefit of a foreign power whose interests are quite different from ours and may be inimical" (77).

75. McClatchy, "Japanese Immigration and Colonization," 87. McClatchy also describes "the urge made upon them constantly by their newspapers and speakers—to maintain a high birthrate and to accumulate lands so they may 'permanently establish the Yamoto race in this country'" (46).

76. Ibid., 86.

77. Ibid., 34, 91.

78. Geraldine Heng and Janadas Devan, "State Fatherhood: The Politics of Nationalism, Sexuality, and Race in Singapore," in Andrew Parker et al., eds., *Nationalisms and Sexualities* (New York: Routledge, 1992), 349.

79. Perhaps reinforcing these fears was the fact that childbearing and mothering in the United States have also been linked to the national interest, as is evident from discourses dating back to the early national period. (See Linda Kerber, "The Republican Mother," in *Women of the Republic* [Chapel Hill: University of North Carolina, 1980], 269–88.) As Molly Ladd-Taylor explains, women's childbearing and mothering have always been central to the functioning of the U.S. political and economic system. Childbearing and mothering are connected to the development and expansion of public health, education, and welfare services. "Indeed, there was no purely 'private' experience of childrearing—both because mothers raised children to be citizens and workers for the nation, and because mothers' working conditions were determined as much by labor and farm policies affecting their family income as by legislation directly concerned with welfare and reproduction." See Molly Ladd-Taylor, *Mother-Work: Women, Child Welfare, and the State, 1890–1930* (Urbana: University of Illinois Press, 1994), 2. Japanese picture brides arrived at a time when U.S. women had organized around their roles as mothers in order to press for a wide range of public policy reforms. While they had some notable degree of success, the resulting programs also institutionalized racial, ethnic, and class differences between women and valorized white middle-class women's childbearing and motherhood in ways that did not extend to women of other groups. See Gwendolyn Mink, *The Wages of Motherhood. Inequality in the Welfare State, 1917–1942* (Ithaca: Cornell University Press, 1995); Evelyn Nakano Glenn, Grace Chang, and Linda Rennie Forcey, eds., *Mothering: Ideology, Experience, and Agency* (New York: Routledge, 1994); Eileen Boris, "The Power of Motherhood: Black and White Activist Women Redefine the 'Political,'" in Seth Koven and Sonya Michel, eds., *Mothers of a New World* (New York: Routledge, 1993); and Mimi Abramovitz, *Regulating the Lives of Women* (Boston: South End Press, 1988) for more information.

80. Glenn, *Issei, Nisei, Warbride*, 45. The term "Issei" refers to first generation immigrants.

81. Mei T. Nakano, *Japanese American Women: Three Generations, 1890–1990* (Berkeley: Mina Press Publishing, 1990), 26.

82. Peter S. Li, "Fictive Kinship, Conjugal Ties, and Kinship Chain among Chinese Immigrants in the United States," *Journal of Comparative Family Studies* 8, no. 1 (spring 1977).

83. Li's analysis also resonates with Teitelbaum's critique of how immigration preference categories are usually viewed and analyzed. Teitelbaum writes, "Many analyses of the effects of immigration policy alternatives implicitly portray them as regulatory and selective mechanisms operating upon exogenously determined demand for immigration slots. . . . Such a construct . . . is becoming less and less defensible . . . immigrant visas to Western high-income countries

clearly are scarce and valued goods. Any given visa allocation scheme, or any changes in such scheme, should be expected over time to evoke behavioral responses designed to improve access to the scarce good." See Michael Teitelbaum, "Skeptical Noises about the Immigration Multiplier," *International Migration Review* 23, no. 4 (winter 1989), 893. My notion of the compelled performance of family in terms that satisfy immigration officials builds from Judith Butler's notion of performance in *Bodies That Matter* (New York: Routledge, 1993).

84. Akemi Kikimura, *Through Harsh Winters: The Life of a Japanese Immigrant Woman* (Novato, Calif.: Chandler and Sharp Publishers, 1981), 25.

85. Barbara F. Kawakami, *Japanese Immigrant Clothing in Hawaii, 1885–1941* (Honolulu: University of Hawaii Press, 1993), 12.

86. For a thorough discussion of how Issei women exercised rich forms of agency within the structure of marriage and the options that legal divorce provided, see Laurie Mengel's excellent "Issei Women and Divorce in Hawai'i, 1885–1908," in *Social Process in Hawaii* 38 (1997): 16–39. My thanks to Laurie for bringing Kawakami's work to my attention.

87. Mirjana Morokvasic has described how the standard image of immigrant women is that they are passive and dependent followers of pioneering migrant men—despite evidence to the contrary. See Mirjana Morokvasic, "Women in Migration: Beyond the Reductionist Outlook," in Annie Phizacklea, ed., *One Way Ticket: Migration and Female Labour* (London: Routledge and Kegan Paul, 1983), 13–31.

88. The State Board of Control of California, in *California and the Oriental* (Sacramento: California State Printing Office, 1920), acknowledged that Japan terminated the migration of picture brides in 1920 but anticipated that they will "circumvent . . . the new restriction" (157). Of the picture brides, the report says, "That their daily occupation as farm laborers has not interfered with the natural increase of the Japanese population in the state is demonstrated by the high birthrate among the Japanese of California" (160). The Commissioner General of Immigration commented negatively on Japanese picture brides in the annual reports of 1912, 1913, 1914, and 1919.

89. The passage was a quotation from *California and the Oriental*, 192.

90. Jacqui Alexander proposes that "loyalty to the nation as citizen is perennially colonized within reproduction and heterosexuality" (64), and that "no nationalism could survive without heterosexuality" (83). See "Erotic Autonomy as a Politics of Decolonization," in M. Jacqui Alexander and Chandra Talpade Mohanty, eds., *Feminist Genealogies, Colonial Legacies, Democratic Futures.*

91. McClatchy, "Japanese Immigration and Colonization," 86.

92. Daniels, *The Politics of Prejudice*, 95. For more on the 1921 Immigration

Act, see John Higham, *Strangers in the Land*, 2d ed. (New Brunswick: Rutgers University Press, 1988).

93. Daniels, *The Politics of Prejudice*, 100–03. See also Ringer, *"We The People" and Others*, 787–837.

94. Candice Lewis Bredbenner, *A Nationality of Her Own: Women, Marriage, and the Law of Citizenship* (Berkeley: University of California Press, 1998), 130. Bredbenner, who focuses largely on binational marriages between white North Americans and the foreign-born, describes how "marrying an alien could be either an act of disloyalty or one of patriotism, depending on the sex and nationality of the actor" (105). While men's marriages to foreign women were valorized, women who married foreign men were stereotyped in an unflattering way. "This woman was a young heiress, and not only did her rich American parents have the bad taste to mimic the ostentatious and insipid lifestyle of Europe's nobility, but they crassly pursued foreign aristocrats for sons-in-law" (61). Furthermore, women who married foreign men faced loss of rights that North American men did not. The gender-disparate impact of marriage to a foreigner makes clear that "snubbing that national icon, the citizen [white] man, was a serious transgression" (74) for which women paid a price.

95. Note that migrants from the Western Hemisphere—who were exempted from most provisions of the 1924 Act—now predominated as *labor* migrants.

96. Beginning in the last decades of the nineteenth century, fears were widely expressed that native-born white middle-class Americans were facing (and committing) "race suicide" because of high birthrates by working-class, culturally different Southern and Eastern European immigrant women. See Linda Gordon, *Woman's Body, Woman's Right*, chapter 7, "Race Suicide"; Carole R. McCann, *Birth Control Politics in the United States, 1916–1945* (Ithaca: Cornell University Press, 1994), chapter 4, "Birth Control and Racial Betterment"; and Angela Y. Davis, *Women, Race and Class*, chapter 12, "Racism, Birth Control and Reproductive Rights."

97. Marion Houston, Roger G. Kramer, and Joan Mackin Barrett, "Female Predominance in Immigration to the United States Since 1930: A First Look," *International Migration Review* 18, no. 4 (1984): 952.

98. Here I have followed the argument that racialization proceeds in different ways for different groups. Thus, although I accept that Southern and Eastern Europeans were racialized, the manner of their racialization offered ways to become part of the majority. Asian immigrants, however, were racialized in a manner that foreclosed this possibility. These distinctions were further encoded in law, for although Southern and Eastern Europeans were racialized, they were not accorded a nonwhite status by law; Asians, however, were constituted as

both nonwhite and as ineligible for citizenship. Sucheng Chan expressed the significance of legal rulings about who belonged to which racial category, and the rights attached to each category, by stating that "what set Asian immigration apart was not the prejudice and violence they encountered but the discriminatory laws that aimed to deprive them of their means of livelihood, restrict their social mobility, and deny them political power." See "European and Asian Immigration into the United States in Comparative Perspective, 1820s to 1920s," in Virginia Yans-McLaughlin, ed., *Immigration Reconsidered* (New York: Oxford University Press, 1990), 61–62.

99. Bredbenner, *A Nationality of Her Own,* 120.

100. This phrase is borrowed from Geraldine Heng and Janadas Devan, who, writing in a different context, analyzed exhortations made by the prime minister of Singapore in 1983 for educated, Chinese-origin women to have more children or risk the state being overwhelmed by lower-class women's offspring (who were, not incidentally, Malay and Indian). These authors write: "Hinging precisely on a wishful fantasy of exact self-replication, this narrative of crisis posits, as the essential condition of national survival, the regeneration of the country's population (its heterogeneous national body) in such ratios of race and class as would faithfully mirror the population's original composition at the nation's founding moment." See Geraldine Heng and Janadas Devan, "State Fatherhood: The Politics of Nationalism, Sexuality, and Race in Singapore," 344.

101. The 1924 Act exempted Filipinos from the general ban on Asian migration, since the United States was colonizing the Philippines. However, the 1934 Tydings-McDuffie Act capped annual Filipino entries at fifty per year.

102. Latino migration, including that by women, was handled under separate provisions governing the Western Hemisphere (the Americas and the Caribbean).

103. *American History in Terms of Human Migration,* Extracts from Hearings before the Committee on Immigration and Naturalization, House of Representatives, 70th Cong., 2nd Sess., 7 March 1928, 11.

104. See my essay in *positions,* which argues that racial and ethnic preferences have been coded in new ways into immigration laws and policies, rather than being entirely abolished.

105. *Time,* special issue, 2. The special issue was subtitled "How Immigrants are Shaping the World's First Multicultural Society."

106. Ibid., 64.

107. Ibid., 64–65. Emphasis added.

108. The "racial and ethnic" categories used to describe these seven pairs are extraordinarily odd: Middle Eastern, Italian, African, Vietnamese, Anglo-Saxon, Chinese, and Hispanic.

109. Lauren Berlant notes that this narrative "situates American posthistory

in prelapsarian time." See Berlant, *The Queen of America Goes to Washington City*, 202.

110. Ibid., 205.

111. Berlant suggests that the special issue "sacrifices the centrality of African American history to American culture by predicting its demise; it sacrifices attention to the concrete lives of exploited immigrant and native people of color by fantasizing the future as what will happen when white people intermarry, thus linking racial mixing to the continued, but masked, hegemony of whiteness; it tacitly justifies the continued ejection of gays and lesbians and women from full citizenship" (207). For other analyses of the special issue see Evelynn Hammonds, "New Technologies of Race," in Jennifer Terry and Melodie Calvert, eds., *Processed Lives: Gender and Technology in Everyday Life* (New York: Routledge, 1997), and Shawn Michelle Smith, "Afterimages: A Brief Look at American Visual Culture in the 1990s," in *American Archives* (Princeton: Princeton University Press, 1999), 222–25.

4. Looking Like a Lesbian

1. Personal interview with Albert Armendariz, Sr., Esq., in El Paso, Texas, on 18 March 1996.

2. Cited in *Matter of LaRochelle*, 11 I&N Dec. 436 (BIA 1965).

3. Senate Report 1515, 81st Cong., 2d Sess., 345 (1950).

4. Senate Report 1137, 82nd Cong., 2d Sess., 46–48 (1952).

5. A significant amount of information about the history of gay and lesbian exclusion has been reconstructed from the records of court cases. To date, *Quiroz* is the only female court case that has been identified.

6. This chapter focuses on the exclusion of lesbians and gay men, specifically, in U.S. immigration. Though the contemporary notion of "queer" also include people who are bisexual and transgendered, as well as various heterosexualities, these were not identities around which the policing of immigration was organized. Rather, the historical record suggests that Congress and the immigration service were specifically concerned with a homosexual threat. Court cases indicate that individuals who were sexually involved with both men and women were considered homosexual, rather than bi- or heterosexual. Indeed, they were considered to be particularly pernicious homosexuals, who deceitfully tried to hide their "condition" by becoming involved with people of the "opposite sex."

7. Kieran Rose, "The Tenderness of the Peoples," in íde O'Carroll and Eoin Collins, eds., *Lesbian and Gay Visions of Ireland: Towards the Twenty-First Century* (London: Cassell, 1995), 74.

8. Foucault, *The History of Sexuality* (Vol. 1), 103. For Quiroz, the density of the relations of power also have to do with the fact that she was a Mexican

woman and, as such, was connected to a larger history of strict immigration monitoring directed at Mexican-origin people attempting to enter the United States. See, for example, Leo Chavez, *Shadowed Lives: Undocumented Immigrants in American Society* (Fort Worth: Harcourt Brace Jovanovich, 1992); Kitty Calavita, *Inside the State;* Roger Rouse, "Making Sense of Settlement: Class Transformation, Cultural Struggle, and Transnationalism among Mexican Migrants in the United States," in Nina Glick Schiller, Linda Basch, and Cristina Blanc-Szanton, eds., *Towards a Transnational Perspective on Migration,* Annals of the New York Academy of Sciences no. 645 (New York: New York Academy of Sciences, 1992).

9. There is a double problem here. Efforts to determine if Quiroz was a lesbian sustain sexual categorizations, even if the efforts are motivated by affirmation of resistant and minority sexual subjects. Furthermore, these sexual categorizations substantially derive their meanings from metropolitan centers, which are materially and ideologically implicated in the production of immigrant women as racial or ethnic minorities. Thus, uncritical application of the term "lesbian" to a woman like Quiroz can easily erase her different historical formation and complex positionality, without revealing anything about her sexuality.

10. Thanks to Judith Butler for this succinct formulation. Two examples may help to illustrate how immigration checkpoints can regulate the terms by which identity is formed. I interviewed a woman who had had a sexual relationship with a woman in her country of origin and thought nothing of it—until she was asked by a State Department official, while applying to immigrate, if she was a homosexual. The fact of being asked, and the manner in which she was asked, made her rethink the significance of that sexual experience. A second, rather different example concerns a woman who came to the United States, lived here for several years, and began to think of herself as a lesbian. But she knew that in order to adjust from immigrant to citizen status she would one day be asked to account for her activities before immigration officials. Therefore, the woman did not feel free to join lesbian groups or activities until she adjusted to citizen status.

11. The fact that certain forms of queer identities were unlikely to be captured by these checkpoints does not make the fact of policing any less salient for all queer people, however.

12. Shannon Minter, "Sodomy and Public Morality Offenses Under U.S. Immigration Law: Penalizing Lesbian and Gay Identity," *Cornell International Law Journal* 26 (1993), 799.

13. But we should not treat this dearth of court cases as further evidence that lesbians were unaffected by immigration policing; instead, we need to remain attuned to the ways that women are historically excluded/unrepresented within

official documents but were present historically and had an impact. See Yolanda Chavez Leyva, "Breaking the Silence: Putting Latina Lesbian History at the Center," in Bonnie Zimmerman and Toni McNaron, eds., *The New Lesbian Studies: Toward the Twenty-First Century* (New York: The Feminist Press, 1996), 145–52.

14. Aside from Quiroz, the only other lesbian immigration case I have ever seen cited is *In re Schmidt*, 56 Misc. 2d 456, 459–60 (N.Y. Sup. Ct.) 1961. This case is cited by Minter, who describes the issue as follows: "a New York court applied Judge Hand's standard to a lesbian seeking naturalization after living and working in the United States for fourteen years. The woman testified to having had a series of relationships with women, both before her entry to the country and after. Citing a New Jersey court that found '[f]ew behavioral deviations . . . more offensive to American mores than . . . homosexuality,' the New York court dismissed the woman's petition for citizenship despite the fact that her behavior was private and violated no law." See Minter, "Sodomy and Public Morality Offenses," 794.

15. Armendariz interview. Armendariz estimates that this officer was single-handedly responsible for the exclusion or deportation of several hundred women for "sexual deviation."

16. Decision of the Special Inquiry Officer concerning case A8 707 653, 25 March 1960, Immigration and Naturalization Service, El Paso, Texas, 3.

17. House Report 1365, 82d Congress, 2d Sess., 1952, 47. Emphasis added.

18. Of course, masculinity and femininity are culturally coded in very specific ways, so when dealing with culturally different and diverse populations of immigrants, this standard would provide only a shaky basis for identifying "deviants."

19. Jennifer Terry, "Lesbians under the Medical Gaze: Scientists Search for Remarkable Differences," *Journal of Sex Research* 27 (1990), 319.

20. Ibid., 321.

21. Ibid., 323, 332.

22. See Siobhan Somerville, *Queering the Color Line* (Durham: Duke University Press, 2000), 17, 25, 27.

23. Nice Rodriguez, "Big Nipple of the North," in Makeda Silvera, ed., *Piece of My Heart: A Lesbian of Colour Anthology* (Toronto: Sister Vision Press, 1992), 35–36.

24. Of course, race and gender are not reducible to "visible marks," either, and the "visible" certainly need not provide an accurate index of an individual's gender or race. In terms of race, this point is most thoroughly developed in writings about people with multiracial heritages. See, for example, the essays in Maria P. P. Root, ed., *Racially Mixed People in America* (Newbury Park, Calif.: Sage, 1992).

25. See Robyn Wiegman, *American Anatomies: Theorizing Race and Gender* (Durham: Duke University Press, 1995), especially 21–42.

26. Timothy J. Dunn, *The Militarization of the U.S.-Mexico Border, 1978–1992* (Austin: CMAS Books, University of Texas, Austin, 1996), 6.

27. Ibid.

28. Since Quiroz crossed the border, U.S.-Mexican border relations have undergone many changes, which are described in more detail in the next chapter.

29. Yvonne Yarbro-Bejarano, "De-constructing the Lesbian Body: Cherríe Moraga's 'Loving in the War Years,'" in Carla Trujillo, ed., *Chicana Lesbians: The Girls Our Mothers Warned Us About* (Berkeley: Third Woman Press, 1991), 146.

30. See "Crime Related Deportation Grounds and Criminal Offenses Under the INA" in *Immigration Law and Crimes*, by the National Lawyers Guild (Deerfield, Ill.: Clark Boardman, 1995), which notes that immigrants who willfully and materially misrepresent their cases are excludable.

31. For example, Attorney Ignatius Bau related that in Russia men accused of homosexuality tend to be jailed, while women accused of lesbianism tend to be hospitalized. Consequently, the mark (or at least, the accusation) of homosexuality is visible in gender-differentiated ways in documents that Russian immigrants submit to the INS. (Personal telephone conversation, April 1995, San Francisco.)

32. When immigrants seemed potentially lesbian or gay, the INS did not always thoroughly investigate them. Instead, it could dispose of them without generating any record at all. This fact means that official records never fully document the extent of lesbian and gay exclusion, deportation, and oppression. Donald C. Knutson, counsel to the National Gay Rights Advocates, explained how suspected lesbians and gays could be excluded without generating an official record: "If the border guard suspects because of that person's appearance or some other reason [that he or she is gay or lesbian], the normal practice has been to inform that person that he or she is not entitled to enter the country, that he or she has two options. One, get on the plane or boat or train or whatever and go back where you came from and you won't have any more trouble. If you persist, however, you must go before an immigration judge. You must go before a psychiatrist for a psychiatric examination, and then you will be excluded from this country, deported, and never permitted to come back again. Well, it is no wonder that statistics do not indicate that many people have taken that [second] course." (See *Exclusion and Deportation Amendments of 1983*, Hearing Before the Subcommittee on Immigration, Refugees, and International Law of the Committee of the Judiciary, House of Representatives, 98th Cong, 2d Sess., on H.R.4509 and H.R.5227, Serial No. 98-72, 28 June 1984 [Washington, D.C.: U.S. Government Printing Office, 1984], 193.) Consequently, although medical

certification provided the means to exclude suspected lesbians and gay men, exclusion could always be implemented more informally, simply by invoking the threat of the medical certification process.

33. Richard Green, "'Give Me Your Tired, Your Poor,'" 140.

34. Robert Poznanski, "The Propriety of Denying Entry to Homosexual Aliens: Examining the Public Health Service's Authority Over Medical Exclusions," 347.

35. David M. Halperin, *St. Foucault: Towards a Gay Hagiography* (New York: Oxford University Press, 1995), 32–33.

36. Foucault refers to such organization and deployment as a discursive economy: "the economy of discourses—their intrinsic technology, the necessities of their operation, the tactics they employ, the effects of power which underlie them and which they transmit—this, and not the system of representations, is what determines the essential features of what they have to say." *The History of Sexuality* (Vol. 1), 68–69.

37. To this day, the PHS remains involved in inspecting the physical and mental health of aspiring immigrants. For more information, see "Inquiry into the Alien Medical Examination Program of the U.S. Public Health Service," Special Series No. 12, Committee of the Judiciary, Subcommittee No. 1, House of Representatives, *Study of Immigration and Population Problems* (Washington, D.C.: U.S. Government Printing Office, 1963).

38. As Foucault phrased it, "the exercise of power is not added on from outside, like a rigid, heavy constraint . . . but is so subtly present in them as to increase their efficiency." See *Discipline and Punish*, 206.

39. Allan Bérubé, *Coming Out Under Fire: The History of Gay Men and Women in World War II* (New York: The Free Press, 1990), 142.

40. Ibid., 266.

41. In the 1950s, when Quiroz became a U.S. resident, discourses of national security constructed gays and lesbians as threats that were analogous to (and sometimes indistinguishable from) the danger of Communist subversion. See John D'Emilio, "The Homosexual Menace: The Politics of Sexuality in Cold War America," in D'Emilio, *Making Trouble* (New York: Routledge, 1992), 57–73; Robert Corber, *In the Name of National Security: Hitchcock, Homophobia, and the Political Construction of Gender in Postwar America* (Durham: Duke University Press, 1993); and Robert Corber, *Homosexuality in Cold War America* (Durham: Duke University Press, 1997). Carl Stychin has remarked on the ways that homosexuality functions as a malleable identity that can be used in the service of nation-building, particularly in times of crisis: "homosexuality has been associated with Communism, fascism, bourgeois capitalism, colonialism, the West and north, the east and south, environmentalism, Europe, and North

America. In the project of nation building, homosexuality is a ready discursive tool that can be conflated with any enemy of the state, in the process of becoming the enemy within." See *A Nation by Rights: National Cultures, Sexual Identity Politics, and the Discourse of Rights* (Philadelphia: Temple University Press, 1998), 194. Of course, in Quiroz's case, she was easily constructed as a national threat not only because the immigration service associated her with homosexuality but also because she was a working-class Mexican woman. Kitty Calavita describes how Cold War paranoia gave rise to fears that Communist subversives were crossing into the United States from Mexico and Latin America, sometimes disguised as farmworkers. The INS assigned top priority to identifying and excluding such "subversive" aliens, and their strategies resulted in the harassment, criminalization, and even deportation of many ethnic Mexicans living legitimately in the United States. See Calavita, *Inside the State,* 49–51, 77–80. See also Gutierrez, "Ethnic Politics, Immigration Policy, and the Cold War," in *Walls and Mirrors,* and Mario T. García, "Mexican American Radicals and the Cold War," in García, *Mexican Americans: Leadership, Ideology, and Identity* (New Haven: Yale University Press, 1989).

42. Bérubé, *Coming Out Under Fire,* 269–70.

43. Ibid., 259.

44. Thanks to Jill Esbenshade, who pointed out to me that there were connections between immigration and military policies during this time period.

45. Foucault, *The History of Sexuality* (Vol. 1), 65.

46. Ibid., 65–67.

47. See n. 29 above.

48. Personal interview, Albert Armendariz, Sr., Esq., El Paso, Texas, 18 March 1996.

49. Decision of the Special Inquiry Officer, 3.

50. Once her testimony had been taken, corroborating testimony had also been obtained from one Celia Rosales, named by Quiroz as one of her lovers during the previous fifteen months—so it was not her speech alone that constructed her as lesbian. However, in many cases, speech about oneself, without such corroboration, was sufficient "proof" of homosexuality—making speech, and the relation of speech to the self, a very contested location. For more on the vexed relationship between self-disclosure and homosexual identity, see Eve Sedgwick, *Epistemology of the Closet* (Berkeley: University of California Press, 1990), especially 69–75.

51. Decision of the Special Inquiry Officer, 3–4.

52. Ibid., 1.

53. The question of using "scientific practice" to "induce" immigrants to speak and to "force a difficult confession" has played out in many ways in immi-

gration monitoring of lesbians and gay men. The PHS suggested, in a 1952 report to Congress, that some people might suffer from a "homosexuality of which the individual himself is unaware." In those cases, "some psychological tests may be helpful in uncovering homosexuality" (House Report 1365, 47). Richard Green speculates that the tests in question were Rorschach "inkblot" tests. (See Green, "Give Me Your Tired, Your Poor," 142, n.7.) PHS psychological tests were not the only means used to force a confession about sexuality—a more dramatic example concerns Jaime Chavez, who was "held incommunicado under armed guard for over twenty four hours [and] subjected to abusive questioning and an abusive search" (*Exclusion and Deportation Amendments of 1983*, 185). Chavez was treated in this way because he was suspected of homosexuality, based on the contents of his luggage.

54. Foucault, *The History of Sexuality* (Vol. 1), 66.

55. Decision of the Board of Immigration Appeals, Case A-8707653, Washington, D.C., 2 June 1960, 7.

56. Foucault, *The History of Sexuality* (Vol. 1), 66–67.

57. Decision of the Special Inquiry Officer, 2.

58. Ibid., 5.

59. Historically, Congress has enjoyed plenary power over immigration matters, such that "Congress has unbounded power to exclude aliens from admission to the United States; Congress can bar aliens from entering the United States for discriminatory and arbitrary reasons, even those which might be condemned as a denial of equal protection if used for purposes other than immigration." See *Matter of Longstaff*, 716 F. 2d 1439 (5th Circuit, 1983). Plenary powers are intended to ensure national sovereignty.

60. Decision of the Board of Immigration Appeals, 4.

61. This argument makes heterosexuality the norm from which all other sexualities are both derivative and deviant; it makes all women's sexual agency derivative of male actions; thus, it implies lesbianism is the result of heterosexuality gone wrong, become spoiled; in this way, it renders impossible the affirmation of women loving women, while constructing lesbians as degraded, sick, and inferior.

62. Decision of the Board of Immigration Appeals, 7.

63. Ibid.

64. Findings of Fact and Conclusions of Law, United States District Court for the Western District of Texas, El Paso Division, in Civil Action No.2175, *Sara Harb Quiroz v. Marcus T. Neelly*, 22 August 1960, 2.

65. United States Court of Appeals for the Fifth Circuit, Case No. 18724, *Sara Harb Quiroz v. Richard C. Haberstroh*, Brief of the Appellant, March 1961, 2. (A more precise date is not given.)

66. Motion to Reopen, in the Matter of Sara Harb Quiroz, Now Sara Harb Escudero, A8 707 653, to the District Director of Immigration and Naturalization Service of El Paso, Texas, 7 August 1961, 1.

67. United States Department of Justice, Immigration and Naturalization Service, "Brief in Opposition," in the Matter of Sara Harb Quiroz, File A8 707 653, 23 August 1961. Emphasis added.

68. See Joseph Carrier, *De los otros: Intimacy and Homosexuality among Mexican Men* (New York: Columbia University Press, 1995).

69. Thomás Almaguer has documented that Chicano men negotiate sexual identity in the intersections of Mexican/Chicano and dominant U.S. sexuality constructions. (See Thomás Almaguer, "Chicano Men: A Cartography of Homosexual Identity and Behavior," in Henry Abelove, Michele Aina Barale, and David M. Halperin, eds., *The Lesbian and Gay Studies Reader*, 255–73.) How that process of negotiation might have occurred for immigrant Mexican women in the late 1950s is something about which we can only speculate. But we know that immigrant lesbians do not easily fit into what Yolanda Leyva calls "the Anglo lesbian paradigm of the modern lesbian identity" ("Breaking the Silence," 149), and other identity formations and traditions must be grasped if we are to theorize the richness of immigrant lesbian history.

70. Oliva M. Espín, "The Immigrant Experience in Lesbian Studies," in Bonnie Zimmerman and Toni McNaron, eds., *The New Lesbian Studies*, 82.

71. Cherríe Moraga, *Loving in the War Years: Lo que nunca pasó por sus labios*, (Boston: South End Press, 1983), 90–142.

72. Leyva, "Breaking the Silence," 145.

73. Espín, "The Immigrant Experience in Lesbian Studies," 79. See also Lourdes Arguelles and B. Ruby Rich, "Homosexuality, Homophobia, and Revolution: Notes Toward an Understanding of the Cuban Lesbian and Gay Male Experience, Part I," in *Signs: Journal of Women in Culture and Society* 9 (1984), 683–99; and Arguelles and Rich, "Homosexuality, Homophobia, and Revolution: Notes Toward an Understanding of the Cuban Lesbian and Gay Male Experience, Part II," in *Signs: Journal of Women in Culture and Society* 11 (1985), 120–35.

74. House Report 101–723, Part I and II, "Family Unity and Employment Opportunity Immigration Act of 1990," 19 September 1990, 101st Cong., 2d Sess., (Washington, D.C.: U.S. Government Printing Office, 1990), 56. The Report is hereafter referred to as HR 101-723.

75. HR 101-723, 56.

76. Green, "Give Me Your Tired, Your Poor," 143. For a more detailed discussion of the APA's decision, see Ronald Bayer, *Homosexuality and American Psychiatry: The Politics of Diagnosis*, 2d ed. (Princeton: Princeton University Press, 1987). Neil Miller mentions that in an effort to contest the automatic labeling of

homosexuality as a mental illness, gay activists "zapped" APA conventions and meetings, and at one panel discussion of the issue, "a psychiatrist . . . created a sensation by announcing that he was gay. It marked the first time that any psychiatrist in the United States had come out publicly; the drama of his revelation was heightened by the fact he found it necessary to wear a mask and speak through a voice altering device." See Neil Miller, *Out of the Past: Gay and Lesbian History from 1869 to the Present* (New York: Vintage, 1995), 256.

77. Thanks to Professor Carolyn (Patty) Blum for her comments on this matter.

78. Memorandum of John M. Harmon, Assistant Attorney General, to David L. Crosland, Acting Commissioner, INS (10 December 1979), 2.

79. Green, "Give Me Your Tired, Your Poor," 143.

80. Minter, "Sodomy and Public Morality Offenses," 780–81.

81. House Report No. 882, 100th Cong., 2d Sess., (Washington, D.C.: U.S. Government Printing Office, 1988), 23–24.

82. Minter, "Sodomy and Public Morality Offenses," 781.

83. Ibid., 787.

84. There are also difficulties with accessing political asylum, especially for lesbians.

85. Katie King, "Local and Global: AIDS Activism and Feminism," in *Camera Obscura* 28 (1992), 80. Note that in the late 1980s HIV became a grounds for immigration exclusion, although it was not specifically listed in the law. In 1993 Congress voted to officially add HIV to the list of grounds for immigration exclusion.

86. HR 100-723, 52–53.

87. This is a project which intersects with the more domestically oriented campaign for "same-sex" marriage.

88. Foucault, *The History of Sexuality* (Vol. 1), 92–93.

5. Rape, Asylum, and the U.S. Border Patrol

1. My argument draws on Saskia Sassen's *Losing Control? Sovereignty in an Age of Globalization* (New York: Columbia University Press, 1996), chapter 3. As Sassen and others note, the nation-state as a mechanism for managing social processes and as a site for affective identification and political mobilization is far from "dead." Global processes materialize in fundamentally national territories, and the nation-state orchestrates key aspects of globalization processes. Of course, although they have not been abolished, there is no question but that nations and nation-states have been transformed by globalization.

2. Susan Brownmiller, *Against Our Will: Men, Women, and Rape* (New York: Bantam, 1975), 8.

3. Kimberle Crenshaw, "Whose Story Is It, Anyway? Feminist and Anti-racist Appropriations of Anita Hill," in Toni Morrison, ed., *Race-ing Justice, En-Gendering Power* (New York: Pantheon, 1992), 409.

4. Crenshaw, "Whose Story Is It, Anyway?" 413. Crenshaw continues, "Historically, a black woman's word was not taken as truth; our own legal system once drew a connection—as a matter of law—between lack of chastity and lack of verity. In other words, a woman who was likely to have had sex could not be trusted to tell the truth. Because black women were not expected to be chaste, they were likewise considered less likely to tell the truth" (413).

5. In a famous interchange, Foucault suggested that rape should be defined as an act of violence, rather than as a sexual crime, and therefore not distinct from other forms of assault. Vikki Bell offers a generous reading of Foucault's suggestion, arguing that he was being consistent with the tenets of *History of Sexuality* (Vol. 1) by refusing to locate sex in specific body parts (85–87). However, French feminist Monique Plaza strongly took Foucault to task for his suggestion. She argued that rape was about sex, not because it necessarily involved the genitals but because it was a technology for *socially* sexing bodies as feminized or masculinized within a violent heteropatriarchal regime. This regime already preexists (but is reinforced by) the rape itself. Plaza also critiqued Foucault's suggestion because it implicitly protected men's sexualities, bodies, and pleasures at the expense of women. On Foucault's comments about rape, and feminist responses to these comments, see Linda Martin Alacoff, "Dangerous Pleasures: Foucault and the Politics of Pedophilia," in Susan J. Hekman, ed., *Feminist Interpretations of Michel Foucault* (University Park: Pennsylvania State University Press, 1996), 99–135; Vikki Bell, "'Beyond the 'Thorny Question': Feminism, Foucault, and the Desexualization of Rape," *International Journal of the Sociology of Law* 19 (1991) 83–100; Ann J. Cahill, "Foucault, Rape, and the Construction of the Feminine Body," *Hypatia* 15, no. 1 (2000), 43–63; Laura Hengenhold, "An Immodest Proposal: Foucault, Hysterization, and the 'Second Rape,'" *Hypatia* 9, no. 3 (summer 1994), 88–107; and Winifred Woodhull, "Sexuality, Power, and the Question of Rape," in Irene Diamond and Lee Quinby, eds., *Feminism and Foucault: Reflections on Resistance* (Boston: Northeastern University Press, 1988), 167–76.

6. Judith Butler, "Contingent Foundations," in Judith Butler and Joan W. Scott, eds., *Feminists Theorize the Political* (New York: Routledge, 1992), 18.

7. The official UN definition is that a refugee is a person who, "owing to a well founded fear of persecution for reasons of race, religion, nationality, membership in a particular social group or political opinion is outside the country of his nationality and is unable or, owing to such fear, is unwilling to avail himself of the protection of that country; or who, not having a nationality and being

outside the country of his former habitual residence as a result of such events, is unable or, owing to such fear, is unwilling to return to it." Quoted in Susan Forbes Martin, *Refugee Women* (London: Zed Books, 1991), 1.

8. The United States did not sign on to the 1951 UN Convention, which defined the international standard, and instead developed its own highly ideological standard of who constituted a refugee. According to Zucker and Zucker, the U.S. Refugee Escapee Act of 1957 "defined refugees-escapees as victims of racial, religious, or political persecution in Communist or Communist-occupied or -dominated countries, or countries in the Middle East. This definition would stand until the Refugee Act of 1980 amended it" to accord with the international standards listed above. The U.S. system's strongly ideological bias meant that those fleeing Communist countries were very likely to be granted asylum, while those fleeing right-wing dictatorships in countries with which the United States was on friendly terms were likely to be denied asylum. See Norman L. Zucker and Naomi Flint Zucker, *The Guarded Gate: The Reality of American Refugee Policy*, 32. Even after the United States adopted the international definition, those fleeing Communist countries remained far more likely to be awarded asylum than anyone else.

9. Jacqueline Bhabha, "Embodied Rights: Gender Persecution, State Sovereignty, and Refugees," *Public Culture* 9, no. 1 (fall 1996), 8. The UN refugee definition has also been criticized for focusing primarily on individuals' civil and political rights to be free from arbitrary state actions, while failing to affirmatively address social, economic, and cultural rights, or the needs of internally displaced people. See, for example, Pheng Cheah, "Posit(ion)ing Human Rights in the Current Global Conjuncture," *Public Culture* 9, no. 2 (winter 1997), 233–66.

10. One reason to press for reinterpretation was the common estimate that women and children comprised 80 percent of the world's refugee population. Only very recently has that assumption been challenged. According to *Refugee Reports,* the assumption "was punctured in a statistical analysis produced by the UN High Commissioner for Refugees (UNHCR) statistical unit in early February [2000]. The statistical unit found that 'there appears little evidence at the aggregate level to suggest that there are considerably more female than male refugees in the world . . . ' UNHCR's statistical unit only analyzed data for the 4.7 million refugees under UNHCR programs, however. . . . Of the 4.7 million refugees in the study, 50.9 percent were female. The even split between males and females was consistently reported in Africa and Asia. Only in Europe was a significantly higher proportion of females reported, 53.2 percent, which was accounted for by a single country, Croatia, with a 59.6 percent female refugee caseload. On the other hand, the percentage of female refugees in Latin America and the

Caribbean (46.8 percent) was considerably lower." See *Refugee Reports* 21, no. 2 (February 2000), 10–11.

11. See for example, Ruth Siefert, "War and Rape: A Preliminary Analysis," in Alexandra Stiglmayer, ed., *Mass Rape: The War Against Women in Bosnia-Herzegovina* (Lincoln: University of Nebraska Press, 1994), 54–72; Catherine N. Niarchos, "Women, War, and Rape: The Challenges Facing the International Tribunal for the Former Yugoslavia," *Human Rights Quarterly* 17, no. 4 (1995), 649–690.

12. Human Rights Watch/Africa, *Shattered Lives: Sexual Violence During the Rwandan Genocide and Its Aftermath* (New York: Human Rights Watch, 1996), 27–28.

13. No doubt many women who had been raped did not mention this, because rape remains underreported and difficult to discuss. There was also no framework in place to ensure that women's accounts of rape would be treated seriously in the asylum system.

14. Political opinion and membership in a particular social group are two of the five grounds on which people are eligible to apply for asylum.

15. *Sofia Campos Guardado v. INS*, 809 F.2d 287; 1987 U.S. App.

16. Ibid.

17. Memorandum from Phyllis Coven to All INS Asylum Officers, "Considerations for Asylum Officers Adjudicating Asylum Claims From Women" (hereafter Gender Guidelines), in 72 *Interpreter Releases* 786 (5 June 1995).

18. *Olimpia Lazo-Majano v. INS* 813 F.2d 1433; 1987 U.S. App.

19. 813 F.2d 1433, 1435.

20. 813 F.2d 1434.

21. 813 F.2d 1435.

22. 813 F.2d 1438.

23. Deborah Anker, with Nancy Kelly and John Willshire-Carrera, "Rape in the Community as a Basis for Asylum: The Treatment of Women Refugees' Claims to Protection in Canada and the United States," *Bender's Immigration Bulletin* (1997), 611.

24. Forbes Martin, *Refugee Women*, 95. The Conclusion says that "states, in the exercise of their sovereignty, are free to adopt the interpretation that women asylum seekers who face harsh or inhuman treatment due to their having transgressed the social mores of the society in which they live may be considered a 'particular social group' within the meaning of Article 1A(2) of the 1951 United Nations Refugee Convention." Quoted in Audrey Macklin, "Cross Border Shopping for Ideas: A Critical Review of United States, Canadian, and Australian Approaches to Gender-Related Asylum Claims," *Georgetown Immigration Law Journal* 13 (fall 1998), 29–30.

25. See Meryem C. Amar, "Boat Women: Piracy's Other Dimension: Rape and its Consequences," *Refugees* (June 1985), 30–31; Forbes Martin, *Refugee Women*, 17.

26. Office of the United Nations High Commissioner for Refugees, *Guidelines for the Protection of Refugee Women*, UN document ES/SCP/67 (1991).

27. Human Rights Watch/Africa, *Shattered Lives*, 29.

28. Canada issued gender asylum guidelines in 1993.

29. Macklin, "Cross Border Shopping for Ideas," 27.

30. Inter American Commission on Human Rights, Organization of American States, *Report on the Situation of Human Rights in Haiti* (Washington, D.C.: Organization of American States, 1995). See also, Human Rights Watch, *Rape in Haiti: A Weapon of Terror* (Washington, D.C.: Human Rights Watch, July 1994).

31. The case was *In Re D-V-*, decided 25 May 1993, BIA Interim Decision 3252. The case concerned a twenty-seven-year-old Haitian woman who had been an active supporter of Aristide through her church group. One evening, soldiers came to her family's house and asked for her. She told them that the person they wanted was not home, but "they identified her by the hair on her feet." They told her that members of her church had already been killed and she was next. One held a gun to her head. Her mother gave the soldiers money, begging them to spare her daughter's life. Three soldiers beat the woman and then raped her. Before leaving, "they warned the applicant that if she talked about them or reported them to the radio station, they would be back." The woman was subsequently examined by a doctor, who told her that she would be unable to have children as a result of the rapes. She went into hiding until she was able to leave Haiti. When she applied for asylum, an immigration judge initially denied her on the grounds that "she had failed to demonstrate a well-founded fear of persecution on the basis of her political opinion because the evidence did not show her to be a prominent supporter of Aristide. . . . the applicant's fear of return to Haiti was based on general conditions of violence in that country, and it was pure speculation on her part that the same attackers would rape and beat her again or kill her." Contrary to the immigration judge, the Board of Immigration Appeals found that "the applicant has a well-founded fear of persecution based on political opinion and religion if she were returned to Haiti." She was granted asylum and thus legally allowed to remain in the United States.

32. For example, the guidelines say that "rape (including mass rape in, for example, Bosnia), sexual abuse and domestic violence, infanticide and genital mutilation are forms of mistreatment primarily directed at girls and women and they may serve as evidence of past persecution on account of one or more of the five grounds." (Gender Guidelines, 782.)

33. Ibid., 785.

34. Ibid.

35. Ibid., 784.

36. Ibid.

37. On the face of it, many domestic violence cases seem to conform to the standards established for gaining asylum. Domestic violence often entails forms of abuse that amount to persecution. As Anker et al. put it, "domestic violence often involves repeated physical assaults, under certain circumstances amounting to torture, frequently resulting in death." Many governments are unable or unwilling to protect women from domestic violence through legal sanction or the provision of services. Even in countries with laws and services, there is often a significant gap between the supposed availability of protection and the reality. Women may experience domestic violence on the basis of various of the five grounds for asylum listed in refugee law, perhaps most obviously on the grounds of their membership in a particular social group, "women." Yet claims for asylum by women who have endured domestic violence are often difficult to win. See Deborah Anker, Lauren Gilbert, and Nancy Kelly, "Women Whose Governments Are Unable or Unwilling to Provide Reasonable Protection from Domestic Violence May Qualify as Refugees Under United States Asylum Law," *Georgetown Immigration Law Journal* 11 (1997), 713.

38. This was the first application for asylum on the basis of domestic violence about which the BIA issued a decision.

39. *In Re R-A-*, BIA interim decision 3403, 11 June 1999, 3.

40. The INS appealed the immigration judge's decision, which is why the BIA was called upon to issue a ruling.

41. *In Re R-A-*, 6.

42. Macklin, "Cross Border Shopping for Ideas," 56.

43. Ibid., 58.

44. Ibid., 59.

45. *In Re R-A-*, 7.

46. Ibid., 3.

47. Ibid., 11.

48. For a critique of the BIA's reasoning, see Mark R. Von Sternberg, "Battered Women and the Criteria for Refugee Status," *World Refugee Survey 2000* (Washington, D.C.: U.S. Committee for Refugees, 2000), 40–47. See also Linda Kelly, "Republican Mothers, Bastards' Fathers, and Good Victims: Discarding Citizens and Equal Protection Through the Failure of Legal Images," *Hastings Law Journal* 51 (March 2000), 557–97. See especially 594–96. For divergent responses by the U.S. media, see the editorial "A Harsh Reality of Immigration," *St. Petersburg Times,* 13 July 1999, A10; Judy Mann, "A Dangerous Precedent for

Abuse Victims," *Washington Post,* 9 February 2000, C15; Susan Sachs, "The Nation: Fears of Rape and Violence; Women Newly Seeking Asylum," *New York Times,* 1 August 1999, Sec. 4, 4; Fredric Tulsky, "Abused Woman Is Denied Asylum: Immigration Ruling Reflects Split over Gender Persecution," *Washington Post,* 20 June 1999, A1.

49. *In Re R-A-,* 6.

50. "Proposed Rule Addrersses Asylum for Victims of Gender-Based Persecution," *Refugee Reports* 22, no. 1 (January 2001), 2.

51. Not in every case, however. See *Angoucheva v. INS* (106 F.3d 781, 1997), which the U.S. Court of Appeals for the 7th Circuit remanded back to the BIA with orders to follow the Gender Guidelines when reanalyzing the case.

52. According to Silva Meznaric, in 1986 the [then] Republic of Serbia modified its penal code to introduce a new criminal offense, "sexual assault on citizens of a different nationality" (86). This category of crime implicitly differentiated rapes committed across ethnic lines from those committed within ethnic groups and penalized the former more severely than the latter. But as Meznaric points out, from the perspective of the rape victim, can we really claim that rape is less offensive, traumatic, and violent when committed by a member of one's own ethnic group rather than by someone of a different ethnicity? Furthermore, this legal distinction may have enabled the use of rape as a brutal weapon of war that created ethnic and national differentiations. Thus, Meznaric rightly questions the consequences of accepting distinctions that construct some rapes as more "serious" or "political" than others. Similarly, I wonder what are the negative consequences of allowing the refugee/asylum system to differentiate among experiences of rape when deciding who can and cannot receive asylum. See Silva Meznaric, "Gender as an Ethno-Marker: Rape, War, and Identity Politics in the Former Yugoslavia," in Valentine M. Moghadam, ed., *Identity Politics and Women: Cultural Reassertions and Feminisms in International Perspective* (Boulder: Westview Press, 1993), 76–97.

53. On this point, see Hengenhold, "An Immodest Proposal."

54. Sherene H. Razack, *Looking White People in the Eye: Gender, Race, and Culture in Courtrooms and Classrooms* (Toronto: University of Toronto Press, 1998), 88.

55. See Chandra Talpade Mohanty, "Under Western Eyes: Feminist Scholarship and Colonial Discourses," in Chandra Talpade Mohanty, Ann Russo, and Lourdes Torres, eds., *Third World Women and the Politics of Feminism,* 51–80; see also Uma Narayan, *Dislocating Cultures: Identities, Traditions, and Third World Feminisms* (New York: Routledge, 1997), especially 81–117.

56. Razack, *Looking White People in the Eye,* 91.

57. Ibid., 107.

58. See "Shifting Grounds for Asylum: Female Genital Surgery and Sexual Orientation," *Columbia Human Rights Law Review* 29 (spring 1998), 516–17.

59. Dr. Nahid Toubia summarizes these contradictions by observing that "the United States wants to talk about women's genitals [in the asylum process], but it does not care if such women die from wars that are created by arms and money supplied through its foreign policy." See "Shifting Grounds for Asylum," 480.

60. Butler, "Contingent Foundations," 18.

61. Jacqueline Bhabha, "Embodied Persecution," 3.

62. See Alex Stepick, *Pride Against Prejudice: Haitians in the United States* (Boston: Allyn and Bacon, 1998), chapter 6; Malissa Lennox, "Refugees, Racism, and Repatriations: A Critique of United States' Haitian Immigration Policy," *Stanford Law Review* 45 (February 1993), 687–724.

63. Stepick, *Pride Against Prejudice*, 102–03.

64. Michael S. McBride notes that "asylum officials and immigration judges are well trained and sensitive to the needs & concerns of asylum seekers. The problem lies with the inspectors who are the first INS officials that a prospective asylum seeker encounters at ports of entry and those who have the authority to carry out the expedited removal process. . . . [A]ccording to Stancill, these inspectors are not as well trained or qualified as asylum officers; few have legal backgrounds, and fewer have college degrees. She believes that their demeanour intimidates many prospective asylum seekers, making them reluctant to put forward what may be legitimate claims. In addition, despite claims to the contrary, applicants are not always given information in a language they can understand, and the outcome of an interview may depend on whether the particular officer takes the 'benefits' or 'enforcement' approach." See Michael S. McBride, "Migrants and Asylum Seekers: Policy Responses in the United States to Immigrants ad Refugees from Central America and the Caribbean," *International Migration* vol. 37, no. 1 (1999): 304–05.

65. *Refugee Reports* 18, no. 1 (January 1997), 2.

66. *Refugee Reports* notes a study of expedited removal, conducted by the Center for Human Rights and International Justice at Hastings College of Law at the University of California, showed that "a high percentage of the sample who were referred from secondary inspection to a 'credible fear' interview were males with high socioeconomic status. More than half had some post secondary education, came from urban areas, and had family ties in the United States and Canada." See *Refugee Reports* 21, no. 5 (summer 2000), 12.

67. Arthur C. Helton and Alison Nicoll, "Female Genital Mutilation as Grounds For Asylum in the United States: The Recent Case of In Re Fauziya

Kasinga and the Prospects for More Gender-Sensitive Approaches," *Columbia Human Rights Law Review* 28 (winter 1997) 391.

68. Wendy A. Young, "U.S. Detention of Women Asylum Seekers: Failing to Practice What We Preach," in *World Refugee Survey* (New York: U.S. Committee for Refugees, 1997), 40.

69. For example, riots in 2000 at the Krome Detention Center in Miami, Florida, highlighted the prevalence of rape, sexual abuse, and sexual coercion that inmates endured. See *Migration News* 7, no. 9 (September 2000) at http://migration.ucdavis.edu.

70. PTSD may occur if someone is exposed to trauma. "The fundamental dynamic underlying PTSD is a cycle of re-experiencing the trauma, followed by attempts to bury the memories of the trauma and the feelings associated with the trauma. . . . During the recall stage of the PTSD cycle, your memories and the emotions associated with them will emerge, in conscious or unconscious awareness, over and over again in a variety of forms. You may have intrusive thoughts or images, dreams and nightmares, even flashbacks about the event. Or you may suddenly find yourself thinking or feeling as if you were back in the original trauma situation" (13). Such experiences of recall are often frightening and emotionally difficult, with the result that people alternate hyperalertness with psychic numbing or shutting down. Note that memories of trauma often emerge in unconscious form. The process of transforming these unconscious memories into consciousness—which in turn may provide the basis for a strong asylum application—can easily take much more than a year. See Aphrodite Matsakis, *I Can't Get Over It: A Handbook for Trauma Survivors* (Oakland: New Harbinger Publications, 1992).

71. IIRIRA also eliminated the Notice of Intent to Deny—notices the INS used to send that explained why they intended to deny a claim and allowing a deadline for response. Such notices served as an articulation of what the INS saw as the problems with a particular case and offered a window within which to respond and sometimes turn the case around.

72. See "Shifting Grounds for Asylum," 503–04. See also Shannon Minter, "Lesbians and Asylum: Overcoming Barriers to Access," in Sydney Levy, ed., *Asylum Based on Sexual Orientation: A Resource Guide* (International Lesbian and Gay Human Rights Commission and Lambda Legal Defense and Education Fund, 1996), 1B/3–1B/13.

73. Anker et al. indicate that other difficulties that have arisen in implementing the Guidelines. They suggest there has been some degree of retreat by courts, the BIA, and certain sectors of the INS in taking the Guidelines seriously. See Anker et al., "Rape in the Community," 614–16.

74. Néstor P. Rodríguez, "Social Construction of the U.S.-Mexico Border," in Juan F. Peres, ed., *Immigrants Out* (New York: New York University Press, 1997), 226.

75. Rodríguez, "Social Construction of the U.S.-Mexico Border," 226–27.

76. For a Foucauldian analysis of how discourses of national security constitute identity, see David Campbell, *Writing Security: United States Foreign Policy and the Politics of Identity* (Minneapolis: University of Minnesota Press, 1992).

77. Rodríguez, "Social Construction of the U.S.-Mexico Border," 227–34.

78. President Bush has said that "his goal was to create seamless borders with Canada and Mexico that would keep out terrorists, drugs, and disease, but more readily let in legitimate entrants and goods." *Migrant News* 9, no. 3 (March 2002).

79. According to Jiménez, the Urban Institute found that only 39 percent of undocumented immigrants in the United States are Mexicans (the INS claims that 55 percent of the undocumented are Mexican). "Yet 90% of the people arrested are Mexican nationals, and 85% of the resources to deal with the 'undocumented problem' are placed in communities along the U.S.-Mexico border." See Maria Jiménez, "The Militarization of the U.S.-Mexico Border," originally published in *In Motion Magazine,* 2 February 1998, available at http://www.inmotionmagazine.com/mj1.html#anchor616739. However, after September 11, 2001, the U.S. government deployed additional personnel to the U.S.-Canada border. On 12 December 2001 Governor Tom Ridge, Director of the Office of Homeland Security, and John Manley, Canada's Minister of Foreign Affairs, signed the "Smart Border Declaration," with a thirty-point action plan to increase border security while maintaining commercial flows. President Bush's proposed 2003 budget included funding to double the number of border patrol agents and inspectors at the U.S.-Canada border. See "Securing America's Borders Fact Sheet: Border Security," at http://www.whitehouse.gov/news/releases/2002/01/20020125.html.

80. This integration continued through the 1990s, with coordinated operations between the Border Patrol and the U.S. Army, Air Force, Marines, National Guard, and local police in various border locations.

81. Maria Jiménez, "War in the Borderlands," *Report on the Americas* 26, no. 1 (July 1992), 30.

82. Jiménez, "War in the Borderlands," 30. Highlighting the integration of border patrol functions with other forms of policing, Jiménez relates, "in December 1989, 100 army and Marine Corps troops began patrolling the Arizona-California border. In early 1990, a Marine drone was deployed to the Laredo sector of the Border Patrol to aid in the interdiction of drugs and undocumented immigrants. . . . in 1991, Marines erected a barrier of corrugated steel plates along 12 miles of the California border" (30).

83. Peter Andreas, "Borderless Economy, Barricaded Border," *NACLA Report on the Americas* 33, no. 3 (November/December 1999): 16.

84. For the year 2000 the INS requested $4.27 billion. This included money for 176 remote video surveillance systems, 20 new or upgraded Border Patrol stations in California, Arizona, and Texas, "enhancements or expansions" of 5 detention facilities, and 155 new detention officers. For 2001, they requested $4.8 billion. A majority of the increase will also be used for increased "control and enforcement" systems. See *Refugee Reports* 21, no. 2 (February 2000) 6.

85. Duncan Hunter, for whom the fence is named, refers to it as the DMZ (demilitarized zone), alluding to the zone that separated North Korea from South.

86. Roberto Martinez, "From Taking Lands to Building Triple Fences," at http://www.inmotionmagazine.com/border.html, 1.

87. Jiménez, "War in the Borderlands," 30.

88. The INS itself argued that this was too rapid a growth and that they could not responsibly absorb that many new personnel in such a brief time period. The General Accounting Office concurred, noting that in 1999, 48 percent of the agency's personnel had less than three years of experience. According to an article in the *San Diego Union Tribune,* "indeed, distress signals have been flaring in the borderlands. In Southern California, over one four day period, three immigrants were shot and killed by Border Patrol agents in separate incidents. . . . Last month a Border Patrol vehicle plunged some 1,200 feet off a mountain cliff, killing the driver and three immigrant detainees. And, recently, a Border Patrol agent fired a pellet gun at a rubber raft occupied by three immigrants attempting to traverse the unfriendly currents of the All-American Canal, with one of the capsized rafters allegedly failing to make it safely back to shore." See Michael Huspek, "Fatal Growing Pains for the Border Patrol," *San Diego Union Tribune,* 22 July 1999, B-13, B-11. Nonetheless, President Bush's proposed border security budget for 2003 included provisions for doubling the number of Border Patrol agents yet again. (*Migration News* 9, no. 3 [March 2002]) at http://migration.ucdavis.edu.

89. Mirta Ojito, "Change in Law Sets off Big Wave of Deportations," *New York Times,* 15 December 1998, A1.

90. See Timothy Dunn, *Militarization of the U.S.-Mexico Border, 1978–1992: Low Intensity Conflict Doctrine Comes Home* (Austin: Center for Mexican American Studies, University of Texas at Austin, 1996), 4.

91. For example, students at Bowie High School in El Paso, Texas, were subject to such regular harassment that they finally resorted to bringing a class action suit against the Border Patrol in federal court. Amnesty International,

Human Rights Concerns in the Border Region with Mexico (New York: Amnesty International, 1998), 6–7.

92. Amnesty International, *Human Rights Concerns in the Border Region with Mexico*, 1, 3. The report further notes, "people who reported they had been ill-treated included men, women, and children, almost exclusively of Latin American descent. They included citizens and legal permanent residents of the USA, and members of Native American First Nations whose tribal lands span the U.S.-Mexico border," 3. See also Jiménez, "War in the Borderlands."

93. Amnesty International, *Human Rights Concerns in the Border Region with Mexico*, 29.

94. Human Rights Watch, *Brutality Unchecked: Human Rights Abuses Along the U.S. Border with Mexico* (New York: Human Rights Watch, May 1992). Human Rights Watch issued four other reports about the U.S.-Mexico border: *Frontier Injustice* (May 1993); *Crossing the Line: Human Rights Abuses Along the U.S. Border with Mexico Persist amid Climate of Impunity* (April 1995); *Human Rights Violations by INS Inspectors and Border Patrol Agents Continue: Attorney General Janet Reno Urged to Address Abuse Problem* (an open letter to Janet Reno, 13 January 1997); and *Slipping Through the Cracks: Unaccompanied Children Detained by the U.S. Immigration and Naturalization Service* (April 1997).

95. American Friends Service Committee (AFSC), U.S.-Mexico Border Program, Immigration Law Enforcement Monitoring Project, *Human and Civil Rights Violations On the U.S.-Mexico Border, 1995–1997* at http://www.afsc.org/ilemp/ilempo4.htm.

96. Ibid. In terms of migrants who have died while attempting to cross the U.S.-Mexico border, activists in 18 cities around the United States held memorials for them in 1999. The number of dead is estimated at some 300 a year. These deaths are not only from shootings, but also drowning, dehydration in the deserts, and so on. According to Roberto Martinez, a study by the AFSC and the University of Houston estimates that some 1,185 people died crossing the border between 1993 and 1996 (Martinez, "From Taking Lands"). See also Pablo Lopez, "'Cemetery,' Procession Honor Dead: Civil-Rights Group Displays Crosses for Immigrants Who Died Crossing Illegally into the United States," *Fresno Bee*, 3 November 1999.

97. The rest of this chapter focuses on the rape and sexual abuse of undocumented women, but it is important to note that documented immigrants, U.S. residents, and U.S. citizens, especially if they are Latina, are also subjected to these practices.

98. Amnesty International, *Human Rights Concerns in the Border Region with Mexico*, 38.

99. Human Rights Watch, *Brutality Unchecked: Human Rights Abuses Along*

the U.S. Border with Mexico, 35. Cited here is the case of a nineteen-year-old who was sexually molested by the Border Patrol when they raided the work camp where she was living, and who was assisted by the AFSC to file a complaint. "She reached a sealed settlement with the INS for money damages; according to the AFSC, the agent involved has not been disciplined" (35).

100. AFSC, *Human and Civil Rights Violations on the U.S.-Mexico Border 1995–1997.*

101. Human Rights Watch, *Crossing the Line,* 2.

102. Amnesty International, *Human Rights Concerns in the Border Region with Mexico,* 5. According to Roberto Martinez of the AFSC and Jose Palafox of National Network for Immigrant and Refugee Rights, there were no substantial changes in accountability in 1999 and 2000. According to Palafox, "at an INS Advisory Panel meeting . . . the INS promised to implement our recommendations but to no avail. Many of the border activists stopped going to the meetings. Waste of time. . . . Now border activists have shifted to try and get the INS/Border Patrol to stop forcing migrants into dangerous crossing areas" (personal communication, 23 April 2000).

103. Julie Light, "Rape on the Border," *The Progressive* 60, no. 9 (September 1996), 24.

104. Ibid.

105. No. CIV-95-491-TUC-FRZ. Memorandum Decision and Order. Findings of Fact and Conclusions of Law. 12 October 1999, 2–3.

106. "Ex-Border Agent Indicted on U.S. Charges," *Arizona Republic,* 9 April 1995, B2.

107. CIV-95-491-TUC-FRZ, "Order Granting in Part and Denying in Part Cross-Motions for Summary Judgment," n.1.

108. This shows that the "choice" he seemingly offered was really no choice at all.

109. "Order Granting . . . " 26–27.

110. H. was given incorrect information by the Santa Cruz County Sheriff's Department, which told her that if she wanted to pursue the case, she would have to pay her own travel and lodging expenses. In fact, it was policy for the Santa Cruz County Attorney's Office to pay these expenses. Nonetheless, due to this misinformation, H. decided to not pursue a charge against Selders. See No. CIV-95-491-TUC-FRZ, Order Granting in Part and Denying in Part Cross-Motions for Summary Judgment, 12 November 1998, 5.

111. OPR investigated allegations of Border Patrol agent misconduct that occurred before 14 April 1989. After that date, the Office of the Inspector General (OIG) did the investigating.

112. No. CIV-95-491-TUC-FRZ. Memorandum Decision and Order. Findings of Fact and Conclusions of Law. 12 October 1999, 20.

113. Ibid, 14.

114. Ibid, 21.

115. Ibid, 11–12.

116. The incident came to OIG attention some five years later because "on or about April 17, 1993, Alma Barajas, a paralegal for the Southern Arizona Legal Aid Office in Nogales testified before a joint meeting of the Arizona and California Committees to the United States Commission of Civil Rights that a Border Patrol agent had sexually assaulted an undocumented Mexican woman" (Ibid., 11). The reasons why D. did not complain are noteworthy. Equally important, though, is the fact that her experience did surface some five years later, and one branch of the U.S. government did make an effort to investigate. That effort was hampered by lack of cooperation from another branch, as we will see.

117. Ibid, 12.

118. Ibid, 8.

119. Ibid, 8.

120. Darlene Clark Hine, "For Pleasure, Profit, and Power," in Geneva Smitherman, ed., *African American Women Speak Out on Anita Hill–Clarence Thomas* (Detroit: Wayne State University Press, 1995), 169.

121. Evelyn Hammonds, "Towards a Genealogy of Black Female Sexuality: The Problematics of Silence," in Chandra Talpade Mohanty and M. Jacqui Alexander, eds., *Feminist Genealogies, Colonial Legacies, Democratic Futures*, 170–82; Clark Hine, "For Pleasure, Profit, and Power"; Patricia Zavalla, "Talk 'n Sex: Chicanas and Mexicanas Theorize about Silences and Sexual Pleasures," paper presented at Sin Vergüenza! An Interdisciplinary Conference on Latino/a Sexuality, 15 April 2000, University of Michigan, Ann Arbor.

122. Clark Hine, "For Pleasure, Profit, and Power," 169. Saidiya Hartman makes clear that the mutually reinforcing violence of the state and the law produce "the pained and burdened personhood of the enslaved" (Saidiya Hartman, "Seduction and Ruses of Power," in Caren Kaplan, Norma Alarcón, and Minoo Moallem, eds., *Between Woman and Nation: Nationalisms, Transnational Feminisms, and the State* [Durham: Duke University Press, 1999], 117). This form of personhood cannot be grasped within traditional liberal narratives of the humanist subject, nor within models of sexuality anchored in notions of white kinship. Instead, racial, gender, and sexual domination interweave in the production of such forms of personhood. Hartman's analysis suggests that we need begin to conceptualize how rape and sexual abuse that are committed both at the border and within the United States generate particular pained forms of embodiment and subjectivity for undocumented women.

123. Hartman, "Seduction and Ruses of Power," 121.

124. Sassen, *Losing Control?*, 66.

125. Chavez, *Shadowed Lives*, 18.

126. Of course, minoritized groups within the United States have historically faced great difficulty in calling on the law for protection, too. The undocumented's difficulties stem from both similar and different causes.

127. Immigrant women, like African American women, are also often stereotyped in highly sexualized ways; in turn, these stereotypes are sometimes inappropriately seen as justifying rape.

128. David Lloyd, *Anomalous States: Irish Writing and the Post-Colonial Moment* (Durham: Duke University Press, 1993), 127.

129. Anne Marie O'Connor, "Border Agent Gets Ten Years for Sexual Assault," *Los Angeles Times*, 20 November 1996, A3. Note that the woman crossed illegally and alone, intending to join her husband and son who were both documented residents and were waiting for her in a motel. After Vinson released her, she was apprehended by other Border Patrol agents. She told then what happened, and they called the police.

130. O'Connor, "Border Agent Gets Ten Years," A3.

131. "Two Women Accuse Border Agents of Rape," *Austin American Statesman*, 30 October 1996, B10. See also Julie Light, "Rape on the Border," 24–25.

132. Other cases reported in the media include a migrant woman who reached a settlement with the U.S. government after reporting that a Border Patrol agent sexually assaulted her near a migrant camp in Encinitas, California. (See Julie Brossy, "FBI Probes Alleged Sexual Assault by Border Agent," *San Diego Union Tribune*, 8 February 1991; Philip J. LaVelle, "Grand Jury to Hear Case against Border Patrol Agent, Lawyer Says," *San Diego Union Tribune*, March 14, 1992.) Also, INS agent James Edward Riley was charged with seventeen counts "including rape, rape under color of authority, kidnapping, and assault" in seven incidents involving Latina migrants. "Riley cruised the streets preying on young undocumented aliens and exploited their fears of the INS. Riley confiscated identification cards and telephoned some women repeatedly after the assaults, the women said. . . . [A] woman said Riley drove her to his Reseda apartment and raped her. Three other women also testified that they were kidnapped and raped by Riley. The others said that they managed to escape after the agent threatened them with deportation and made sexual advances." (See Sebastian Rotella, "INS Agent to Stand Trial in Rape of Latinas," *Los Angeles Times*, 31 January 1991, B3.) Riley was eventually found guilty of false imprisonment but was acquitted of charges of rape and kidnapping. The defense portrayed the women as willing sexual partners, and the jury found their testimony inconsistent. The prosecuting attorney said "she was 'disgusted' by the jury's

decision. She said that, while finding Riley guilty of false imprisonment for holding one victim in his car against her will, the jury also found him not guilty of
kidnapping for the same incident." She also believed that "the immigration status of the victims may have played a role in the verdict." Riley was sentenced to
two years in prison for false imprisonment but was then immediately paroled
for time served. The INS said it would begin termination proceedings against
Riley when they received proof of his conviction. (See Michael Connelly, "INS
Officer Acquitted of Rapes," *Los Angeles Times,* 29 February 1992, A3, A34.) Finally, Calexico Border Patrol Agent Luis Santiago Esteves faced eighteen sex charges
from an alleged attack on a seventeen-year-old Mexican woman. A day before
the hearing, Border Patrol agents arrested and deported two members of the
girl's family. The immigration service characterized the arrests as a "coinci-
dence." (See Chet Barfield, "Arrests Called Border Patrol Retaliation," *San Diego
Union Tribune,* 11 October 1991, B3.)

133. Sharon Marcus, "Fighting Bodies, Fighting Words: A Theory and Politics of Rape Prevention," in Judith Butler and Joan Scott, eds., *Feminists Theorize
the Political,* 385–403. See also Ann S. Cahill, *Rethinking Rape* (Ithaca: Cornell
University Press, 2001).

134. For discussion of this point, see Robyn Wiegman's "Anatomy of Lynching" in John C. Fout and Maura Shaw Tantillo, eds., *American Sexual Politics*
(Chicago: University of Chicago Press, 1993), 223–45. See also Hyunah Yang, "Re-
membering the Korean Military Comfort Women: Nationalism, Sexuality, and
Silencing," in Elaine H. Kim and Chungmoo Choi, eds., *Dangerous Women: Gender and Korean Nationalism* (New York: Routledge, 1998), 123–39.

135. Hine, "For Pleasure, Profit, and Power," 175.

136. The fact that Latino citizens and legal residents are continually subjected
to the violence of border control, to the extent that they are even denied entry to
or are deported from their own country, further underscores how border control substantially results in the reproduction of social borders *within* the United
States itself.

137. Robert Chang, *Dis-Oriented* (New York: New York University Press,
1999), 39.

138. See Pierette Hondagneu Sotelo, *Gendered Transitions: Mexican Experiences of Immigration* (Berkeley: University of California Press, 1994), 150–51;
Rita J. Simon and Margo Corona DeLey, "Undocumented Mexican Women:
Their Work and Personal Experience," in Rita J. Simon and Caroline B. Brettell,
eds., *International Migration: The Female Experience* (New Jersey: Rowman and
Allanheld, 1986), 118–19; Lourdes Arguelles, "Undocumented Female Labor in
the United States Southwest: An Essay on Migration, Consciousness, Oppression, and Struggle," in Adelaida R. Del Castillo, ed., *Between Borders* (Encino,

Calif.: Floricanto Press, 1990), 304; Chris Hoagland and Karen Rosen, *Dreams Lost, Dreams Found: Undocumented Women in the Land of Opportunity* (San Francisco: Coalition for Immigrant and Refugee Rights and Services, 1990), 10, 30, 43, 45, 56–58; Gilberto Cardenas and Estevan T. Flores, *The Migration and Settlement of Undocumented Women* (Austin: CMAS Publications, University of Texas at Austin, 1986), 25.

139. Though no one has been able to reliably estimate the likely rates of rape and sexual abuse of undocumented domestic workers, we can reasonably assume that the problem is at least as pervasive as among documented domestics. On rape and sexual abuse of documented domestics, see, for example, Human Rights Watch, *Hidden in the Home: Abuse of Domestic Workers with Special Visas* (New York: Human Rights Watch, 2001), which describes the experiences of legal immigrant domestics employed by diplomats and high-ranking officials on Embassy Row in Washington, D.C., and New York.

140. Ironically, the firm's name is abbreviated to T & A.

141. "EEOC and Tanimura and Antle Settle Sexual Harassment Case in the Agricultural Industry," at http://www.eeoc.gov/press/2-23-99.html.

142. This sector also employs a significant number of Latina/o workers. According to Maria Dominguez, "the hired farm work force in 1992 was about 60 percent white, 30 percent Hispanic, and 10 percent Black or other." This is despite the fact that Hispanics comprise a mere 8 percent of the U.S. workforce overall. See Maria M. Dominguez, "Sex Discrimination and Sexual Harassment in Agricultural Labor," *American University Journal of Gender and Law* 6 (fall 1997), 234. Dominguez further notes that women comprise perhaps 16 percent of the agricultural workforce (238). Estimates of the number of undocumented women in agriculture are very difficult to derive.

143. According to Dominguez, women working in agriculture are also subjected to discrimination, such as employers who "give them fewer hours of work than their male counterparts, or pay them less for the same work as their male counterparts. Employers sometimes refuse to hire or promote women based solely on their gender. They limit women to certain kinds of work. . . . Finally, employers may discriminate against women by refusing to provide them with housing that is otherwise provided to men" ("Sex Discrimination," 240).

144. "EEOC and Tanimura."

145. Dale Rodebaugh, "Sexual Harassment Costly," *The Gazette* (Montreal), 24 February 1999, E14.

146. Ilana DeBare, "Record Settlement in Farmworkers' Suit," *San Francisco Chronicle,* 24 February 1999, B1.

147. Dominguez, "Sex Discrimination," 255.

148. Ibid., 255–57.

149. Tanimura and Antle underscore that in agreeing to such a settlement, they were admitting no wrong, and that "we were never able to substantiate the allegations made by the EEOC in this case." But it's hard to imagine why they would have agreed to such a large settlement if there were no problems. See "EEOC and Tanimura."

150. For instance, sexual abuse in domestic service work has long been recognized as a problem that workers face. Perhaps the most spectacular, distressing example in recent years was provided by the case of Sarah Balabagan, a fifteen-year-old from the Philippines who worked in the United Arab Emirates. When her employer raped her at knifepoint, she grabbed the knife and killed him. She was sentenced to death, but after international protests the sentence was amended to require that she pay $41,000 to the dead man's family, spend a year in jail, and endure one hundred lashes. Balabagan was just one among hundreds of thousands of immigrant women working as domestics in countries including the United States who endured rapes by employers.

151. Julinne Malveaux, "The Year of The Woman or The Woman of The Year: Was There Really an 'Anita Hill Effect?'" in Geneva Smitherman, ed., *African American Women Speak Out on Anita Hill–Clarence Thomas,* 161.

152. Ironically, the INS workplace has also been characterized as a place where women employees face sexual harassment. For instance, in 1993 the director of immigration services at Los Angeles International Airport, Arthur Alvarez, was accused of engaging in sexual harassment and assault of many women employees under his supervision. He was initially transferred from Los Angeles to another INS facility in San Pedro while the charges were being investigated. Then he was placed on leave "after the LA city attorney charged him with sexual battery, lewd conduct, and indecent exposure" in connection with a complaint filed by Rosa Esther Arauz, an employee. "Arauz said Alvarez made persistent efforts to kiss her and exposed himself to her twice while she was in his office, including once when he began masturbating in her presence." See Marcus Stern, "INS Workers Tell of Sexual Misconduct," *San Diego Union Tribune,* 20 July 1993. The INS has also been charged with racial discrimination toward its own employees. See House of Representatives, *Enforcement of Equal Employment Protection at Immigration and Naturalization Service: A Broken Promise,* Hearing Before the Legislative and National Security Subcommittee of the Committee on Government Operations, 103rd Cong., 2d Sess., 15 November 1994 (Washington, D.C.: U.S. Government Printing Office, 1994).

153. Instead, as Lowe puts it, we need to analyze "all the sites of bodily exploitation as constitutive parts of the value of [the women's] labor," as well as of the process through which they become politically subjected. See Lisa Lowe, *Immigrant Acts,* 156.

154. See Anannya Bhattacharjee, "Public/Private Mirages," in Chandra Tal-

pade Mohanty, and M. Jacqui Alexander, eds., *Feminist Genealogies, Colonial Legacies, Democratic Futures,* 309–29.

155. The terms of the IMFA are gender neutral, but "women comprise a majority of applicants for spouse based visas," and women are also the ones rendered most vulnerable by the terms of IMFA. See Bhattacharjee, "Public/Private Mirages," 314.

156. Leti Volpp, *Working with Battered Immigrant Women: A Handbook to Make Services Accessible* (San Francisco: The Family Violence Prevention Fund, 1995), 37.

157. Michelle J. Anderson, "A License To Abuse: The Impact of Conditional Status on Female Immigrants," *Yale Law Journal* 102 (1993), 1401.

158. According to Bernal's attorney, the government eventually agreed to withdraw its appeal and pay $700,000.

159. Ironically, although the distinction between refugee/asylum seekers and undocumented women may be clear-cut in law, in practice numbers of undocumented women are actually refugees who have been unable to obtain recognition through the refugee/asylum system and thus resort to unauthorized entry.

160. Feminists have frequently remarked on the connections between rape and the reproduction of dominant nationalism. This chapter has extended these feminist analyses by examining the connections between rape, migrant women's ability to legally or illegally cross the territorial borders of the United States, and the reproduction of dominant nationalism. Scholarship that further theorizes these connections in a variety of locations would be very valuable.

161. For a related analysis of the ways that rape and the construction of borders are implicated—in this case, in Mexico—see Ursula Biemann's video *Performing the Border* (1999). The video draws connections between the emergence of maquiladora industries at Mexico's northern border, which employ primarily young women under extremely exploitative conditions, and the crimes of a serial rapist-murderer who has been primarily targeting these young women. Biemann suggests that there are powerful links between industrial mass production at the border, to which women migrate for work, and the compulsive, repetitive rapes and killings of women. See also Lourdes Portillo's documentary, *Señorita Extraviada: Missing Young Women* (2002), or contact Lorena Mendez, director of Justice for Women in Juarez, at Mendez@fox11a.com or Azul Medina, founder of Viejaskandalosas, at unasviejas@yahoo.com.

Conclusion

1. Aristide Zolberg is one of a few migration scholars who has also addressed this point; he writes, "categoric distinctions between immigrants and migrants, and between guest workers and undocumented aliens, reflect

administrative practices rather than economic and sociological realities." See Aristide Zolberg, "Contemporary Transnational Migration in Historic Perspective: Patterns and Dilemmas," in Mary Kritz, ed., *U.S. Immigration and Refugee Policy* (Lexington, Mass.: Lexington Books, 1983), 36.

2. See Richard Handler, "Is 'Identity' a Useful Cross-Cultural Concept?" in John Gillis, ed., *Commemorations: The Politics of National Identity* (Princeton: Princeton University Press, 1994), 27–40; Roger Rouse, "Questions of Identity: Personhood and Collectivity in Transnational Migration to the United States," *Critique of Anthropology* 15, no. 4 (1995), 351–80; John Torpey, *The Invention of the Passport.*

3. Eve Sedgwick, *Epistemology of the Closet,* 30.

4. Michael Warner, "Introduction," in Warner, ed., *Fear of a Queer Planet* (Minneapolis: University of Minnesota Press, 1993), xxi.

5. See Eithne Luibhéid and Sasha Khokha, "Building Alliances Between Immigrant Rights and Queer Movements," in Jill M. Bystydzienski and Steven P. Schact, eds., *Forging Radical Alliances across Difference* (New York: Rowen and Littlefield, 2001), 77–90.

6. For discussion of this issue, see Yolanda Chavez Leyva, "Breaking the Silence: Putting Latina Lesbian History at the Center," in Bonnie Zimmerman and Toni McNaron, eds., *The New Lesbian Studies: Toward the Twenty-First Century,* 145–52; and Martin F. Manalansan IV, "In the Shadows of Stonewall: Examining Gay Transnational Politics and the Diasporic Dilemma," in Lisa Lowe and David Lloyd, eds., *The Politics of Culture in the Shadow of Capital* (Durham: Duke University Press, 1997), 485–505.

7. David Eng and Alice Hom, "Introduction," in Eng and Hom, eds., *Q & A: Queer in Asian America,* 12.

8. The framing of immigrant men's sexualities proceeds somewhat differently.

9. Manalansan, "In the Shadows of Stonewall"; Mirjana Morokvasic, "Women in Migration: Beyond the Reductionist Outlook," in Annie Phizacklea, ed., *One Way Ticket: Migration and Female Labour,* 13–31; Chandra Talpade Mohanty, "Under Western Eyes," in Chandra Talpade Mohanty, Ann Russo, and Lourdes Torres, eds., *Third World Women and The Politics of Feminism,* 51–80.

10. Morokvasic, "Women in Migration," 17.

11. For decades after gender and migration became recognized as a legitimate topic for research, gender was also usually analyzed within an evolutionary model. For a discussion of this problem, see Morokvasic, "Women in Migration." For examples of a different way of theorizing gender and migration, see Pierrette Hondagneu-Sotelo, *Gendered Transitions: Mexican Experiences of Immigration* (Berkeley: University of California Press, 1994), and Nazli Kibria, *The*

Family Tightrope: Changing Contours of Vietnamese American Lives (Princeton: Princeton University Press, 1993).

12. Manalansan, "In the Shadows of Stonewall," 486.

13. But important dimensions of immigrant women's agency cannot be traced unless official documents are supplemented by other kinds of inquiry, including ethnographic research.

14. Judith Butler, *Bodies That Matter*, 10.

15. Furthermore, repetition is always, in some way, new.

16. Butler, *Bodies That Matter*, 124.

17. See Lucy Salyer, *Laws Harsh as Tigers*, 44, and Him Mark Lai, Genny Lim, and Judy Yung, *Island*, 114.

18. "Immigration Marriage Fraud," A Hearing Before the Subcommittee on Immigration and Refugee Policy of the Committee of the Judiciary, U.S. Senate, 99th Congress, 2d Sess., 26 July 1985 (Washington, D.C.: U.S. Government Printing Office, 1986) 13.

19. This is fueled by the fact that immigration is, in one sense, basically a business. As John Salt and Jeremy Stein explain, "International migration . . . [can be] regarded as a diverse international business, with a vast budget, providing hundreds of thousands of jobs world-wide, and managed by a set of individuals and institutions, each of which has an interest in how the business develops. . . . The global migration business is not homogenous. Most obviously, it may be divided into legitimate (legal/regular) and illegitimate (illegal/irregular) components, each of which may be further subdivided, differently valued, and represent a particular business niche" John Salt and Jeremy Stein, "Migration as a Business: The Case of Trafficking," *International Migration* 35, no. 4 (1997), 468–69.

20. For example, the 1986 Immigration Reform and Control Act, which established penalties for employers who *knowingly* hire undocumented workers, has given rise to complex performances during which employers try to stage their unknowingness, in complicity with immigrants and sellers of forged documents. At the same time, the fact that employers *have* to demand documentation of work eligibility from all employees, in order to avoid fines, has driven up the price that immigrants must pay for even poorly forged documents. Furthermore, these poorly manufactured documents signal the immigrant's exploitability to the employer.

21. Historical reconstruction is particularly difficult because this subversive play is characterized by DeCerteau as a "tactic," belonging to those without power to directly confront or challenge the dominant, and its success depends on the ability to become literally unrecognizable. See Michel DeCerteau, *The Practice of Everyday Life* (Berkeley: University of California Press, 1984), 29–44.

22. David Lloyd's analysis of violence and the state, mentioned in chapter 5, is

surely applicable here, if we substitute the word "fraud" for the word "violence." Lloyd writes that from the perspective of the state, the actions of the subaltern must be represented as violent/fraudulent. "'Must' in two senses: that which cannot be assimilated to the state can only be understood as outside the law, disruptive and discontinuous, unavailable for narration; secondly, the history of the state requires a substrate which is counter to its laws of civility and which it represents as outrageous and violent [fraudulent], in order that the history of domination and criminalization appear as a legitimate process of civilization and the triumph of law." See David Lloyd, *Anomalous States* (Dublin: Lilliput, 1993), 27.

23. Butler, *Bodies That Matter,* 125.

24. Oliva Espín, *Latina Realities: Essays on Healing, Migration, and Sexuality* (Boulder, Colo.: Westview, 1997), 175.

Appendix

1. Norman L. Zucker and Naomi Flink Zucker, *The Guarded Gate,* 48.

2. See "Description of U.S. Refugee Processing Priorities, FY 2002," *Refugee Reports* 27, no. 12 (December 2001), 13, for a description of the priorities.

3. Zucker and Zucker, *The Guarded Gate,* 141.

4. *Refugee Reports* 22, no. 12, 5. At the end of fiscal year 2001, an estimated 324,438 asylum applications were waiting to be processed.

5. In reality, people facing persecution often experience economic difficulties as well. Consequently, no neat distinction can be drawn between political refugees and economic migrants.

6. Jacqueline Bhabha, "Embodied Rights: Gender Persecution, State Sovereignty, and Refugees," 8.

7. Nancy Kelly, "Gender-Related Persecution:Assessing the Asylum Claims of Women," *Cornell International Law Journal* 26 (1993), 630–31, n.24.

8. Bhabha, "Embodied Rights," 11.

9. For more information, see Elisa Mason, "The Protection Concerns of Refugee Women: A Bibliography," *Texas Journal of Women and the Law* (fall 1999), 95–116.

10. *In re Oluloro,* No. 172-147-491, Washington, D.C., EOIR Immigration Court, 23 March 1994.

11. Since 1996, suspension of deportation is no longer available as a judicial remedy.

12. According to Bhabha, "the first FGM asylum case to come to Western attention was that concerning a Malian woman, Aminata Diop, who sought asylum in France in 1991. Though the French asylum adjudication body (OFPRA) refused her asylum application on the basis that she had not effectively exhaust-

ed the domestic remedies available to resist mutilation, it did decide that FGM was a form of persecution and that the threat of it could found an asylum claim." See Bhabha, "Embodied Rights," 28, n.75.

13. *Matter of J.* (1995), No. A72 370 565 (IJ Baltimore, 28 April), reported in *Interpreter Releases* 72 (1995), 1375. Quoted and cited in J. Bhabha, "Embodied Rights," 28, n.72.

14. In re Fauziya Kasinga, Interim Decision No. 3278 (BIA, 1996).

15. Kasinga's account of her experiences, including her detention by the INS, is available in Fauziya Kassindja and Layli Miller Bashir, *Do They Hear When You Cry?* (New York: Delacorte Press, 1998). (Clearly, the BIA misspelled her name, but I have kept their spelling so that interested researchers will be able to locate the appropriate legal sources about her case.) Hope Miller and Isabelle Gunning note that she was "shackled, kept in unsanitary conditions, and placed in isolation for washing herself at dawn before her morning prayers, according to her religious traditions. She, along with other inmates and detainees, were teargassed and beaten during an insurrection at one of the facilities in which she was being held." See Hope Lewis and Isabelle R. Gunning, "Cleaning Our House: 'Exotic' and Familial Human Rights Violations," *Buffalo Human Rights Law Review* 123 (1998), 129.

16. Arthur C. Helton and Alison Nicoll, "Female Genital Mutilation as Grounds for Asylum in the United States: The Recent Case of In Re Fauziya Kasinga and the Prospects for More Gender-Sensitive Approaches," *Columbia Human Rights Law Review* 28 (winter 1997), 37.

17. Quoted in Bhabha, "Embodied Rights," 30.

18. Nonetheless, their decision that a cultural practice could constitute persecution was helpful to other applicants whose asylum claims were refused on the grounds that what they fled and objected to was "merely cultural." The decision was also important because it recognized that family members—not just direct agents of the state—could be agents of persecution. The case also established that a persecutory *intent* was not necessary in order for a practice to amount to persecution. For more discussion, see Deborah Anker, Lauren Gilbert, and Nancy Kelly, "Women Whose Governments are Unable or Unwilling to Provide Reasonable Protection from Domestic Violence May Qualify as Refugees Under United States Asylum Law," *Georgetown Immigration Law Journal* 709 (1997).

19. Professor Asha Samad has said, "Many people from our affected community have said that they do not like to be targeted as 'mutilated, primative people.' . . . Most feminists and most conscious, thinking people do not want to be seen only on one level, for example, as sex objects. However, in this case [the discussion of FGM] it has reached the point (perhaps not because anyone

wanted it to, but because of the previous sterotyping of Africa and also of women) that today African women are often seen principally and primarily in relation to this issue. Often they are thought of mainly as genitalia. In fact, one organization that is working on this issue has as its symbol black genitalia, black female genitalia. . . . Many people neglect the fact that our communities and their women are infinitely more affected by massive poverty, natural disasters, malnutrition, wars, and environmental hazards such as toxic waste dumping than by female circumcision/FGM. Due to these massive and widespread hazards, female circumcision/FGM is of secondary or tertiary priority to most African women and their communitites. Thus, female circumcision/FGM is pushed to the back burner, and it cannot be addressed fully, equally, or effectively in the sense of eradicating the custom fully until the critical problems (listed above) that affect us more severely are addressed. In fact, the countries that seem to have had the most success in addressing female circumcision/FGM have been those that are also addressing other socioeconomic problems and issues." See "Shifting Grounds For Asylum: Female Genital Surgery and Sexual Orientation," *Columbia Human Rights Law Review* (spring 1998), 490.

20. Lewis and Gunning, "Cleaning Our House," 132.

21. Quoted in *Refugee Reports* 18, no. 1 (31 January 1997), 6.

22. Charles E. Schulman, "The Grant of Asylum to Chinese Citizens Who Oppose China's One-Child Policy: A Policy of Persecution of Population Control?" *Boston College Third World Law Journal* (spring 1996), 320, emphasis added. Schulman goes on to list these various policy reversals.

23. Audrey Macklin, "Cross-Border Shopping for Ideas," 55.

24. Ibid., 55–56.

25. See "U.S. Congress Extends Asylum to Refugees Fleeing Coercive Reproduction Policies," *Reproductive Freedom News* 5, no. 17, 25 October 1996, 7.

26. Gender Guidelines.

27. Ibid.

28. The case is *In Re D- V-*, Interim Decision 3252 (BIA, 1993), elevated as precedent on 25 April 1995.

29. For example, in a landmark Canadian decision, an Argentinian gay man was awarded asylum after establishing that he had been persecuted in ways that included being raped by the police. See Daniel Raymond, "Aylum," *San Francisco Sentinel*, 16 January 1992, 7. See also *Hernandez-Montiel v. INS* #98-70582 and Katrina C. Rose, "When Is an Attempted Rape *Not* an Attempted Rape? When the Victim Is Transsexual," *American University Journal of Gender, Social Policy, and the Law* 9 (2001): 505–40.

30. Quoted in David Tuller, "Gay Foreigners Try New Ways to Stay," *San Francisco Chronicle*, 29 September 1992, A8.

31. *In re Toboso-Alfonso*, 20 1. & N. Dec. 819 (BIA, 1990).

32. See "Shifting Grounds for Asylum," 500.

33. See Shannon Minter, "Lesbians and Asylum: Overcoming Barriers to Access," in Sydney Levy, ed., *Asylum Based on Sexual Orientation: A Resource Guide* IB/31B/13. For more information, contact Dusty Aráujo, Asylum Project Coordinator, International Gay and Lesbian Human Rights Commission, 1360 Mission St., Suite 200, San Francisco, CA 94103, USA, tel. (415) 255-8020, http://www.iglhrc.org/asylum/index.html, or Lesbian and Gay Immigration Rights Taskforce, (212) 818-9639, http://www.lgirtf.org/.

34. Fatima Mohyuddin, "United States Asylum Law in the Context of Sexual Orientation and Gender Identity: Justice for the Transgendered?" in *Hastings Women's Law Journal* 12 (summer 2001): 387–410, 392–393.

35. Moreover, according to Currah and Minter, transgender people may be deemed nonhuman because they do not conform to conventional gender categories. As nonhumans, at least in the eyes of some courts, they remain unprotected from violence, discrimination, and persecution. See Paisley Currah and Shannon Minter, "Unprincipled Exclusions: The Struggle to Achieve Judicial and Legislative Equality For Transgender People," *William and Mary Journal of Women and Law* 7 (fall 2000): 37–60.

36. *Hernandez-Montiel v. INS,* Case No.98-70582, 24 August 2000, Ninth Circuit Court, 225 F. 3d 1084; 1089.

37. Taylor Flynn, "Transforming the Debate: Why We Need to Include Transgender Rights in the Struggle for Sex and Sexual Orientation Equality," *Columbia Law Review* 100 (March 2001): 392–420, 405.

38. See Mohyuddin for a description of some transgender asylum cases that have been granted in the United States. For more information, contact Chris Daley, Transgender Law Project, National Center for Lesbian Rights, 870 Market Street, Suite 570, San Francisco, CA 94102, USA, tel. (415) 391-6257 ext. 308, email Daley@nclrights.org; and Dusty Aráujo, Asylum Project Coordinator, International Gay and Lesbian Human Rights Commission, 1360 Mission St., Suite 200, San Francisco, CA 94103, USA, tel. (415) 255-8020, http://www.iglhrc.org/asylum/index.html.

39. Michael Ratner, "How We Closed the Guantanamo HIV Camp: The Intersections of Politics and Litigation," *Harvard Human Rights Journal* 11 (spring 1998), 191.

40. Ibid., 195.

41. Quoted in ibid., 201, n.56.

42. *Haitian Centers Council Inc. v. Sale,* 823 F. Supp. At 1045.

43. Peter Barta, "Lambskin Borders: An Argument for the Abolition of the United States' Exclusion of HIV-positive Immigrants," *Georgetown Immigration Law Review* 12 (winter 1998), 336.

44. Since 1996 HIV is described as a ground for "inadmissibility."

45. According to the San Francisco AIDS Foundation Web site, the INS applies a three-part test to all HIV-positive people seeking legal permenant residence. "Although this test does not not appear in the immigration law or in the regulations implementing the HIV ground of inadmissibility, INS policy is that it is part of the HIV waiver process." The applicant has to show that acquiring permanent residence will pose (1) minimal danger to public health, (2) minimal possibility of the spread of HIV, and (3) no cost to a government agency without that agency's prior consent. "The third part of the test has become increasingly problematic. Private health insurance can be enough, but not everyone can get private insurance, especially with a 'pre-existing condition' like HIV. . . . Many legal advocates believe the extra INS test is an unlawful expansion of INS authority." See the SF AIDS Foundation Web site, www.sfaf.org, or contact the HIV Assistance Project of the Bar Association of San Francisco, (415) 764-1600.

46. Margaret A. Somerville and Sarah Wilson, "Crossing Boundaries: Travel, Immigration, Human Rights, and AIDS," in *McGill Law Journal* (December 1998), 804.

47. *Refugee Reports* 21, no. 10 (October 2000), 4.

48. See "Crossing Borders," in *The Hindu,* 8 October 2000.

49. *Refugee Reports* 21, no. 10 (October 2000), 5.

50. Ibid., 4.

51. See Dan Eggen, "Proposal Broadens Asylum," *Washington Post,* 8 December 2000, A4; Patrick J. McDonnell, "California and the West: Changes Planned in Asylum Rules on Domestic Abuse," *Los Angeles Times,* 7 December 2000, A1.

52. Michel Foucault, *The History of Sexuality* (Vol. 1), 103.

Index

Eithne Luibhéid is assistant professor of ethnic studies at Bowling Green State University in Ohio. Her research focuses on the connections among immigration control, sexual regulation, and racial formation in a globalizing world.